TEACHER RESEARCH AND
EDUCATIONAL REFORM

TEACHER RESEARCH AND EDUCATIONAL REFORM

Ninety-third Yearbook of the
National Society for the Study of Education

PART I

Edited by
SANDRA HOLLINGSWORTH AND HUGH SOCKETT

Editor for the Society
KENNETH J. REHAGE

19 | NSSE | 94   70877

Distributed by THE UNIVERSITY OF CHICAGO PRESS ● CHICAGO, ILLINOIS

The National Society for the Study of Education

Founded in 1901 as successor to the National Herbart Society, the National Society for the Study of Education has provided a means by which the results of serious study of educational issues could become a basis for informed discussion of those issues. The Society's two-volume yearbooks, now in their ninety-third year of publication, reflect the thoughtful attention given to a wide range of educational problems during those years. In 1971 the Society inaugurated a series of substantial publications on Contemporary Educational Issues to supplement the yearbooks. Each year the Society's publications contain contributions to the literature of education from more than a hundred scholars and practitioners who are doing significant work in their respective fields.

An elected Board of Directors selects the subjects with which volumes in the yearbook series are to deal and appoints committees to oversee the preparation of manuscripts. A special committee created by the Board performs similar functions for the series on Contemporary Educational Issues.

The Society's publications are distributed each year without charge to members in the United States, Canada, and elsewhere throughout the world. The Society welcomes as members all individuals who desire to receive its publications. Information about current dues may be found in the back pages of this volume.

This volume, *Teacher Research and Educational Reform*, is Part I of the Ninety-third Yearbook of the Society. Part II, published at the same time, is entitled *Bloom's Taxonomy: A Forty-Year Retrospective*.

A listing of the Society's publications still available for purchase may be found in the back pages of this volume.

Library of Congress Catalog Number: 92-063305
ISSN: 0077-5762

Published 1994 by
THE NATIONAL SOCIETY FOR THE STUDY OF EDUCATION

5835 Kimbark Avenue, Chicago, Illinois 60637
© 1994 by the National Society for the Study of Education

First Printing

Printed in the United States of America

iv

v

Acknowledgments

The support of many people has made possible the publication of this volume. We are especially indebted to the teacher researchers in the United States and the United Kingdom who have educated us over these years, specifically, Anthony Cody, Mary Dybdahl, Sharon Jeffrey, Leslie Turner Minarik, Marian Mohr, Ann Sevcik, Jennifer Davis-Smallwood, and Karen Teel.

We also acknowledge with thanks the support of members of the Board of Directors of the National Society for the Study of Education, especially Ann Lieberman, A. Harry Passow, and David C. Berliner.

Our thanks are due to Kenneth J. Rehage for his careful editing and his advice. We also deeply appreciate the work of Patricia Noell at Michigan State University. Her administrative assistance was invaluable.

SANDRA HOLLINGSWORTH
HUGH SOCKETT

The contributors to this volume have all had experiences in one way or another with teacher research. From their various perspectives they bring their experience to bear on the challenges confronting those who engage in teacher research either as individual researchers or in a collaborative relationship with other researchers. The result is an informative book that will surely help to clarify many of the issues that arise when teaching is seen as research and research as teaching.

We are grateful to all who have had a part in producing this book. We particularly appreciate the work of the editors, Sandra Hollingsworth and Hugh Sockett, who have assiduously attended to the many detailed tasks that must be performed in seeing a book through to publication.

As she has done for the past three years, Margaret Early, a former member of the NSSE Board of Directors and a professor at the University of Florida at Gainesville, has again assisted with the editing of this volume. Her helpful suggestions reveal her concern for high standards for NSSE Yearbooks and especially her concern for clarity in writing.

Christopher A. Shinn, assistant in the NSSE office, has prepared the name index with his usual meticulous attention to detail.

KENNETH J. REHAGE
Editor for the Society

Table of Contents

Section One
Overview

Section Two
Epistemological Issues for Teacher Research

Section Three
The Socio-Political Context of Teacher Research

Section Four

Prospects for the Profession through Teacher Research

Section Five

Conversations and Critiques
of Teacher Research and Educational Reform

Section One
OVERVIEW

CHAPTER I

Positioning Teacher Research in Educational Reform: An Introduction

SANDRA HOLLINGSWORTH AND HUGH SOCKETT

Movements toward educational reform since the late 1950s have often been polarized between positions of control and autonomy. By 1986, with the creation of the National Board for Professional Teaching Standards, the emphasis of reform proposals shifted away from a period of increasing control over teaching and the form and content of schooling toward an emphasis on decentralization, professionalization, and improved teacher education. These two positions illustrate the tension between public control and teacher autonomy with each implying a different stance, ideology, and style for educational improvement.

Many discussions of characteristic differences in these positions on educational reform appropriately refer to the accompanying ideological stances on educational research. For example, the dominant "scientific" paradigm in educational research has historically been both an ally and a tool of the ideology of improvement through public control. John Goodlad has shown how its institutional legacy is embodied in the hierarchical and bureaucratic character of relations between universities and schools. The control view of educational reform and improvement has been a matter of "what works." Scientific conclusions are discovered by university researchers, tested in the Heraclitan fire of the refereed journal, and

Sandra Hollingsworth is an Associate Professor in the Department of Teacher Education at Michigan State University. Hugh Sockett is President of the Institute for Educational Transformation at George Mason University.

handed down to efficient classroom technicians. This view of improvement creates and feeds teacher-practitioners who are "hungry for technique"; in so doing, it may actively hinder their engagement in understanding and challenging what is being offered rather than merely imitating it in classrooms. Given the rapidly changing nature of "science" itself, this dependence on scientifically controlled solutions fosters an occupation which relies on "fads, fashions, and rituals"[1] for both its substantive and evaluative components, and becomes manifest in waves of workshops and courses based on "hot topics" in research. Where the short two-day course provides practical tips for immediate implementation, the longer courses (e.g., master's degree programs) provide bouts of theory and "what the research says," but rarely do either find a place for teachers' practical wisdom. Instead teachers are initiated into research typically done outside the context of the classroom, and they too often return to the classroom wondering either what is wrong with them as teachers or their students as learners when the prescribed treatments fail to work (see chapter 3). In short, the view of educational reform and improvement implicit in the control paradigm appears to be described by its commitment to (a) generalization about contexts rather than to contexts themselves, (b) a hierarchical view of theory/theorists and practice/practitioners, and (c) agenda driven by bureaucracies rather than by teaching professionals.

Discussions of the ideological and methodological underpinnings of reform based on teacher autonomy will be cast in opposite terms. However, transformative educational reform (or "reformation" to use Jonas Soltis's term[2]) may require a discussion that goes beyond the positionings of methodologies or paradigms and into the power relations which position the teacher (see chapter 13). Indeed, those who see teacher autonomy and decentralization as an alternative to the control ideology and see that alternative as a necessary route to the professionalization of education *also* find themselves struggling with an epistemology, a dynamic social reality, and a politics of educational research which serve inadequately as vehicles for that aspiration. Emerging from that struggle is a third stance toward educational improvement which challenges the dichotomous debate between control and autonomy by introducing professional, epistemological, and sociopolitical critique. It is in such postmodern groundings, which we will examine later in this chapter, that we can locate prospects for the profession within the contemporary teacher research movement.

The title of this Yearbook is not, therefore, accidental. The positioning of "teacher" in research and the potential for transformative educational reform are intimately and profoundly related. This relationship is explored here in historical, contemporary, possible, and problematic terms. In this introductory chapter, we provide brief historical accounts of teacher research which locate it in both national and international developments of action research—and within the control/autonomy stances on education reform. Second, we give a reading on contemporary teacher research, which stresses the significance of epistemological and feminist critique, and we briefly assess the impact and potential of the movement on professionalization and educational reform. Finally, we provide a review of the volume's chapters organized around the three central themes of epistemology, sociopolitics, and professionalization.

A Brief Historical Overview of Teacher Research

Action research is a most important ancestor of teacher research. Many historical accounts, including Susan Noffke's and James McKernan's, support the conventional wisdom that action research was the creature of social psychologist Kurt Lewin.[3] With roots in the nineteenth-century science in education and the group dynamics movements, Lewin focused on a methodology and a style of experimental inquiry with *groups* facing specific problems, as a way of bringing social science directly into social practice. For Lewin, the problems of society did not involve the epistemology, but who worked with it. He sought to find ways to involve social actors (school teachers and others) with researchers through group decision making and elaborate problem-solving procedures as ways of implementing social and cultural changes.

Within the context of a continuing debate on progressive education, post-1945 curriculum development activity was influenced by Lewin and other social reconstructionists. Stephen Corey, with colleagues at the Horace Mann-Lincoln Institute at Teachers College, Columbia University, conducted a variety of projects in the belief that action research would improve curriculum because practitioners would use the results of their own investigations to bring about that reconstruction. Hilda Taba's intergroup education projects in the early 1950s engaged schools in a form of action research derived from John Dewey, rather than Lewin, in the belief that not only could such involvement improve teachers' own practices, but that research findings would then pragmatically contribute to general theoretical knowledge. The history of the action research movement of the 1950s in education, however, was unhappy first because the quality of the output by classroom teachers was judged on conventional research criteria, and second because the Lewin model demanded controlled participation by the whole of a given group, assigning to many teachers a role they did not want. The small experiment with action research in education quietly fizzled. Only the idea of collaboration was to remain—in varying forms.

The Revival of Action Research as Teacher Research and Reflective Practice

The Woods Hole Conference of September 1959 was the post-Sputnik occasion to improve schools through innovative discipline-based curriculum programs and a government-sponsored research, development, and dissemination model of educational innovation.[4] The curriculum reform movement in the ideology of public control was thus renewed by discipline-based academics and educational researchers who envisioned research and practice as separate entities. The earlier questions raised by progressive educators about educational reform were by-passed in this high-profile, expensive intervention.

Across the water, partnerships in England and Wales gave more emphasis to professional development and autonomy. The Schools Council for Curriculum and Examinations was a central government initiative, promoted by liberal civil servants, which brought teacher unions and educational administrators into the reform process as well, at the same time as British progressive education was being revitalized through publication of the Plowden Report, *Children and Their Schools*.[5] The political and social climate encouraged radical innovation, especially for average and below-average students, as they were then called.

The path to educational improvement in the United States adopted in the decade after Woods Hole was, paradoxically, more concerned with academically talented students, although the social reality of schooling in the 1960s was more dominated by Vietnam and civil rights issues. By the 1980s the U.S. curriculum reform movement had faltered, partly because of the disjuncture between educational theories of research and social realities, partly because of the economic constraints of the 1970s, and partly because of the reform movement's systemic faults, including its gap between research and practice.

Attention was once again devoted to collaboration between researchers and teachers in what came to be called *interactive* research and development. Such interactive collaboration picked up both Lewin's and Corey's action-research strategies, then used them to disseminate research results through in-service training.[6] This path to reform provided a framework where teachers were encouraged to investigate topics related to their practice, but did not address the epistemological problems of the nature of curricular models, nor the social, contextual, and political problems surrounding the generation of those models.

A VIEW OF PROFESSIONALISM AS TEACHER RESEARCH

In the British curriculum reform process in the late 1960s and early 1970s, Lawrence Stenhouse and John Elliott began to articulate the deep significance of teacher participation in improvement and reform at the classroom level. The recreation and development of action research in education therefore took place in Britain, then spread to Australia and to some countries in Europe. A tradition of collective teacher autonomy assisted this work. Stenhouse, Director of the Center for Applied Research in Education at the University of East Anglia, was the first to write about teachers as researchers, an advocacy which arose directly from his work as Director of the Humanities Project from 1967 to 1972. He asked teachers to engage in a "process model" of curriculum innovation where professional development and curricular development became the same enterprise. Like Lewin and Corey, Stenhouse did not ignore the use of the scientific method in developing and testing curricular hypotheses, but he did question the ethical stance of separating the performance from the performer (or activities of "making" in Aristotle's terms). Teacher researchers, according to Stenhouse, engaged in activities of "doing" where the ends included ethical qualities which were realized in the activities themselves rather than quantities produced as a result of the activities. A decade or more of growth for this fledgling movement, notably through Elliott's Classroom Action Research Network,[7] was also possible because there were limited political constraints: it was not until the *late* 1970s and early 1980s that the kind of tough-minded accountability apparent in the United States in the *early* 1970s influenced Britain. Many curriculum and other projects sought to foster good relations between the school and the university and between the teacher/practitioner and the academic in Britain, although such relationships were not widespread.

Interinstitutional partnership being developed in the United States in the late 1970s seemed radical and unusual, particularly as the separatism of the curriculum reform movement had repelled it. Educational research monies were provided more for researchers to criticize practices in schooling rather than for developers who would support them. The traditional educational research paradigm supporting public control remained virtually unchallenged in the United States, even among teachers who had begun to do research in their work places. The British movement had been challenging that paradigm from the late 1960s, primarily because both Stenhouse and Elliott, in different ways, focused on the practical business of teaching. Both read philosophical critiques of positivism and its heirs as undermining the empirical and intellectual basis of educational research. Elliott characterized teaching as an unremittingly theoretical activity, and Stenhouse came to see it as a research activity. For both, the centrality of teacher-selves in research necessarily undermined the kind of objectivity espoused by traditional researchers working with a natural science model, and it also challenged hierarchical models in professional workplaces.

Action research in the professional or "process model" was seen as a viable alternative in the United States during the late 1970s and early 1980s because of the difficulties of applying quantitative experimental methodologies to local and social educational settings. Two other factors favoring action research were the growing acceptance of the concept of curriculum as integrated with human deliberation—particularly in the work of Joseph Schwab—and the professional and political reaction against the regulatory accountability movement. Soon after Donald Schön published *The Reflective Practitioner* in 1983[8] the American educational reform movement began to build collaborative partnerships with teams sharing in planning, analysis, execution, and dissemination of particular projects. Differences of perspective brought by different professionals from different roles had ensured a better understanding of issues for social change.

A VIEW OF PROFESSIONALISM AS REFLECTIVE PRACTICE

Schön's importance in the United States cannot be underestimated. It lies in his trenchant and clear-headed rejection of the dominant epistemology as able to provide a coherent account of the theory-practice relationship for all professions, not just teaching—a problem which philosophers as different as John Dewey and Michael Oakeshott had long since articulated. To Schön, the alternative epistemology is knowing-in-action—as opposed to the "trickle-down" view of the relationship of theory to practice. The professional is a reflective practitioner as opposed to a technician. For the American movement, putting the activities of those engaged in collaborative groups in an epistemological framework was a major stimulus and a profound innovation in educational thought. *The Reflective Practitioner* thus proved to be a source around which many teachers and academics could rally, even though it lacked the depth of experience in the education profession, and hence the range of relevant ideas, which characterized Stenhouse's *An Introduction to Curriculum Research and Development* (1975), where the notion of the teacher as researcher was established so clearly.[9]

Reflective practice in teacher research is also grounded in other critiques of the profession. In the United Kingdom and, more recently, in the United States, Hugh Sockett has developed a strong argument for teacher professionalism within a moral account of what Schön calls an epistemology of practice.[10] Sockett takes professionalism to mean a focus on the quality of practice (not the status of the occupation)—a focus that demands an extended conception of what constitutes a career in teaching. Involvement in research activity as a process of teacher education and teachers' work is a sine qua non of the professional educator. Other critiques of the profession and reflective practice involve the relational aspect of knowledge about teaching. For example, Peter Posch in Austria sees knowledge about teaching being acquired in the negotiated risk between teacher and student in a local context. Teacher research is a necessary activity to delineate that knowledge.[11] From the roots of action research, therefore, both reflective practice and teacher research have emerged, each giving strong support to the ideology of educational improvement through developing professional autonomy.

CRITICAL PRAXIS IN TEACHER RESEARCH

Beyond the notions of teacher research and reflective practice, a third derivative of action research—critical praxis—is important background to a contemporary understanding of the movement in the United States. This societal focus was a response to needs of diversity in its international population, both as a moral indignation toward the increasing gap between the concept of democracy and the reality of domination and oppression, and as the active rejection of that reality. Alternately fueled by the Civil Rights and Women's Movements during the 1960s and 1970s, philosophers, scientists, and teachers questioned the firm modernist belief in rationalist science—and the unfragmented and politically silencing nature of knowledge that "science" assumes. Even popular teacher-promoted curricular projects which challenged static views of knowledge and societal norms (but from a singular philosophic stance, such as the Bay Area Writing Project) were not free from scrutiny.[12]

Instead of the local pragmatic focus of simply improving practice in social situations, critical praxis was intended also to disrupt social environments or conditions of practice. Similar to the grounded rationale of Elliott, who critiqued the ways schools reproduced inequitable social hierarchies, Stephen Kemmis and his colleagues at Deakin University, Australia, articulated a model of an educational science based upon a critical-interpretive-activist philosophy which had more in common with Jürgen Habermas and the community of philosophers and social scientists of the "Frankfurt School."[13] The critical stance clearly rejects as illusory the view of objective, publicly controlled reality in which the individual has no control, and which undermines the capacity of individuals to reflect upon their own situations and change them through their own actions. An overriding concern of the Frankfurt School, therefore, has been to articulate a view of theory that has the central task of emancipating people from the positivist "domination of thought" through their own understandings and actions. Thus seen as intrinsically related to the professional development of teachers, the development of a critical educational science implies not only engaging in "doing" education, but learning about it and changing its structure, and simultaneously changing teachers' roles within the institution.

This critical stance for teachers-as-researchers focuses on desired and possible changes within the structure and profession of education. It has moved from Australia into the United States, the United Kingdom, and other countries, and it has taken new forms. Critical teacher research may or may not involve collaboration with university faculty. In the United States, for example, the Boston Women's Teachers' Group met for three years to help each other cope with the isolated struggle of their daily work. At the same time, they studied how their work conditions affected them as teachers. They noted the important paradox that teachers work in institutions preparing children for adulthood but they are regarded as incapable of mature judgment.[14] These teacher-researchers challenged that "objective reality" by creating their own professional structure where critical judgment of epistemic privilege (i.e., that some ways of knowing are more powerful than others) was possible.

Adopting this sociopolitical stance to educational improvement suggests that teachers must be prepared to become critical professionals able and willing to challenge institutional structures as well as curriculum to change. Examples in the United States include colleges where inquiry orientations to teaching are developed, where social studies methods courses emphasize teachers critiquing school and societal contexts of education, and where the supervision of student teachers has been reframed within an emancipatory approach.[15] In Canada, both teacher research and research on teachers' knowledge of their craft point to the transformative nature of that work in challenging the structure of institutions and serve as challenges to teacher preparation programs which are based on codified knowledge from university research alone.[16]

Thus a third view of educational improvement through critical praxis or sociopolitical critique has emerged to characterize the contemporary teacher research movement. A disenchantment with the view of control as a means of improving education, a concern with teacher autonomy, and a growing understanding of knowledge as a source of power in society created an ideological convergence which provides a clearer realization of the interconnected nature of knowledge, research, and practice. What makes this diversity of national and international interest a movement? Even though each separately allows for different definitions and interpretations, five fundamental criteria appear to bind the separate dimensions of action research, reflective practice, and critical praxis together into a contemporary movement for teacher research:

1. Collaborations and partnerships are created across school and university roles.
2. Research starts from where the action is.
3. The practitioner's practical wisdom is a central source of knowledge.
4. Research leads to personal and social change, as well as curricular and instructional change.
5. There can be no single, privileged way of knowing.

A Contemporary Overview of Teacher Research

In the United States, a strong contemporary emphasis in teacher research is on how schools and teaching are shaped and institutionalized in society, what knowledge is privileged, and what epistemological views are important for their transformation. Challenges to the view of improvement through control have also been enriched by the growth and sophistication of feminist theory, which, though it does not often address educational issues, has important implications for emancipation from education as, *pari passu*, "a woman's profession." We deal with each of these critiques in turn before assessing the impact of the teacher research movement on the reform of the educational profession.

EPISTEMOLOGICAL CRITIQUES

Societal positions based on privileged conceptions of knowledge are the focus of epistemological critique. Jerome Bruner, for example, questions the power ascribed to the paradigmatic or "rational" view of knowledge and the power which might be attributed to its antitheses. One such antithesis is the narrative view of knowledge explored by Michael Connelly and Jean Clandinin who see the concept of narrative inquiry in education as informing and reforming.[17] Sandra Harding questions natural science's position on objectivity as too limited to the power of the dominant white, male society. Mary Belenky, Blythe Clinchy, Nancy Goldberger, and Jill Tarule raise questions about alternative ways of knowing which might privilege some women over others, while Susan Laird questions competing views of understanding teaching problematically as a "woman's profession." Culturally diverse and third-world ways of knowing and representing knowledge, such as those pointed out by Audrey Lourde and bell hooks, also represent critiques of societally accepted knowledge.[18] All these writers question the separation of hierarchically powered social structures and inquiry methods, a position shared in the contemporary movement for teacher research.

FEMINIST CRITIQUES

For the authors of this chapter, the contemporary teacher research movement has increasingly not only taken on an epistemological critique, but is also grounded in and contributes to feminist theory and praxis. One of us, Sandra Hollingsworth, has written extensively about this area.[19] Feminist critiques argue against privileged positions of personhood: race, class, gender, sexual orientation, and handicapping conditions. Feminist teachers are conscious of the problematic reality of their perspectives and positions (i.e., most American teachers are white, middle-class, heterosexual, able-bodied women administratively "controlled" by white, middle-class, heterosexual, able-bodied men). Yet feminist teachers also understand their abilities to construct and critique knowledge, and the problematic nature of "outsider" knowledge in directing their work. It is important not to slip into dichotomous modernist thinking that teachers' knowledge should now become privileged. However, it *is* important to support, hear, and acknowledge teachers as practitioners and researchers of educational knowledge. It is also important to understand the different standpoints of teachers of color with regard to teacher research and feminist theory. Although it is not a simple feat, given the persistent and inequitable socialized position of teachers as less than powerful, many feminist researchers, including Corrine Glesne, show how teachers who do engage in teacher research come to trust their own abilities to construct knowledge, to be meaning makers, and to improve their practices. "Buoyed by trust in themselves, they gather confidence to take new risks. The impact expands like concentric circles around the stone thrown in water."[20]

The work of such teachers contributes to a feminist critique of education and those critiques then further support professionalization in a sociopolitical mode. Weiner, for example, contrasts teacher research in the Schools Council Sex Differentiation Project with mainstream professional development in England. She argues that teacher research on gender takes on a perspective of social justice within a professional development framework. Weiner admits that both types of teacher research endorse emancipatory purposes which could "liberate teachers and pupils from a system of education which denied individual dignity and was predicated upon external authority and control."[21] Rather than convince teachers of the need for changes in their practices, however, feminist researchers such as Weiner and her school-based colleagues wish to bring about improvements in the social and economic position of women (see also chapter 4). Rather than trying to improve existing professional development models, feminist researchers attempt to rewrite the notion of professionalism.

Similar research is being conducted in the United States. Janet Miller, for example, favors teachers as the researchers of their own underlying assumptions "as connected to [their] particular biographical, cultural, and historical situations, and as manifested in classroom processes and interactions." Teachers must be involved in interpreting as well as conducting their own research, must be wary of teacher-as-researcher formats which simply reproduce the procedures and intentions of prevailing norms in educational research. Such forms of teacher research give power to the "expert" who enters the classroom. Though appearing to be collaborative, most of this work excludes the teacher from determining the research focus or interpretation especially when the definition of what is researchable is set in terms which validate exclusive norms. Miller looks for collaborative approaches that "recognize the capacities of educators to challenge and to change existing situations that limited their students as well as themselves."[22]

It is important to remember that feminist critique is not the essential domain of women. Many male researchers also offer suggestions for educational reform from feminist perspectives. Citing Michael Apple, for example, Kenneth Zeichner reminds us that "Teaching is not just work; it is gendered work. Work dominated by women has been particularly vulnerable to the kind of rationalization and standardization seen in teaching."[23] Zeichner, however, also writes about the potential "down side" of teacher empowerment and school reform. He points out that because teachers are asked to take on new demands such as research, the schools' academic missions could be undermined unless their expanded responsibilities are incorporated into instead of added onto their work.

THE IMPACT OF TEACHER RESEARCH ON EDUCATIONAL REFORM

What is the impact of teacher research on prospects for the reform of the educational profession? The Bay Area Writing Project and its national affiliates sponsor and promote a network of teacher research activities. The numbers of conferences devoted to the themes of action research and teacher research are increasing, particularly as they inform current efforts to create school-university collaborations. The American Educational Research Association has included a special interest group on Teacher Research since 1989. Excellent examples of first-order or teacher-generated research reports, grounded not only in an ideology of teacher autonomy, but in epistemological and feminist critique, are being published in increasing numbers.[24]

There is a sense, then, that the range of teacher research activities is capturing international attention on reform issues in all areas of the educational enterprise: research, teaching, the profession, its moral purpose, its impact on society. Important questions remain. Are these changes fundamentally different, leading to a reformation in education? Might the political implications of teacher empowerment and societal reform lead us to a new and unknown world with unfamiliar epistemological and social norms? Does it include the voices of teachers of color? Is the growing popularity of the teacher research movement leading to a new form of power and hierarchy inside schools? Might it now become mandated, measured, and ineffectual in improving practice, and simply a new label for existing school structures and resultant societal outcomes? The trends found in the literature fail to resolve these worries. What is clear is that the movement is part of the larger evolution of society into the postmodern age and that teachers as researchers are less marginally involved. ˎ

Yet it is difficult to assess with any accuracy the present level of commitment across the United States. Led by the Holmes Group, many universities have established collaborative partnerships with schools, but academics face unhelpful promotion and tenure criteria, hostility from colleagues, and insufficient resources for collaborative work which involves, at times, a critique of the academy itself. The shifting of focus from the university to the classroom may also be hindered by the university's heavy emphasis on publication rather than service in action. At the same time, there is increasing attention to the need for inquiry and reflective practice in teacher preparation programs and among teacher educators. In Noffke and Hursh's words, teacher educators become "not only people who assist others in their efforts to understand and act in their worlds, but also ones whose sphere of action is equally problematic."[25] The breadth of those efforts can only be impressionistically captured here, but the editors and contributors to this book are united by the ambition to serve as a common focus for these efforts.

We are not, however, promoting teacher research as the "new enlightenment." We see this volume as raising nagging questions about the nature of education, schooling, professionalism, research, reform, and knowledge itself and not as the new canon for educational reform. By pulling together this collection of essays, we hope to contribute to a conversation on the positioning of "teacher" in research and reform and to develop "theories and practices and practical circumstances which are more rather than less justified in their own understanding, more rather than less comprehensive, more rather than less alert to contradiction."[26] In this volume we attempt to show that the contemporary teacher research movement defines a different character for the close and intimate link between not only an ideology of collective teacher autonomy, but an epistemological and sociopolitical view of educational improvement. Instead of viewing professionalism just in terms of control versus autonomy, the feminist reminder of the multiple and changing standpoints of knowledge (and the personal as political) encompasses prospects for the profession and educational reform. Teacher research has thus emerged as both a root and branch alternative to modern reform movements. Its implications reach into every aspect of professional work in education—into the quality of teaching in universities and schools, into matters of respect for the practical wisdom of teachers, into perceptions of educational improvement, into social and institutional relationships, and it is also beginning to influence how university study and degree work is constructed. The task of this yearbook is to portray this variety and breadth of commitment, which require varied and new (for example, in chapters 7 and 12) forms of discourse and intellectual exchange.

Martha Nussbaum has argued trenchantly that it is the obligation of the intellectual to encourage inquiry into, and commitment to, new or emerging forms of study, and that is, of course, a highly political business.[27] Not that there should be an eleemosynary attitude toward such upstarts. The new forms of study deserve, and they want, tough-minded intellectual engagement, free and unfettered with institutional or political clout. Ideas turn into movements and many kinds of change become necessary. We should not simply do educational research, as Elliott puts it, but our research should itself be (normatively) educational. Teacher research equally seeks educational reform and improvement which is itself educational—governed by moral criteria and self-consciously providing opportunities for learning. We see the potential and the promise of teacher research in terms of four primary elements: the epistemologies that underpin it, the sociopolitical contexts which frame its futures, its prospects inside the education professions, and the critiques and conversations appropriate to its characterizations. These four issues are examined in depth in the remainder of this volume.

Teacher Research and Educational Reform:
A Contemporary Analysis

EPISTEMOLOGICAL ISSUES FOR TEACHER-RESEARCH

Three of the epistemologically centered major problems teacher research faces as it tackles educational improvement are discussed in Section Two. In chapter 2, Susan L. Lytle and Marilyn Cochran-Smith propose a theoretical framework for teacher research which centers around questions of knowledge production, research methodology, and the politics of school and university relationships. They suggest that a reconceptualization of how and by whom knowledge can be constructed would lead to a different epistemology of teaching. Such a reconceptualization, they argue, has profound implications for the construction and reconstruction of teacher learning in schools and universities and across the professional lifespan.

In chapter 3, Olga Welch takes up the complex problem of what is known and who can know it in the practice of teaching in multicultural settings. In her essay on "The Case for Inclusive Dialogue in Knowing, Teaching, and Learning about Multicultural Education," Welch describes the problems and possibilities of culturally inclusive pedagogy through varying perspectives or standpoints on research in culturally diverse classrooms. She shows the need, challenges, and promises of connecting issues of academic excellence and equity in classroom instruction. She implies that teachers' inquiry into inclusive dialogue can provide powerful alternatives to Euro-American approaches to multicultural education.

In chapter 4, Kenneth Zeichner examines the role of knowledge produced through teacher research in promoting individual teacher development and a higher quality of teaching, in institutionalizing changes in schools, in making educational policy, and in building a more democratic and decent society. In doing so, he argues against uncritical glorification of knowledge produced through teacher research and for acknowledging the social and political implications of teacher-produced knowledge. Zeichner's chapter becomes a bridge between the epistemological and the sociopolitical features of teacher research.

THE SOCIOPOLITICAL CONTEXT OF TEACHER RESEARCH

The sociopolitical issues involved in contemporary views of teacher research are discussed from various standpoints in Section Three. In chapter 5, Michael Connelly and Jean Clandinin view collaboration as a political act in the sense that two or more participants are engaged in a shared task which implies mutuality and equality. The political nature of those individual relationships is important. In addition, they suggest that collaborative research is most often engaged in by participants from different institutional structures, usually a research institution and an institution of practice (school). Connelly and Clandinin then show how these institutional contexts shape the nature of the research process and raise issues of voice, ownership, and community.

J. Myron Atkin's essay (chapter 6) addresses "Research by Teachers to Change Education Policy" by asking how teachers, working collaboratively, can direct their inquiry toward modification of state and local policy that affects them. Based on the case of a group of mentor teachers who conducted a study designed to illuminate the development of California's Mentor Teacher Program, this chapter shows how the group identified trends they viewed as problematic and then set out to influence state policy. Atkin speculates on both the political problems in such a development and how teachers might move toward still greater influence in the arena of educational policy.

Sandra Hollingsworth and Janet Miller illustrate the personal and complex questions they face as researchers of their own teaching and collaborative research within the academy. In chapter 7 they consider, personally and problematically, the issue of rewriting gender equity and other feminist framings for teacher research. From varying feminist standpoints, the authors engage in a conversation about the role of shifting values, relations, and political imperatives in accomplishing the social and political changes afforded by teacher research.

PROSPECTS FOR THE PROFESSION THROUGH TEACHER RESEARCH

Section Four illustrates the professional applications of the arguments presented in Sections Two and Three. The authors here question the traditional structures in which educational knowledge is applied. Two chapters investigate the structures of preservice education and staff development programs which would encourage teacher researchers to engage in self- or codirected-inquiry. Another chapter suggests a way that curriculum and instruction might be examined and rewritten by professional teachers, using the processes of teacher research. The final chapter focuses on appropriate institutional structures that would support teacher research as part of professional life.

In chapter 8, Marilyn Cochran-Smith takes up the issue of "Teacher Education and Preservice Teacher-Research." Can prospective teachers learn to be both educators and activists? Can they learn to regard themselves as agents for change and to regard reform as an integral part of the social, intellectual, ethical, and political activity of teaching? Cochran-Smith argues that the only way student teachers can learn to reform teaching, or "teaching against the grain" as she puts it, is by working in the company of experienced teachers who are themselves struggling to be reformers in their own classrooms, schools, and communities. She provides an analysis of two approaches to preparing preservice teachers to teach against the grain, each representing a variation in teacher research, and she suggests that differences between them can be understood as the result of different underlying assumptions about knowledge, power, and language in teaching.

Chapter 9 provides an example of how curriculum could be rewritten by teacher researchers who take into account epistemological and sociopolitical aspects of the movement. Susan Noffke, Linda Mosher, and Christine Maricle studied the knowledge that was made available in Linda's and Christine's high school classrooms and the factors that affected its selection, organization, and treatment. The authors explore not only substantive issues arising from the teachers' curriculum-in-use, but also the process by which the analysis of curriculum might take place.

Chapter 10 addresses "Teacher Inquiry as Professional Staff Development." Virginia Richardson briefly analyzes the traditional literature on staff development and suggests that the conclusions emanating from this literature are based on a concept of staff development that is different from, perhaps antithetical to, the empowering concepts of teacher research. Richardson then develops an alternative concept of staff development that is based on critical inquiry and teacher research, using the results of a recent study of such a staff development process. Her analysis suggests that the traditional staff development literature may not be an appropriate guide for this different approach to staff development.

In chapter 11, Ann Lieberman and Lynne Miller write about the "Problems and Possibilities of Institutionalizing Teacher Research." Although many are embracing the idea of teacher research as a part of the move to further professionalize teaching and rethink their schools, the authors show how certain conditions must be in place (or at least developing) if such inquiry is to become an integral part of the school's norms and not just another "innovation" that will fade with the times. Lieberman and Miller describe how these conditions get built, what forms they take, and the persistent problems of time, leadership, context, and teachers' learning in context.

CONVERSATIONS AND CRITIQUES OF TEACHER RESEARCH AND EDUCATIONAL REFORM

If teacher research is concerned with the practical wisdom of professional teachers, their voices, and their articulation of the reality of understanding students and schools, then those voices have to be heard across the academy. Chapter 12 represents some classroom teachers' conversations around the issue of teacher research and educational reform. Eight teachers, led by Susan Threatt, ground their critical remarks in their particular teacher research activities.

In the final chapter of the book, Jonas Soltis responds to the areas of challenge the teacher research movement brings to educational reform and provides a thoughtful analysis not only of the various discourses represented in the descriptive chapters, but also of the movement's epistemological, sociopolitical, and professional implications.

NOTES

1. Herbert M. Kliebard, "What Happened to American Schooling in the First Part of the Twentieth Century?" in *Learning and Teaching the Ways of Knowing*, edited by Elliot Eisner, Eighty-fourth Yearbook of the National Society for the Study of Education, Part 2 (Chicago: University of Chicago Press, 1985), pp. 1-22.

2. Jonas F. Soltis, "Reform or Reformation?" *Educational Administration Quarterly* 24, no. 3 (1988): 241-245.

3. Susan E. Noffke, "The Social Context of Action Research: A Comparative and Historical Analysis" (Paper presented at the Annual Meeting of the American Educational Research Association, San Francisco, 1989); James McKernan, *Curriculum Action Research: A Handbook of Methods and Resources for the Reflective Practitioner* (New York: St. Martin's Press, 1991).

4. Jerome Bruner, *The Process of Education* (New York: Vintage Books, 1963).

5. Central Advisory Council for Education (England), *Children and Their Primary Schools*, A Report of the Central Advisory Council under the chairmanship of Lady Plowden (London, England: Her Majesty's Stationery Office, 1967).

6. Leslie Huling, "The Effects on Teachers of Participation in an Interactive Research and Development Project" (Paper presented at the Annual Meeting of the American Educational Research Association, New York, 1982); Beatrice Ward and William Tikunoff, "Collaborative Research" (Paper presented at a conference sponsored by the National Institute of Education on "The Implications of Research on Teaching for Practice," San Francisco, 1982).

7. John Elliott, *Action Research for Educational Change* (Buckingham, U.K.: Open University Press, Milton Keynes, 1991).

8. Donald Schön, *The Reflective Practitioner: How Professionals Think in Action* (New York: Basic Books, 1983).

9. Lawrence Stenhouse, *An Introduction to Curriculum Research and Development* (London: Heinemann Educational Books, 1975).

10. Hugh Sockett, *The Moral Basis for Teacher Professionalism* (New York: Teachers College Press, 1993).

11. Peter Posch, "Teacher Research and Teacher Professionalism" (Presentation at the International Conference on Teacher Research, Stanford University, April, 1992).

12. See, for example, Lisa Delpit, "Skills and Other Dilemmas of a Progressive Black Educator," *Harvard Educational Review* 56, no. 4 (1986): 379-385.

13. Wilfred S. Carr and Stephen Kemmis, *Becoming Critical: Education, Knowledge, and Action Research* (London: Falmer Press, 1986).

14. Boston Women's Teachers' Group (Sara Freedman, Jane Jackson, and Katherine Boles), "Teaching: An Imperilled 'Profession'," in *Handbook of Teaching and Policy*, edited by Lee S. Shulman and Gary Sykes (New York: Longman, 1983), pp. 261-269.

15. Marilyn Cochran-Smith, "Learning to Teach against the Grain," *Harvard Educational Review* 61, no. 3 (1991): 279-310; Andrew Gitlin, Karen Bringhurst, Mari Burns, Valerie Cooley, Beth Myers, Kathy Price, Robyn Russell, and Pat Tiess, *Teachers' Voices for School Change: An Introduction to Educative Research* (New York: Teachers College Press, 1992); Jesse Goodman, "Using a Methods Course to Promote Reflection and Inquiry among Preservice Teachers," in *Issues and Practices in Inquiry-oriented Teacher Education*, edited by B. Robert Tabachnick and Kenneth M. Zeichner (London: Falmer, 1991), pp. 56-76; John Smyth and Andrew Gitlin, *Teacher Evaluation: Educative Alternatives* (London: Falmer, 1989); Kenneth M. Zeichner and Daniel Liston, *Traditions of Reform and Reflective Teaching in U.S. Teacher Education*, Issue Paper 90-1 (E. Lansing, MI: National Center for Research on Teacher Education, 1990).

16. D. Jean Clandinin, Annie Davies, Pat Hogan, and Barbara Kennard, *Learning to Teach, Teaching to Learn: Stories of Collaboration in Teacher Education* (New York: Teachers College Press, forthcoming); Peter Grimmett and Alan McKinnon, "Craft Knowledge and the Education of Teachers," in *Review of Research in Education*, vol. 18, edited by Gerald Grant (Washington, DC: American Educational Research Association, 1992).

17. Jerome S. Bruner, "Narrative and Paradigmatic Modes of Thought," in *Learning and Teaching the Ways of Knowing*, edited by Elliot Eisner, Eighty-fourth Yearbook of the National Society for the Study of Education, Part 2 (Chicago: University of Chicago Press, 1985), pp. 97-115; F. Michael Connelly and D. Jean Clandinin, "Stories of Experience and Narrative Inquiry," *Educational Researcher* 19, no. 4 (1990): 2-13.

18. Mary F. Belenky, Blythe McVicker Clinchy, Nancy R. Goldberger, Jill M. Tarule, *Women's Ways of Knowing: The Development of Self, Voice, and Mind* (New York: Basic Books, 1986); Sandra Harding, *Whose Science? Whose Knowledge? Thinking from Women's Lives* (Ithaca, NY: Cornell University Press, 1991); bell hooks, *Talking Back* (Boston: South End Press, 1989); Susan Laird, "Reforming 'Women's True Profession': A Case for 'Feminist Pedagogy' in Teacher Education," *Harvard Educational Review* 56, no. 4 (1987): 449-463; Audrey Lourde, *Sister Outsider* (Freedom, CA: Crossing Press, 1984).

19. Sandra Hollingsworth, "Learning to Teach Literacy through Collaborative Conversation: A Feminist Approach," *American Educational Research Journal* 29, no. 2 (1992): 373-404.

20. Corrine Glesne, "Yet Another Role? The Teacher as Researcher," *Action in Teacher Education* 13, no. 1 (1991): 11.

21. Gaby Weiner, "Professional Self-knowledge versus Social Justice: A Critical Analysis of the Teacher-Researcher Movement," *British Educational Research Journal* 15, no. 1 (1989): 45.

22. Janet L. Miller, *Creating Space and Finding Voices: Teachers Collaborating for Empowerment* (Albany: State University of New York Press, 1990), p. 17.

23. Kenneth M. Zeichner, "Contradictions and Tensions in the Professionalization of Teaching and the Democratization of Schools," *Teachers College Record* 92, no. 3 (1990): 366.

24. Though this volume provides few examples of first-order teacher research, there are many excellent examples available. See Alaska Teacher Researchers, *The Far Vision: The Close Look* (Juneau: Alaska Teacher Research Network, 1991); Nancy Atwell, *In the Middle: Writing, Reading, and Learning with Adolescents* (Portsmouth, NH: Boynton/Cook, 1987); Louise M. Berman, Francine H. Hultgren, Diane Lee, Mary S. Rivkin, Jessie A. Roderick, and Ted Aoki, *Toward Curriculum for Being: Voices of Educators* (Albany: State University of New York Press, 1991); Robert Fecho,

"The Way They Talk: An English Teacher Ponders His Role" (Paper presented at the Ethnography in Education Research Forum, University of Pennsylvania, February 1991); M. R. Goodman and Jim Hahn, *Visions and Revisions: Research for Writing Teachers*, vol. 2, no. 1 (Davis, CA: Center for Cooperative Educational Research, University of California, Davis, 1990); Dixie Goswami and P. Stillman, *Reclaiming the Classroom: Teacher Research as an Agency for Change* (Upper Montclair, NJ: Boynton/ Cook, 1987); Sandra Hollingsworth, Mary Dybdahl, Anthony Cody, Leslie Minarik, Lisa Raffel, Jennifer Smallwood, and Karen Teel, *Sometimes I'd Rather Show Them Some Love: Relations, Conversations, and Feminist Research on Urban Literacy Education* (New York: Teachers College Press, forthcoming); Charles Naylor and Linda Coplin, *"Snap to It": A Teacher Union/Researcher Collaboration Using Photography* (Vancouver: British Columbia Teachers' Federation, 1992); J. D. Newman, ed., *Finding Our Own Way: Teachers Exploring Their Assumptions* (Portsmouth, NH: Heinemann, 1990); E. Sachar, *Shut Up and Let the Lady Teach: A Teacher's Year in a Public School* (New York: Poseidon Press, 1991); Kathleen Weiler, *Women Teaching for Change: Gender, Class, and Power* (South Hadley, MA: Bergin and Garvey, 1988).

25. Susan E. Noffke and David H. Hursh, "Action Research and Teacher Development: Some Unresolved Issues" (Paper presented at the Second Spencer Hall Invitational Conference on Teacher Development, London, Ontario, October 1992), p. 9.

26. Stephen Kemmis, "Emancipatory Action Research and Postmodernisms," *Curriculum Perspectives* 11, no. 4 (1991): 64.

27. Martha Nussbaum, "The Softness of Reason," *New Republic* 207 (July 13 and 20, 1992): 26-35.

Section Two
EPISTEMOLOGICAL ISSUES FOR TEACHER RESEARCH

Introduction

The authors of the chapters in this section set the tone for the volume by situating teacher research as a movement which raises the questions about issues of power and relations in models of knowing and knowledge. They question basic issues such as acceptable demonstrations of knowledge in the world of education, who gets to know, and for what purposes knowledge is used. They question the appropriate methods for educational research across research sites, purposes, and usages. They question the exclusion of teachers, people of color, and teacher educators from what gets to be known about learning in classrooms. They suggest that by situating the teacher research movement within such epistemological questions, it will become less of a new approach to knowledge in education and more of a process for determining not only the worth but the ethics and uses of that knowledge.

CHAPTER II

Inquiry, Knowledge, and Practice

SUSAN L. LYTLE AND MARILYN COCHRAN-SMITH

Over the past decade there has been renewed interest among teachers, teacher educators, and researchers in exploring the potential of teacher research as a mode of professional development, an avenue for generating practice-based knowledge about teaching, and a catalyst for social change in schools, universities, and communities. In the literature and in popular usage, terms such as "research," "action," "collaborative," "critical," and "inquiry" have been combined with one another and/or with the term "teacher" to signal a wide range of meanings and purposes. These terms and the various ways they are connected reflect surface as well as deeper differences—contrasting paradigms for research, conflicting conceptions of professional development for beginning and experienced teachers, and different assumptions about teachers' roles in the production and use of knowledge. This admixture of terms is not surprising given the complex ideological, multinational, and sociocultural history of efforts by teachers and their school- and university-based colleagues to document, understand, and alter practice. Considered together, the diverse initiatives and conceptions in the burgeoning teacher research movement prompt new questions about how teachers understand their work, how they create and use interpretive frameworks, and how inquiry functions to inform and alter classroom practice as well as the cultures of teaching. In short, current iterations of teacher research have helped to reopen and reframe basic epistemological questions about the relationships that obtain among inquiry, professional knowledge, and teaching practice and about the implications of these for school reform and social change.

As we have argued,[1] the concept of teacher research itself invites us to question the common assumption that knowledge for and about

---

Susan L. Lytle is an Assistant Professor in the Graduate School of Education, University of Pennsylvania. Marilyn Cochran-Smith is an Associate Professor of Education at the same institution.

teaching should be primarily "outside-in," that is, generated at the university and then used in schools, a position that suggests the unproblematic transmission of knowledge from a source to a destination. Rather, implicit in all versions of teacher research, no matter how disparate, is the notion that knowledge for teaching is "inside/outside," a juxtaposition that calls attention to teachers as knowers and to the complex and distinctly nonlinear relationships of knowledge and teaching as they are embedded in local contexts and in the relations of power that structure the daily work of teachers and learners in both the schools and the university.

The growing complexity in the field of teacher research and the fundamental epistemological questions it engenders make it clear that we need theoretical frameworks that elaborate and interrogate these and other questions as played out in particular school and university communities. Certainly there are a variety of disciplinary and interdisciplinary perspectives from which theoretical frameworks for teacher research might emerge. However, we are working from the premise that, like other forms of action- and practitioner-based research,[2] teacher research is or has the potential to be a kind of praxis,[3] or a research process embedded in the critical intersections of theory and practice wherein the relationships between knowers and known are significantly altered. It follows, then, that theoretical frameworks and other analytical tools for understanding and interrogating teacher research must also be grounded in practice and emerge from these intersections.

In this chapter we propose a theoretical framework for teacher research—a framework that has evolved from the dialectic of university-based research, teaching, and teacher education over a relatively long period of time. Our framework centers around the questions that are made visible when the boundaries of research and practice are blurred: questions about the definition and types of teacher research, the status of teacher research as a form of research on teaching, the nature and function of the knowledge that is created when teachers do research, and the implications of teacher research for the construction of a knowledge base, for teacher education and professional development, and for the politics of school and university relationships. The framework we propose also suggests a research agenda for further conceptual and empirical study, particularly for examining in local contexts the relationships among teacher inquiry, professional knowledge, and practice.

Teacher Research: Toward a Theoretical Framework

DEFINING AND POSITIONING TEACHER RESEARCH

Process-product research, which has dominated research on teaching over the last two decades, foregrounds the actions of teachers and attempts to capture the activity of teaching by identifying a set of discrete behaviors reproducible from one teacher and one classroom to the next. Qualitative or interpretive studies of teaching, on the other hand, provide detailed descriptive accounts of customary school and classroom events that shed light on their meanings for the participants involved. Although these two paradigms for research on teaching diverge in many ways, they are strikingly similar in the sense that neither foregrounds the teacher's role in the generation of knowledge about teaching and learning, and both, at times, even make that role invisible. The *Handbook of Research on Teaching*,[4] described on its book jacket as "the definitive guide to what we know about teachers, teaching, and the learning process," does not contain a single research review written by a school-based teacher, nor are published accounts of teachers' work cited. In most of the studies included, teachers are the objects of researchers' investigations. Missing from the field of research on teaching, then, are the voices of teachers themselves, the questions that teachers ask, and the interpretive frames that teachers use to understand and improve their own classroom practices. Those who have daily access, extensive expertise, and a clear stake in improving classroom practice have no formal ways for their knowledge of classroom teaching and learning to become part of the literature on teaching.

Teacher research: A definition. Teacher research, which we define as systematic and intentional inquiry carried out by teachers in their own schools and classrooms, has the potential to make accessible some of the expertise of teachers and to provide the university and the school communities with unique perspectives on teaching and learning. We base our definition in part on the work of Lawrence Stenhouse,[5] who defines research in general as "systematic, self-critical enquiry," and in part on an ongoing survey of the literature of teacher writing. In many of its recent iterations, teacher research has been thought of almost exclusively as classroom- or school-based studies[6] conducted by teachers and resembling university-based studies in conventions, methods, and forms.[7] We wish to emphasize, however, that there already exists a wide array of both empirical and conceptual work initiated by teachers that is appropriately regarded as research. In the typology we have proposed, we include teachers' empirical research, which involves the collection, analysis, and interpretation of data gathered from their own schools and classrooms and which takes the form of journals, oral inquiries, or studies, as well as teachers' conceptual research, which consists of theoretical work or the analysis of ideas and which typically appears in the form of essays on classroom and school life or on the nature of research itself.

Journals are accounts of classroom life in which teachers record observations, analyze their experiences, and reflect on and interpret their practices over time.[8] Similar in some ways to ethnographic field notes, they capture the immediacy of teaching, and because they stand as a written record of practice, they provide teachers with a way to revisit, reanalyze, and reevaluate their experiences. In dramatic contrast to the certainty of some of the instructional principles asserted in the literature on effective teaching, journals also reveal the inherent uncertainty and tentativeness of teaching. Clearly more than anecdotal records or loose chronological accounts of particular classroom activities, teachers' journals provide access to the ways teachers construct and reconstruct interpretive perspectives using rich data about many of the central issues of teaching, learning, and schooling. As systematic intentional inquiry, journals are made up of a unique juxtaposition of classroom vignettes and more general assertions and interpretations through teachers' eyes and in teachers' voices.

Teachers' oral inquiries are unique in our typology of teacher research in that they are by definition collaborative, oral, and social. These are procedures in which two or more teachers jointly research their experiences by examining particular educational concepts, texts, examples of students' work, and other classroom and school data.[9] The primary outcome of oral inquiries, during which teachers build on one another's insights, is the conjoined understanding of the participants. Not simply synonymous with teacher talk, oral inquiries follow specific, theoretically grounded procedures and routines, require extensive preparation and collection of data, and rely on careful documentation. When documentary records of oral inquiries are preserved, they reveal the ways teachers relate particular cases to theories of practice and construct perspectives for problem posing and problem solving.

The category of classroom studies most closely resembles university-based research and encompasses most of what others currently term teacher research. In classroom studies, teachers and their students "formulate questions about language and learning, design and carry out inquiries, reflect on what they have learned, and tell others about it."[10] Although our definition of classroom studies is essentially the same as this one and others common in the teacher research literature, we see studies as one among four types of teacher research. Studies often address significant issues that academics are also researching, among them: discrepancies between the intended and the enacted curriculum; authority, power, and autonomy in classrooms; and the culture of the classroom as a social construction of students and teachers. Teachers' evolving questions in these areas often suggest avenues of inquiry that the university community has not considered or found important.

In conceptual research, teachers recollect and reflect on their experiences to construct an argument about teaching, learning, or schooling. Drawing on students' work and classroom observations, for which there may or may not be complete or written records, teachers theorize about students' learning and development, the school as workplace, professional growth across contexts, and sources of knowledge for teaching. Unlike journals and oral inquiries, which are initially intended only for the participating teachers themselves, essays select examples that provide for a more public audience a kind of "evidentiary warrant" for the general assertions that are made.[11] Rather than disqualifying this work because it is often personal, retrospective, and based on the "narrow" perspective of a single teacher, it is our view that these characteristics are part of what recommends it. The essay form itself, which builds on the dialectic between argument and evidence, provides a unique context for teacher research.

Teacher research and research on teaching. Comparison of teacher research with university-based research involves a complicated set of assumptions and relationships that often act as barriers to enhancing our knowledge base about teaching. Researchers in the academy tend to equate "knowledge about teaching" with the high-status information attained through traditional modes of inquiry. Teacher research, if simply compared with university research, can easily be found wanting. We want to argue here, however, that such a comparison is not only not useful but also ultimately condescending. Instead, we have argued that we need to explore the ways that teacher research is both like and unlike traditional research on teaching without assuming at the outset that the goals, conventions, and evaluative criteria of the two are necessarily the same.

Research on teaching is generally conducted by professional researchers based at universities or research and development centers.

Although some teacher researchers are university-based teachers who study their own teaching,[12] most are classroom teachers in K-12 or adult programs and student teachers. Some teacher researchers work on collaborative research projects with university-based researchers or teacher educators;[13] others form research partnerships with their teacher colleagues[14] or with their own students.[15] Unlike the academic research community which is organized to provide formal and informal structures to support research on teaching, however, the community of teacher researchers is disparate, and there are few structures that on the one hand encourage teacher autonomy and initiative, but on the other hand also recognize that teacher research occurs within the context of broad-based efforts of school improvement. Variations in the efforts of the Office of Educational Research and Improvement, the National Council of Teachers of English, and other organizations reflect the complexity of the problem.

In university-based research on teaching, questions generally emerge from careful study in a discipline or multiple disciplines and from analysis of the existing theoretical and empirical literature. Although questions are sometimes negotiated with teachers when classroom data are collected, they are referenced to the relevant major published work in the field. The questions of teacher researchers, on the other hand, generally emerge from problems of practice—from discrepancies between intention and reality or between theory or research and practice. As such, they are highly reflexive and referenced primarily to the immediate classroom and school context.

University-based research on teaching is intended to produce findings for application and use outside of the context in which they were developed. These are often reported either as specific teaching procedures that have been correlated with increased student learning or as interpretations and analyses of the social and cultural construction of teaching and learning. The findings of teacher research, on the other hand, are chiefly intended for application and use within the contexts in which they were developed; they generally take the form of enhanced conceptual frameworks, altered practices, and reconstructed curricula. Although these findings are not necessarily motivated by a need to generalize beyond the immediate case, they are in fact often relevant to a wide variety of contexts. Teachers are uniquely situated to observe learners over long periods of time and in a variety of academic and social situations, to analyze events in terms of insider knowledge about the culture of the community, school, and classroom, and to connect the events of classroom life to the roles and responsibilities of teachers. These conditions set the perspectives of teacher researchers apart and make it possible for their findings to be both more general than those that concentrate on the effectiveness of specific techniques, materials, or instructional methods and more specific than those that explore the meanings of customary school and classroom events.

Not only is the status of teacher questions and findings at issue, but there is also considerable disagreement about the way in which teacher research is theoretically grounded.[16] In university-based research on teaching, theoretical frameworks are both derived from and intended to generate theories related to teaching, learning, and schooling within a discipline or multiple disciplines such as psychology, linguistics, anthropology, sociology, and literature. In teacher research, on the other hand, theoretical frameworks are derived from professional practice as well as from disciplines related to teaching, learning, and schooling. If we regard teachers' theories as sets of interrelated conceptual frameworks grounded in practice, then teacher researchers are revealed as both users and generators of theory.

In university-based studies of teaching, standard paradigms of quantitative and interpretive research are employed, as are conventional norms for data collection, analysis, and evidence. The objectivity and relative detachment of the researcher are assumed. In many respects the forms of documentation in teacher research resemble those of interpretive research: field notes and mechanical recordings of classroom events, interviews with classroom and school participants, and collection of documents and artifacts. A strength of teacher research, like university-based qualitative research, is that it entails multiple data sources that can be used to confirm and/or illuminate one another. In teacher research, however, the position of the researcher relative to the researched is not detachment, but long-term, intense, and direct professional involvement. This means that the goal of the researcher is not objectivity but systematic subjectivity, a position that leads to new paradigms for research on teaching and to the construction of alternative modes of discourse and analysis.

RETHINKING THE KNOWLEDGE BASE

Since John Dewey's[17] writings at the beginning of this century, scholars and researchers have devoted considerable attention to understanding the relationships of knowledge and teaching. From various disciplinary perspectives and research paradigms, scholars have asked what it means to know about teaching—what can be known, how it can be known, who has the authority to know, and how knowledge can or should be used for theoretical and practical purposes. Over the past several decades there have been a variety of efforts to codify a knowledge base for teaching, as is evidenced by the plethora of "knowledge base" handbooks that has appeared. While we are not suggesting that the knowledge contained in these handbooks or other similar volumes is of no use to teachers, we have argued that underlying volumes like these is a theory of knowledge that privileges one source of knowledge—that of university researchers—over others. The implication that the knowledge that makes teaching a profession comes from authorities outside the profession itself and that what makes teachers professional is using this knowledge base in their daily practice is exclusionary and disenfranchising. It stipulates that knowing the knowledge base for teaching—what university researchers have discovered—is *the* privileged way to know about teaching and is that which "distinguishes more productive teachers from less productive ones."[18]

If, however, we take seriously the idea that teacher research is a legitimate form of research on teaching, then we need to develop a different theory of knowledge for teaching, a different epistemology that regards inquiry by teachers themselves as a distinctive and important way of knowing about teaching. From this perspective, fundamental questions about knowing, knowers, and what can be known have different answers. Teachers are among those who have the authority to know, and what is worth knowing includes what teachers who are researchers in their own classrooms can know through systematic inquiry. With this different epistemology, teacher research, which is currently marginalized in the field, can contribute to a fundamental reconceptualization of the notion of knowledge for teaching, and through inquiry teachers can play a role in reinventing the conventions of interpretive social science, just as feminist researchers and critical ethnographers have done, by making problematic the relationships of researcher and researched, knowledge and authority, and subject and object.[19] Teacher researchers are uniquely positioned to provide a truly emic (or insider) perspective on teaching, a perspective that makes visible the ways students and teachers together construct knowledge. When teachers do research, they draw on interpretive frameworks built from their own histories and intellectual interests, and, because the research process is embedded in practice, the relationship between knower and known is significantly altered. This obviates the necessity of "translating findings" in the conventional sense, and moves teacher research toward praxis, or critical reflection on practice.[20]

In order to theorize about teacher research, then, we need to consider the contribution of teacher inquiry to a different epistemology of teaching. We have been trying to make the case that research by teachers is a significant way of knowing about teaching that generates both *local knowledge* developed and used by teachers for themselves and their immediate communities as well as *public knowledge* useful to the larger school and university communities.

TEACHER RESEARCH AND LOCAL KNOWLEDGE

In his volume of essays on interpretive anthropology, Geertz[21] writes about the difficulties involved in representing emic, or insider, knowledge and meaning perspectives. He suggests that ultimately anthropologists can not really represent "local knowledge"—what native inhabitants see—but only what they see through, that is, their interpretive perspectives on their own experiences. Borrowing Geertz's term, we use local knowledge to signal both what teachers come to know about their own knowledge through teacher research and also what communities of teacher researchers come to know when they build knowledge collaboratively.

Individual teachers: Knowing one's own knowledge. In arguing for an epistemology of teaching that includes the knowledge generated by teacher researchers, we begin with the assumption that through their interactions, teachers and students together construct classroom life and the learning opportunities that are available. Essentially, then, regardless of stance or pedagogy, teachers and students negotiate what counts as knowledge in the classroom, who can have knowledge, and how knowledge can be generated, challenged, and evaluated. Through analysis of a series of cases of teacher research across institutional levels and school cultures, we have demonstrated in detail elsewhere that teacher research is a way for teachers to understand how this happens in their own classrooms and how their own interpretations of classroom events are shaped—essentially, we have argued that teacher research is a way for teachers to come to know their own knowledge.

When teacher researchers initiate and conduct classroom research, for example, they often invite their students to conduct classroom inquiries that bring unexpected insights into their own work.[22] Whether experienced teachers or student teachers, teacher researchers see their classrooms as sites of inquiry into students' learning, and they approach the planning of curriculum and instruction with central questions about the teacher's role.[23] As they analyze data collected over time, teacher researchers may discover that their assumptions about students have been largely incorrect.[24] Research allows them to expand their interpretive frameworks and their ideas about where to look and what to look at in order to understand students' efforts to respond and revise their classroom efforts. When teachers treat classroom occurrences as data, they see discrete and sometimes disparate events as parts of larger patterns of behavior and interpretation. Rereading the texts of their classrooms allows teacher researchers to make visible their own characteristic ways of interpreting students' behavior and makes it possible for them to revisit and revise them.

Teacher researchers also study interventions that take place over time as groups of teachers and students construct and reconstruct the curriculum.[25] They explore the dynamic relationships that evolve among talk, writing, choice and access, changing roles, and student achievement. Inquiries of this kind involve working with students to renegotiate the meaning of student ability, construct new routes to textual understanding, and alter views about knowers and knowing in schools and classrooms.[26] They diminish traditional distinctions between researcher and researched by making the agenda for the class public and by involving students in ongoing analysis of the data.[27] In this way teachers both research their own teaching and teach as a way of doing research. Classrooms with a feminist view of critical pedagogy, which explicitly makes issues of knowledge, authority, and institutional hierarchies parts of the curriculum,[28] are particularly important as strategic sites for understanding what it means for teachers to know their own knowledge through inquiry.

In contrast to the implications of "knowledge base" efforts, then, we argue here that what distinguishes more productive from less productive teachers may *not* be mastery of a knowledge base, but rather standing in a different relationship to one's own knowledge, to one's students as knowers, and to knowledge generation in the field. Freire has argued that educators and their students are "knowing subjects," constantly learning from the process of teaching. For him, "education is a pedagogy of knowing."[29] There is a dynamic interaction among teachers' stances toward themselves as knowers, their students as knowers and learners, and their knowledge of disciplinary subject matter.[30] When teachers redefine their own relationships to knowledge about teaching and learning, they often begin to reconstruct their classrooms and to offer different invitations to their students to learn and know. When they change their relationships to knowledge, they may also realign their relationships to the brokers of knowledge and power in schools and universities.

Teacher research communities: Knowing collectively. We have defined intellectual communities of teacher researchers as networks of individuals who enter with others into a search for meaningful work lives[31] and who regard their research as part of larger efforts to transform teaching, learning, and schooling. Through inquiry, groups of teachers conjoin their understandings to create local knowledge in and for their own communities. Because teachers in different settings have diverse goals, activities, and ways of doing research, there is considerable variation in the knowledge constructed in different groups. We are arguing here that just as the knowledge generated by individual teachers ought to count in an epistemology of teaching, so should the knowledge generated by particular communities of teachers.

Teacher research functions as a way of knowing for the local community in a variety of ways within single institutions and within groups who come together from several institutions to form a community. Groups of teachers from the same institution may use inquiry as a way to develop curriculum, for example, moving back and forth between collaborative curriculum building and data gathering in individual classrooms. Through co-teaching and mentoring arrangements, descriptions of students' work, reflections on key concepts, descriptive reviews, task forces and working groups on curriculum, and analyses of other classroom data, groups explore their own values and assumptions about learners' appropriate behavior, develop new and revised curriculum, rethink the learning tasks set for students, and make specific recommendations for working with individual students or classes. Developing curricula through analysis of data is radically different from the process of curriculum typically used by many schools and school districts. When groups of teachers develop curriculum through inquiry, they use data from their own classrooms (e.g., students' work, actual lesson and unit plans, descriptions of individual learners, syllabi, texts, and teacher-made materials and assignments) to pose problems, sort out commonalities and differences in perspectives and values, and build instructional frameworks. Any time groups of teachers from the same institution come together to consider issues of curriculum and instruction, there is the potential for building knowledge for the local community. This is similar to earlier propositions that schools and school systems have the potential to be centers for inquiry,[32] and to recent calls for school-university partnerships wherein experienced and beginning teachers work together with university faculty in professional development schools.[33] And of course the notion that curriculum construction is a form of knowledge making is an essential part of the history of teacher research. As Stenhouse reminds us, curriculum is the medium through which the teacher can learn about the art of teaching.[34]

Rather than having a shared physical and institutional context, other teacher groups cross institutional boundaries and share a broad intellectual agenda, which sometimes sets them apart from one another. Cross-institutional communities of teachers pose distinctive problems for themselves, and hence build knowledge in domains different from one another. Often this is a reflection of their origins and their affiliations with various programs, universities, and institutes or with particular ideologies. In each case, the community of teachers constructs knowledge for its own consideration and use. By investigating a variety of topics, teachers build knowledge and develop local criteria for evaluating questions, evidence, and interpretive frameworks.

TEACHER RESEARCH AND PUBLIC KNOWLEDGE

In addition to its function as a way of knowing for teacher researchers in their local communities, teacher research has the potential to be a significant way of knowing for the larger communities of both school-based teachers and university-based researchers and teacher educators, as well as policymakers and school administrators. Teacher research has particular potential for transforming the university-generated knowledge base. As Philip Jackson argued in a recent address to the American Educational Research Association, we have recently witnessed "a decline of interest on the part of many of us in what used to be looked upon as our main business, which was the discovery of rules and principles of teaching and of running schools that would prove to be universal or nearly so in application and invariant or nearly so over time. . . . In its place we have substituted the much more modest goal of trying to figure out what's happening *here and now* or what went on *there and then*."[35]

Jackson's discussion suggests to us that there may be several ways that teacher research is a way of knowing for the larger community of both school-based and university-based teachers and researchers. The teacher researcher is a native inhabitant of the research site—not a participant observer over a bounded period of time but a permanent and "observant participant"[36] who knows the research and context in its richest sense of shared "webs of significance."[37] Because it often investigates from an emic perspective topics that are already widely researched by university-based researchers, teacher research is a source of new knowledge in many of the domains of teaching and learning, and it also has the potential to open up new areas of study. Further, because teaching requires simultaneous attention to many agendas and because it also provides the opportunity for constant observation of particular phenomena, such as children's drawing or writing, teacher-researchers' analytic frameworks are extraordinarily rich and complex. Teacher research is well positioned to produce precisely the kind of knowledge currently needed in the field.

Almost by definition, teacher research is case study—the unit of analysis is typically the individual child, the classroom, or the school. Whether and how case studies function in knowledge generation is part of a larger set of questions about the relationships between qualitative research and practice, which have long been topics of considerable debate. As Eisner points out, this debate hinges on what is meant by the accumulation of knowledge in a field—on whether we mean that knowledge accumulates in the sense that dollars and garbage do, a view that presumes that knowledge is an "inert material" that can be collected, stored, and stockpiled, or whether we see knowledge growth in the social sciences as "more horizontal than vertical,"[38] not at all like building with blocks but yielding multiple conceptual frameworks that others use to understand their own situations. We think that with teacher research, knowledge will accumulate as communities of school-based and university-based teachers and researchers read and critique each other's work, document and perhaps disseminate their responses, and create a network of citations and allusions, and hence begin to build a different kind of interpretive universe.

The domain in which teacher-researchers in K-12 and adult programs have been most active is language and literacy, where teachers have studied their own and their students' experiences reconstructing the traditional language/literacy curriculum. What we know from each domain of teacher research is not simply a series of discrete findings, but instead a sense of the multiple perspectives teachers bring to their work, which together generate unique interpretive universes. None of these examples of teacher research is what Calkins has referred to as "field-testing" research in which practitioners test out new ideas that they are already convinced are exemplary. The goal of teacher research is not product testing, but "the development, assessment, and revision of theories that inform practice."[39] Teacher research, then, is a way of knowing for the larger communities of teachers and researchers because it contributes both conceptual frameworks and important information about some of the central domains of the knowledge base.

Finally, research conducted by preservice and in-service teachers provides a window into the nature of their perspectives on teaching, learning, and schooling. This method of data collection contrasts with some of the more common methods for exploring teachers' thinking and knowledge including stimulated recall, policy capturing, and repertory grid techniques, which are often supplemented by interviews, observations, and narrative descriptions.[40] Of necessity, these methods typically focus on simplified and researcher-created tasks, constructs, or a priori categories. Consequently, these techniques do not account for the ways in which teacher inquiry is mediated by, and essentially embedded in, the cultures of classrooms, schools, school districts, and teacher research communities. Because teacher research emerges from praxis and because it preserves teachers' own words and analyses, it has the potential to be a particularly robust method for understanding whether and how preservice and in-service teachers construct their knowledge and theories of practice, how these may change and develop over time, and the impact of these on teaching and learning.

KNOWLEDGE AND POWER

As teacher research of various kinds accumulates and is more widely disseminated, it presents a more and more radical challenge to current assumptions about the relationships of theory and practice, schools and universities, and inquiry and reform. Research by teachers represents a distinctive way of knowing about teaching and learning that over time will alter, not just add to, what we know in the field. Because we see teacher research as both interpretive and critical, however, we do not anticipate that its contribution is likely to be in the form of generalizations about teaching (this time from the "inside" perspective), nor is it the case that teacher research will be benign and evolutionary, a process of accumulating new knowledge and gradually admitting new knowers to the fold. Rather the different theory of knowledge, upon which teacher research is predicated and to which it contributes, will fundamentally redefine the notion of knowledge for teaching, altering the locus of the knowledge base and realigning the practitioner's stance in relationship to knowledge generation in the field.

Legitimating the knowledge that comes from practitioners' research on their own practice is a critical dimension of change in both school and university cultures. In challenging the university's hegemony in the generation of expert knowledge for the field, teacher research also challenges dominant views of staff development and preservice training as the transmission and implementation of knowledge from outside to inside schools. These transformations will inevitably cause conflict as those traditionally disenfranchised begin to play increasingly important roles in generating knowledge and in deciding how it ought to be interpreted and used. Furthermore, because teacher research makes visible the ways teachers and students negotiate power, authority, and knowledge in classrooms and schools, it has the potential to alter profoundly the cultures of teaching—how teachers work with their students toward a more critical and demo-cratic pedagogy, how they build intellectual communities of col-leagues who are both educators and activists, and how they position themselves in relationship to school administrators, policymakers, and university-based experts as agents of systemic change.

In the preceding theoretical framework, we have defined and positioned teacher research as a powerful form of research on teaching, and we have argued that because it is a distinctive way of generating both local and public knowledge, it has far-reaching implications for the epistemology of teaching. In the section that follows, we argue that this conception of teacher inquiry also has profound implications for the construction and reconstruction of teacher education in both schools and universities and across the professional lifespan. Drawing on the work of teachers and teacher educators in two programs, one at the preservice and one at the in-service level, we describe some of the features of teacher education that is teacher-research centered and congruent with this conception. Programs of this kind function as strategic research sites[41] for examining over time the complex interrelationships of inquiry, knowledge, and practice.

Reconstructing Professional Development:
Implications of Teacher Research for
Teacher Education across the Lifespan

Implicit in the notion of teacher research is a view of teaching as primarily an intellectual activity that hinges on what Zumwalt[42] calls the "deliberative" ability to reflect on, and make wise decisions about, practice. From this perspective, teaching is assumed to be complicated and intentional—an activity requiring a great breadth and depth of professional knowledge and judgment in conditions that are inherently uncertain.[43] In contrast to a more technical view that teaching hinges on the use of particular techniques applied in various situations, a deliberative view of teaching regards teachers as professionals who use their knowledge to construct perspectives, choose actions, manage dilemmas, interpret and create curricula, make strategic choices, and to a large extent define their own teaching responsibilities.[44] Teacher researchers regard these tasks as opportunities for systematic, intentional inquiry and regard the inquiries of others in their communities as opportunities for rethinking their own assumptions and practices.

Treating teaching as an inquiry process means that teacher researchers stand in a different relationship to their own knowledge, to their students as knowers, and to knowledge generation in the field. Early in the century Dewey emphasized the importance of teachers' reflecting on their practices and integrating their observations into their emerging theories of teaching and learning.[45] He urged educators to be both consumers and producers of knowledge about teaching, both teachers and students of classroom life. Dewey's notion of teachers as students of learning prefigures the concept of teachers as reflective practitioners more recently developed in the work of Schön and others. Unlike those who characterize teaching as the acquisition of technical skills, Schön[46] depicts professional practice as an intellectual process of posing and exploring problems identified by teachers themselves.

When teachers redefine their own relationships to knowledge about teaching and learning, they reconstruct their classrooms and begin to offer different invitations to their students to learn and know. A view of teaching as research is connected to a view of learning as constructive, meaning-centered, and social. What we are emphasizing here is the reciprocal relationship between theories about teaching and theories about learning. Teachers who are actively researching their own practices provide opportunities for their students to become similarly engaged.[47] Researching teachers create classroom environments in which there are researching students[48]—students ask, not just answer questions; pose, not just solve problems; and help to construct curriculum out of their own linguistic and cultural resources, rather than just receive preselected and predigested information. As Britton reminds us, "every lesson should be for the teacher, an inquiry, some further discovery, a quiet form of research."[49]

This view of teaching and knowledge for teaching has profound consequences for teacher education and professional development. When the generation of a knowledge base is primarily associated with a technical view of teaching, and when it is assumed to be constructed only by university-based researchers, then the teacher's role is clear. She is expected to learn the skills of effective teaching and also learn how to apply them to her practice. When the professionalization of teaching is linked to this technical view, staff development is regarded as a vehicle for transmitting skills to teachers rather than as a process for collaborative inquiry, and the teacher has no role to play in the generation of a knowledge base. In contrast, an inquiry-based view of teaching and professional development is premised on the notion that learning from teaching ought to be regarded as the primary task of teacher education across the professional lifespan.[50] By "learning from teaching" we mean that inquiry ought to be regarded as an integral part of the activity of teaching and a critical basis for decisions about practice. Further, we mean that classrooms and schools ought to be treated as research sites and sources of knowledge, which are most effectively accessed when teachers collaboratively interrogate and enrich their theories of practice. This argument is based in part on the assumption that the increasing diversity of America's schools and schoolchildren and the increasing complexity of the tasks educators face render global solutions to problems and monolithic strategies for effective teaching impossible. Hence what is required in both preservice and in-service teacher education programs are processes that prompt teachers and teacher educators to construct their own questions and then begin to develop courses of action that are valid in their local contexts and communities.

When learning from teaching is taken to be the primary task of teachers across the lifespan, a distinctive set of assumptions about knowledge, collaboration, and inquiry obtains. Because teachers are assumed to be among those who have the authority to know—that is, to construct knowledge about teaching, learning, and schooling—and because their research becomes a significant part of a redefined knowledge base for teaching, knowledge from the academy is not accepted unproblematically but rather is taken to be rich and generative, providing conceptual frameworks, detailed information from other contexts, new problems and dilemmas, confirming and disconfirming evidence, and grist for further deliberations. This stance on knowledge is interdependent with a concept of teachers as collaborators[51] rather than simply co-workers or cooperators. More and less experienced teachers as well as teacher educators labor together to construct their understandings of individual learners, classroom interactions, and the cultures of schooling by closely observing students, reflecting on experiences, and reading and writing widely in content and pedagogy.

If inquiry is to be an integral part of teaching across the professional lifespan, then we need intellectual, social and organizational structures supportive of beginning and experienced teachers' learning and collaboration. A teacher education curriculum that is based on teacher research at both the preservice and in-service levels provides this critical link between inquiry and professional development. Using examples from preservice education (Project START) and in-service education (The Philadelphia Writing Project), the sections that follow provide a model of the goals, the social and organizational structures, and the learning opportunities that can provide the context for teachers to learn from their teaching across the professional lifespan.

ORGANIZATIONAL GOALS AND STRUCTURES

Teacher education programs based on teacher research assume that teachers make curricular and instructional decisions, construct their own interpretations through the processes of inquiry, and play significant roles in the shaping of policy and practice. Project START (Student Teachers as Researching Teachers), a fifth-year program in elementary education for liberal arts graduates, was conceived five years ago by Philadelphia area teachers and teacher educators at the University of Pennsylvania to provide intensive, year-long student teaching experiences and closer links between university and schools. Working within long-standing traditions of research-based and theory-based methods and foundations courses in teacher education, project designers took what Dewey calls a "laboratory" view of the practical work in teacher education, which emphasizes the intellectual strategies of teachers, in contrast with an "apprenticeship" view, which has the more immediate goal of training students to perform as efficient workers in the classroom. In Project START, each student teacher works in the same classroom over the course of one school year, beginning on the first teaching day and working two days per week for the first four months, and then working five days per week for the next four months.

In preservice programs such as Project START, student teachers are invited into a community of school-based and university-based learners and, essentially, into a way of life as teachers that emphasizes reform and inquiry across the professional lifespan. Prospective teachers are assumed to be part of a larger struggle with a responsibility to reform, not just replicate, standard school practices by "teaching against the grain,"[52] a skill learned by struggling along with experienced teachers to be reformers in particular schools and classrooms. Toward this end, students progress through the program as a cohort, participating simultaneously in university-based coursework and school-based fieldwork experiences. Courses are designed to prompt critical perspectives on teaching, learning, and schooling as well as theoretical frameworks for learning from children and constructing subject matter curriculum.

In this approach to preservice teacher education, critical program activities are organized at both the university and school sites. Project START provides monthly university seminars as a context for student teachers, experienced teachers, and teacher educators to meet over the course of a year to raise questions about teaching and learning across grades, schools, and school systems. Student teachers also attend school-based and outside-school professional development activities such as in-service workshops, faculty meetings, parent-teacher conferences, and teacher collaboratives with their cooperating teachers. The key school-site structure in Project START is the teacher-researcher team meeting, a weekly session of each sub-cohort of student teachers, cooperating teachers, and university supervisor. In these meetings, which feature classroom and school inquiries on topics selected by the individual group, participants share observations, raise questions, and suggest different ways of looking at, and thinking about, the social life of classrooms.

In teacher-research based in-service education such as The Philadelphia Writing Project (PhilWP), organizational structures are designed to connect the goals of the university and the schools, to create the context for teacher collaboration over time, and to emphasize the roles of teachers as writers, researchers, and reformers. Located at a graduate school of education at a research university in a major urban area, PhilWP is a school-university partnership and a site of the National Writing Project that reflects its origins and ongoing affiliation with a national model as well as the distinctive and dynamic features of a local culture. Begun by School District of Philadelphia teachers, University of Pennsylvania faculty, and other educators working to build a writing-across-the-curriculum initiative in the city schools, the project is a teacher collaborative, designed primarily to provide an intellectual community for urban teachers in the city system and to strengthen the district's efforts to reform and restructure schools. It shares with the national model fundamental assumptions about teacher-to-teacher in-service education, collaboration between schools and universities as partners, cross-grade and cross-discipline writing, staff development across the professional lifespan, teachers as writers, and practice as an important source of knowledge for teaching. As the project has evolved, participants have come to include not only K-12 teachers but also college teachers, school administrators, and adult literacy practitioners as well.

Such an approach to in-service professional development focuses on building an enduring intellectual community for teacher inquiry wherein teachers' explorations support the gradual transformation of the cultures of teaching and schooling for children, adolescents, and adults. In these communities, teachers' own classrooms, schools, and collegial relationships with other teachers provide critical sites for observation and inquiry; their ongoing research functions as a powerful medium for sharing daily experiences, for learning from one another, and for generating both local and public knowledge.

These PhilWP structures are intended ultimately to realign relationships between the schools and the university and to strengthen avenues for collegial learning within schools and districts. Summer and year-long institutes, for example, provide a unique environment for diverse groups of teachers to engage in intensive talking, reading, and writing about practice. Drawing on the prior knowledge and experience of teachers in the group and on the writings of other teachers, these institutes also use the research literature as a source of knowledge. This juxtaposition enables participants to investigate deeply their own histories as learners with a particular focus on what they have experienced as readers and writers of a particular race, class, and gender. To counter the isolation of experienced teachers, participants in teacher-research based in-service programs may also need periodic access to each others' classrooms during the school day through some program of cross-visitation.[53]

Designed with these goals and organizational structures, both preservice and in-service programs invite teachers into communities of learners and build and sustain professional networks. In turn, these communities emphasize reform, research, and renewal across the professional lifespan and thus support the restructuring and reform of schools and programs.

Teacher-research based preservice teacher education interrupts the role expectations of the novice-expert model common to many programs. Rather than imitating the instructional styles of their mentors, student teachers are expected to construct their own knowledge of teaching and learning, question theory-practice relationships, write about their work, and participate with their experienced mentors as inquiring professionals. Likewise, the primary role of cooperating teachers is not to demonstrate model teaching techniques and effective language. Cooperating teachers, who are selected for their commitment to curricular redesign, teacher research and publication, progressive education, grass-roots parent-teacher community groups, teacher collaboratives, or other teaching and school reform efforts, are expected to bring an inquiry-centered perspective to their roles as mentors and to articulate their own questions and frameworks to student teachers as they support students' initial forays into inquiry. Finally, the university supervisor, who spends considerable time learning the culture of the school site, getting to know school personnel, and observing in classrooms, is expected to function as co-learner and colleague rather than evaluator and broker of knowledge. In addition to regular consultations with students and cooperating teachers, supervisors share resources, facilitate weekly teacher-researcher meetings, and meet regularly with the other university staff members to inquire into their own work as teacher educators. Working with school and university mentors who inquire about their own work, call policies and procedures into question, and seek out ways to meet regularly with their colleagues provides student teachers with powerful role models for learning from teaching across the lifespan.

Similarly, in approaches to professional development at the in-service level, educators from schools, programs, and universities work together to redefine and restructure their roles in both the field and the university. Such programs deliberately interrupt role expectations associated with teachers as isolated practitioners and recipients or implementors of expert knowledge and thus alter the roles of university researchers as generators of knowledge and transmitters or trainers of others. In programs involving teachers, administrators, university faculty, and students, all participants—both school-based and university-based—construct and reconstruct their own knowledge of teaching and learning, question theory-practice relationships, and contribute to the creation of a new image of professionalism and scholarly work that makes activist inquiry fundamental in both schools and the university. In-service teachers, university professors, and other educators thus mediate the daily life of teaching or administering in schools and programs and their commitment to the larger political project of educational reform.

Teachers in research-based professional development programs regard restructuring their own roles in classrooms as central, so that students and their teachers as well as parents and others function as active and critical inquirers and constructors of knowledge and curriculum. At the university and in the school districts, teachers play new roles by designing and facilitating institutes for their peers, mentoring new teachers, presenting their research in graduate courses, offering their own classrooms as sites for collaborative inquiry, and contributing to the literature of the field by disseminating their own research on practice. In accord with their emphasis on teachers as researchers, such programs offer opportunities for teachers to assume new roles as writers and collaborators on grants, proposals, curricula, and school-university research projects. In preservice and in-service teacher-research based programs, participants at both schools and universities interrogate their practices, realign their relationships to knowledge and the brokers of knowledge, and assume leadership in advocating for school and university reform. By presenting and publishing their work in local, regional, and national forums, participants in these programs have the potential to inform others beyond their immediate community and to build networks of practitioners with common concerns and issues.

LEARNING OPPORTUNITIES, THEMES, AND STRATEGIES

In teacher research communities, groups of teachers engage in joint construction of knowledge through reading, writing, and oral inquiry. For example, through conversation they make their tacit knowledge more visible,[54] call into question assumptions about common practice, and generate data that make possible the consideration of alternatives. Some teacher research groups regularly conduct oral inquiries, while others do not use formal structures but talk in distinctive ways about their teaching. Teacher research communities use a wide range of texts, not all of which are published or disseminated. But the texts are essential to teachers' individual and collective gathering, recording, and analyzing data. They include teacher-researcher reports in the form of journals, essays, and studies as well as selections from the extensive theoretical and research literatures in the fields related to teaching and learning. Texts used by teachers in their communities also include the written records of teachers' deliberations, informal writing used to facilitate the talk of these groups, transcripts of class-room interactions and interviews, notes made of classroom observations, as well as drafts of teachers' plans and work in progress.

Course assignments, school- and university-site activities, in-house and regional publications and professional forums, and the larger professional community give participants in preservice teacher education programs opportunities to engage in many kinds of inquiry about schools and schooling.[55] Inquiry strategies in an elementary pre-service program, for example, may include critical discussion of com-mon readings, descriptive reviews of individual children, reflective conversations, cross-grade and cross-school observations, literature studies, journal writing, and collaborative analysis of children's work, anecdotal records, and excerpts from essays. Through structures such as weekly school-site meetings and monthly university-site seminars, student teachers have the chance to be both close observers and par-ticipants in the inquiry process. Student teachers can conduct small-scale classroom studies that provide opportunities for both active teaching and research on teaching. Small scale studies like these offer students opportunities to construct curriculum and develop pedagogy.

In in-service projects that are based on teacher research the most common structures for collaborative inquiry are smaller school-site or cross-school communities within the larger community which emerge from particular project affiliations and commitments.[56] Participants may include teachers and others who share an interest in topics such as interdisciplinary thematic curriculum, whole language as a theory of practice, issues of cultural and linguistic diversity, critical and inter-generational literacy and pedagogy, performance-based assessment, and/or collegial learning and teaching. Teacher inquiry groups vary in size, duration, leadership, activities, and supportive structures; they have in common participatory organization and collaborative teacher leadership, often with a particular emphasis on writing and inquiry as powerful modes of learning about teaching, students, and school and program improvement.

Preservice and in-service programs thus have in common many similar themes for inquiry, such as language and literacy, curriculum and pedagogy, issues of race, class, and gender, modes of assessment, community-school relationships, and the cultures of teaching, schooling, and reform. To promote an inquiry stance on teaching across the professional lifespan, both engage participants in a range of strategies for research including documentary processes[57] (critical discussion/writings about experiences and common readings, collaborative analyses of classroom data, cross-grade, cross-school, and cross-school system observations, discussions and writings, individual and collaborative journals, as well as case studies of students, classrooms and schools).

LEARNING FROM TEACHING

What is clear in teacher research-centered teacher education programs at both the preservice and in-service levels is that teacher research is not simply one in a diverse array of activities or techniques. Rather, the central ideas that underlie the framework that we have proposed in this chapter—that teaching is an intellectual activity and that teacher research is a way of knowing about teaching across the professional lifespan—require a concurrent and fundamental transformation of the institutional and curricular arrangements of teacher education. In keeping with this framework, the relationships of knowledge and power that structure traditional relationships of schools and universities would be altered. The inquiries conducted by teachers influence not only their own professional knowledge and practice, but also enable them to play increasingly important roles in the reform of schools. Finally, the reconstruction of teacher education as communities for inquiry has far-reaching implications for, and indeed requires, the parallel and reciprocal transformation of universities. Legitimating the knowledge that comes from practitioners' research on their own practice—whether in schools or universities—is thus a critical dimension of change in both cultures.

Toward a Research Agenda: Teacher Inquiry, Professional Knowledge, and School Reform

Limiting the official knowledge base for teaching to what academics have chosen to study and write about contributes to a number of problems, including discontinuity between what is taught in universities and what is taught in classrooms, teachers' ambivalence about the claims of academic research, and a general lack of information about classroom life from the inside. It is widely agreed that instructional reform depends upon tapping into, and supporting, teachers' potential to be thoughtful and deliberate architects of teaching and learning in their own classrooms, and is contingent upon members of the teaching profession developing their own systematic and intentional ways to scrutinize and improve their practices. Teacher research may function as one of the critical ways that teachers access and interrogate their own knowledge and thus shape the larger reform agenda.

Traditionally, scholars have not explored teacher inquiry as a way to generate knowledge about teaching or as a way to examine teachers' thinking. An important agenda for research on the nature and function of teacher inquiry itself would examine both how teachers learn from inquiry into practice—that is, how they generate knowledge from practice by conducting systematic inquiry into their own classrooms and schools, and how that knowledge can be used by teacher researchers as well as the wider community of educators to understand and ultimately improve teaching, learning, and schooling. The aim would be to examine the roles of teacher inquiry in the generation, adaptation, and utilization of knowledge for teaching and for the improvement of teaching in individual classrooms and in local communities of teachers. Understanding these complex interrelationships among individual teachers' efforts, the local knowledge of teacher research communities, and the more public knowledge of the profession requires both case studies of individual teacher researchers who work at various grade levels in urban and suburban public and independent schools and other educational programs and case studies of teacher researcher groups that function within schools or as part of university-sponsored programs and school-university partnerships. This research agenda would contribute to the field by illuminating how inquiry informs classroom instruction, curriculum development, collegial relationships, and school policies, particularly relationships between teacher inquiry and student inquiry in classrooms, the interrelationships of inquiry and practice within and across sites, and the functions of teacher inquiry at various points in the professional life cycles of teachers.

Although we are arguing for a research agenda in which university-based researchers join with school-based teacher researchers to investigate the relationships of teacher inquiry, professional knowledge, and practice, we also want to emphasize that there are both possibilities and problems inherent in such an agenda. Such research requires innovative and collaborative arrangements that take seriously issues such as the differential power and status of school-based and university-based researchers, the politics of representation, and the reward and support structures that are in place in different institutions. As school and university colleagues join together in this endeavor, it is essential to remember that teachers are not committed to teacher research for its own sake; their task is not simply to produce research, as some have argued is true in the academic research community. Rather, the commitment of teacher researchers is to change—in their own classrooms, schools, districts, and professional organizations. At the base of this commitment is a deep and often passionately enacted responsibility to students' learning and life chances. It is the synergy that comes from close collaborative work, then, that will make it possible to renegotiate the boundaries of research and practice and reconfigure relationships inside and outside schools and universities.

NOTES

1. The arguments we make throughout this chapter draw on and synthesize our work in a series of articles designed to construct a theoretical framework for teacher research. See Marilyn Cochran-Smith and Susan L. Lytle, "Research on Teaching and Teacher Research: The Issues that Divide," *Educational Researcher* 19, no. 2 (1990): 2-11; idem, "Communities for Teacher Research: Fringe or Forefront?" *American Journal of Education* 100, no. 3 (May 1992): 298-324; idem. eds., *Inside/Outside: Teacher Research and Knowledge* (New York: Teachers College Press, 1993); Susan L. Lytle and Marilyn Cochran-Smith, "Toward Clarifying the Concept," *National Writing Project Quarterly* 11, no. 2 (1989): 1-3, 22-27; idem, "Learning from Teacher Research: A Working Typology," *Teachers College Record* 92 (1990): 83-104; idem, "Teacher Research as a Way of Knowing," *Harvard Educational Review* 62 (1992): 447-474.

2. Wilfred Carr and Stephen Kemmis, *Becoming Critical* (London: Falmer Press, 1986); Joe L. Kincheloe, *Teachers as Researchers: Qualitative Inquiry as a Path to Empowerment* (London: Falmer Press, 1991); Kurt Lewin, *Resolving Social Conflicts* (New York: Harper and Row, 1948).

3. Patti Lather, "Research as Praxis," *Harvard Educational Review* 56 (1986): 257-277.

4. Merlin C. Wittrock, ed., *Handbook of Research on Teaching*, 3rd ed. (New York: Macmillan, 1986).

5. Lawrence Stenhouse, *Research as a Basis for Teaching* (London: Heinemann, 1985).

6. For example, Glenda Bissex and Richard Bullock, *Seeing for Ourselves: Case Study Research by Teachers of Writing* (Portsmouth, NH: Heinemann, 1987); Dixie Goswami and Peter Stillman, eds., *Reclaiming the Classroom: Teacher Research as an Agency for Change* (Upper Montclair, NJ: Boynton/Cook, 1987); Marian Mohr and Marion Maclean, *Working Together: A Guide for Teacher-Researchers* (Urbana, IL: National Council of Teachers of English, 1987).

7. Miles Myers, *The Teacher-Researcher: How to Study Writing in the Classroom* (Urbana, IL: National Council of Teachers of English, 1985).

8. For a variety of quite diverse but equally compelling examples of teachers' journals, see the following articles in Cochran-Smith and Lytle, eds., *Inside/Outside*: Mickey Harris, "Looking Back: 20 Years of Teachers' Journals," pp. 130-140; Deborah Jumpp and Lynne Y. Strieb, "Journals for Collaboration, Curriculum, and

Assessment," pp. 140-149; Lynne Y. Strieb, "Visiting and Revisiting the Trees," pp. 121-130. See also, L. G. Natkins, *Our Last Term: A Teacher's Diary* (Lanham, MD: University Press of America, 1986); Stuart B. Palonsky, *900 Shows a Year: A Look at Teaching from a Teacher's Side of the Desk* (New York: Random House, 1986); Lynne Y. Strieb, *A Philadelphia Teacher's Journal* (Grand Forks, ND: North Dakota Study Group Center for Teaching and Learning, 1985).

9. For the best-developed examples of oral inquiry processes as teacher research, see descriptions of the Prospect School Documentary Processes developed over time by Patricia Carini and her teacher colleagues at the Prospect School (North Bennington, VT) found in Patricia Carini, *Prospect's Documentary Processes* (Bennington, VT: The Prospect School Center, 1986). See also, Philadelphia Teachers Learning Cooperative, "On Becoming Teacher Experts: Buying Time," *Language Arts* 6 (1984): 731-735; Cecelia Traugh, Rhoda Kanevsky, A. Martin, A. Seletzky, K. Woolf, and Lynne Y. Strieb, *Speaking Out: Teachers on Teaching* (Grand Forks, ND: University of North Dakota, 1986); and two articles in Cochran-Smith and Lytle, eds., *Inside/Outside*: Rhoda Kanevsky, "Descriptive Review of a Child: A Way of Knowing about Teaching and Learning," pp. 150-162, and Penny Colgan-Davis, "Learning about Learning Diversity," pp. 163-169.

10. Goswami and Stillman, eds., *Reclaiming the Classroom*, "Preface."

11. Frederick Erickson, "Qualitative Methods in Research on Teaching," in Merlin Wittrock, ed., *Handbook of Research on Teaching*, 3rd ed. (New York: Macmillan, 1986).

12. For example, Eleanor Duckworth, *The Having of Wonderful Ideas* (New York: Teachers College Press, 1987); Ellie Kutz, "Preservice Teachers as Researchers: Developing Practice and Creating Theory" (Paper presented at the Ethnography in Education Forum, University of Pennsylvania, Philadelphia, 1989).

13. Judy Buchanan and Katherine Schultz, "Looking Together: Communities of Learners in an Urban Third-Fourth Grade Classroom" (Paper presented at the spring conference of the National Council of Teachers of English, Charleston, SC, 1989); Carole Edelsky and Chris Boyd, "Collaborative Research" (Keynote address presented at the spring conference of the National Council of Teachers of English, Charleston, SC, 1989); Susan L. Lytle and Robert Fecho, "Meeting Strangers in Familiar Places: Teacher Collaboration by Cross-visitation," *English Education* 23 (1991): 5-28.

14. Philadelphia Teachers Learning Cooperative, "On Becoming Teacher Experts"; Boston Women's Teachers' Group (Sara Freedman, Jane Jackson, and Katherine Boles), "Teaching: An Imperiled 'Profession'," in *Handbook of Teaching and Policy*, edited by Lee Shulman and Gary Sykes (New York: Longman, 1983).

15. Amanda Branscombe, Dixie Goswami, and Jeffrey Schwartz, eds., *Students Teaching, Teachers Learning* (Portsmouth, NH: Boynton/Cook, Heinemann, 1992); Marilyn Cochran-Smith, Elizabeth Garfield, and Rachel Greenberger, "Student Teachers and Their Teacher: Talking Our Way into New Understandings," in *Students Teaching, Teachers Learning*, edited by Branscombe, Goswami, and Schwartz.

16. Gary D Fenstermacher, "Philosophy of Research on Teaching: Three Aspects," in *Handbook of Research on Teaching*, ed. Wittrock; Stephen North, *The Making of Knowledge in Composition: Portrait of an Emerging Field* (Upper Montclair, NJ: Boynton/Cook, 1987); Donald P. Sanders and Gail McCutcheon, "The Development of Practical Theories of Teaching," *Journal of Curriculum and Supervision* 2 (1986): 50-67.

17. John Dewey, "The Relation of Theory to Practice in Education," in *The Relationship of Theory to Practice in the Education of Teachers*, edited by Charles A. McMurry, Third Yearbook of the National Society for the Scientific Study of Education, Part 1, pp. 9-30 (Chicago: University of Chicago Press, 1903).

18. Maynard C. Reynolds, ed., *The Knowledge Base for the Beginning Teacher* (New York: Pergamon Press, 1989).

19. Mary Crawford and Jeanne Marecek, "Feminist Theory, Feminist Psychology: A Bibliography of Epistemology, Critical Analysis, and Applications," *Psychology of Women Quarterly* 13 (1989): 477-491; Susan Noffke, "Knowers, Knowing, and Known in Action Research" (Paper presented at the Annual Meeting of the American Educational Research Association, Boston, 1990).

20. Lather, "Research as Praxis."

21. Clifford Geertz, *Local Knowledge: Further Essays in Interpretive Anthropology* (New York: Basic Books, 1983).

22. Robert Fecho, "On Becoming Mean and Sensitive: Teacher to Student Writing Conferences in the Secondary Classroom," Report prepared for the National Council of Teachers of English Research Foundation (Philadelphia: University of Pennsylvania, 1989); idem, "Reading as a Teacher," in Cochran-Smith and Lytle, eds., *Inside/Outside*.

23. Madeleine Rawley Crouse, "Fantastic Mr. Fox: What about the Farmers?" Unpublished manuscript, Philadelphia, PA, 1990.

24. Shelley Baum-Brunner, "Talking about Writing and Revision of Rough Drafts" (Doctoral dissertation, University of Pennsylvania, 1990); idem, "Stepping In and Stepping Out," in Cochran-Smith and Lytle, eds., *Inside/Outside*.

25. Joan Cone, *Untracking Advanced Placement English, Creating Opportunity is Not Enough—Research in Writing: Working Papers of Teacher Researchers* (Berkeley, CA: Bay Area Writing Project, University of California, 1990).

26. Jessica Howard, "On Teaching, Knowledge and 'Middle Ground'," *Harvard Educational Review* 59 (1989): 226-239.

27. Magda Lewis, "Politics, Resistance, and Transformation: The Psycho/Social/Sexual Dynamics in the Feminist Classroom" (Paper presented at the Annual Meeting of the American Educational Research Association, San Francisco, 1989).

28. Elizabeth Ellsworth, "Why Doesn't This Feel Empowering? Working through the Myths of Critical Pedagogy," *Harvard Educational Review* 59 (1989): 297-324; Patti Lather, *Getting Smart: Feminist Research and Pedagogy with/in the Postmodern* (London: Routledge, Chapman, and Hall, 1991); Lewis, "Politics, Resistance, and Transformation"; Janet Miller, "Points of Dissonance in Teachers/Researchers: Openings into Emancipatory Ways of Knowing" (Paper presented at the Bergamo Conference on Curriculum Theory and Classroom Practice, Dayton, OH, November, 1987).

29. Paulo Freire, *Pedagogy of the Oppressed* (New York: Herder and Herder, 1971), p. 217.

30. Nona Lyons, "Dilemmas of Knowing: Ethical and Epistemological Dimensions of Teacher Work and Development," *Harvard Educational Review* 60 (1990): 159-180.

31. J. H. Westerhoff, "The Teacher as Pilgrim," in *Teacher Renewal*, edited by Frances S. Bolin and J. M. Falk (New York: Teachers College Press, 1987).

32. Miles Myers, "Institutionalizing Inquiry," *National Writing Project Quarterly* 9 (1987): 1-4; Robert J. Schaefer, *The School as a Center of Inquiry* (New York: Harper and Row, 1967).

33. Holmes Group, *Tomorrow's Schools: A Report of the Holmes Group* (East Lansing, MI: Holmes Group, Inc., 1990).

34. Lawrence Stenhouse, *Research as a Basis for Teaching* (London: Heinemann, 1985), p. 98.

35. Philip Jackson, "The Functions of Educational Research," *Educational Researcher* 19, no. 7 (1990): 7.

36. Susan Florio-Ruane and M. Walsh, "The Teacher as Colleague in Classroom Research," in *Culture and the Bilingual Classroom: Studies in Classroom Ethnography*, edited by Henry Trueba, Grace Guthrie, and Kathryn Au (Rowley, MA: Newbury House, 1981).

37. Clifford Geertz, *The Interpretation of Cultures* (New York: Basic Books, 1973).

38. Elliott Eisner, *The Enlightened Eye* (New York: Macmillan, 1991), p. 210.

39. Lucy M. Calkins, "Forming Research Communities among Naturalistic Researchers," in *Perspectives on Research and Scholarship in Composition*, edited by Ben W. McClelland and Timothy R. Donovan (New York: Modern Language Association, 1985), p. 143.

40. Christopher Clark and Penelope Peterson, *"Teachers' Thought Processes,"* in *Handbook of Research on Teaching*, ed. Wittrock.

41. Sharon Feiman-Nemser, "Growth and Reflection as Aims in Teacher Education: Directions for Research," in *Exploring Issues in Teacher Education: Questions for Further Research*, edited by G. E. Hall (Austin, TX: Research and Development Center in Teacher Education, University of Texas at Austin, 1980).

42. Karen K. Zumwalt, "Are We Improving or Undermining Teaching?" in *Critical Issues in Curriculum*, edited by Laurel N. Tanner, Eighty-seventh Yearbook of the National Society for the Study of Education, Part 1 (Chicago: University of Chicago Press, 1982); idem, "Research on Teaching: Policy Implications for Teacher Education," in *Policy Making in Education*, edited by Ann Lieberman and Milbrey W. McLaughlin, Eighty-first Yearbook of the National Society for the Study of Education, Part 1 (Chicago: University of Chicago Press, 1982).

43. Lee Shulman, "Paradigms and Research Programs in the Study of Teaching: A Contemporary Perspective," in *Handbook of Research on Teaching*, ed. Wittrock; idem, "Those Who Understand: Knowledge Growth in Teaching," *Educational Researcher* 15, no. 2 (1986): 4-14; idem, "Knowledge and Teaching: Foundations of the New Reform," *Harvard Educational Review* 51 (1987): 1-22; idem, "Teaching the Disciplines Liberally" (Paper presented at the Third Annual Meeting of the Holmes Group, Atlanta, GA, January, 1989).

44. Marilyn Cochran-Smith, "Of Questions, Not Answers: The Discourse of Student Teachers and Their School and University Mentors" (Paper presented at the Annual Meeting of the American Educational Research Association, San Francisco, April 1989); Linda Lambert, "The End of an Era of Staff Development," *Educational Leadership* 18 (1985): 78-83.

45. Dewey, "The Relation of Theory to Practice in Education," p. 16.

46. Donald A. Schön, *The Reflective Practitioner* (San Francisco: Jossey-Bass, 1983); idem, *Educating the Reflective Practitioner* (San Francisco: Jossey-Bass, 1987).

47. Patricia Johnson, "A Shift in Paradigm: As Teachers Become Researchers So Goes the Curriculum" (Paper presented at the Ethnography in Education Forum, University of Pennsylvania, Philadelphia, February 1990); Jeffrey Schwartz, "The Drudgery and the Discovery: Students as Research Partners," *English Journal* 77 (1988): 37-40.

48. Branscombe, Goswami, and Schwartz, eds., *Students Teaching, Teachers Learning*.

49. James Britton, "A Quiet Form of Research," in Goswami and Stillman, eds., *Reclaiming the Classroom*.

50. Lytle and Fecho, "Meeting Strangers in Familiar Places."

51. Susan Florio-Ruane, "Taking a Closer Look at Writing Conferences" (Paper presented at the Annual Meeting of the American Educational Research Association, San Francisco, April 1986); Judith Warren Little, "Teachers as Colleagues," in *Educators' Handbook*, edited by Virginia Richardson-Koehler (New York: Longman, 1987).

52. Cochran-Smith, "Reinventing Student Teaching"; idem, "Learning to Teach against the Grain."

53. PhilWP has such a program of cross-visitation supported by the School District of Philadelphia. See Lytle and Fecho, "Meeting Strangers in Familiar Places."

54. Michael Polanyi, *Personal Knowledge: Towards a Post-Critical Theory* (Chicago: University of Chicago Press, 1958).

55. The learning opportunities described here are based on those developed at Project START over the past five years.

56. The Communities referred to here include the Seminar in Teaching and Learning for Restructuring Comprehensive High Schools (Sponsored by PhilWP through the Philadelphia Schools Collaborative), the Philadelphia site of the Urban Sites Writing Network, and the Adult Literacy Practitioner Inquiry Project (Sponsored by PhilWP and the National Center for Adult Literacy).

57. Carini, *Prospect's Documentary Processes.*

CHAPTER III

The Case for Inclusive Dialogue in Knowing, Teaching, and Learning about Multicultural Education

OLGA M. WELCH

This chapter represents a challenge to epistemological norms in American education. Some norms favor learning opportunities for culturally mainstreamed students which lead to academic excellence, while other norms exclude such perspectives for culturally diverse students in the name of equity. The research reported here will argue for connecting such norms—especially in classrooms where students are largely from minority groups, in programs for the preparation of their teachers, and in the community of educational researchers, all of which help establish epistemological and instructional norms.

At the outset, it is important to notice that the intellectual thought of minorities, students, and teachers has been marginalized or ignored in educational research. Beverly Gordon, for example, argues that there is no absence of discourse and literature produced by minorities, particularly African-American scholars and practitioners.[1] However, this work has limited influence on the prevailing paradigms and ideology within the scholarly community. Instead it receives lip service under the broad rubric of multicultural and/or cross-cultural studies while Anglo scholarship actually dominates educational practice. This marginalizing is viewed as a major factor in the lack of overall improvement in the academic preparation of working or underclass African-American and other children who are "at risk" for school failure.

Inherent in this marginalization is the devaluing of the importance of knowledge possessed by minorities and their ways of knowing. It is perpetuated in teacher education through program designs which include attention to instructional "options" for African-American,

Olga M. Welch is Professor of Special Education, College of Education, University of Tennessee at Knoxville.

Latino, and American Indians—options which are in contrast to the "regular business" of education for Anglo-European students. For example, issues of "academic" excellence are assumed to be pertinent only for "students who are already academically successful as well as members of the racial majority group, while issues of equity are identified with racial minorities, the unsuccessful, poor, and other nonmainstream students."[2] Moreover, when multicultural education is viewed by teachers in preparation as lessons in human relations, cultural characteristics, and ethnic holidays, or as information relevant only to inner-city schools, opportunities diminish for teachers to develop wider, more substantive, and more inclusive perspectives on pluralistic education.

Given the current epistemological climate in which educators claim to value the social construction of knowledge, the time is right to make such changes. In support of such change, I use here a nested set of cases to point out the need for inclusive dialogue and the challenges and the promises of establishing the kind of inclusive dialogue needed to eradicate the marginalizing of non-Anglo perspectives. "Inclusive dialogue" is used here to mean that the voices of all students, teachers, and researchers are heard (including those from minority groups) and that genuine attention must be paid to what those voices are saying. Thus, rather than try to remediate and silence culturally different voices by dissolving them into mainstream norms which separate equity from excellence, inclusive dialogue is an awareness, a set of environmental conditions, and an epistemological process which affirms pluralism (ethnic, racial, linguistic, religious, and economic, among others): a pluralism of voice and virtue.[3]

The Silence of Exclusion

A brief but compelling illustration of the need for inclusive dialogue in multicultural education can be found in Michelle Fine's ethnography of a Manhattan high school with a largely Latino and African-American student body. In an exploration of conditions and processes which can stifle critical analysis of educational practice, Fine, a Euro-American ethnographer, describes the "silencing" of debate she discovered between and among the school's multiple and culturally diverse constituencies. There is substantial evidence, she writes, that many of the students in the study, who were judged by their teachers as low in skill and motivation, were also eager to choreograph their own learning, to generate a curriculum of lived experience, and to engage in a participatory pedagogy. Therefore, every attempt by administrators and teachers to undermine or stifle their autobiographical writing sacrificed another chance to connect with students and their communities.[4]

The ambivalence about the educational process and credentials displayed by many of the students, even as they verbalized a support for and an understanding of the importance of a diploma, underscored this loss of connection. Financial security had been achieved by others in their community without the diploma. Administrators and teachers regardless of race or position desired "the best" for the students, but this attitude was tempered by their participation in "silencing" various forms of discourse, thus perpetuating the very academic ambivalence they sought to eradicate. Consciously and unconsciously, responses of administrators and teachers to the students, their parents, and the community, imposed the "silences" reflected in their collective and individual stances toward the educational process. Fine's study demonstrates that even the *concept* of inclusive dialogue was clearly missing from the multicultural environment.

Reflections on the Education of African-American Students and their Teachers

Educators of color have long realized the silencing of students through the preponderance of Eurocentric perspectives and disparate norms in the educational process for students of color and in the preparation of teachers who will work with them. Lisa Delpit raises these concerns as she reflects on her experiences as both an African-American teacher and a teacher educator researching her own practices in a narrative reflection. As a product of preparation programs de-emphasizing "skill-based" approaches to writing for disadvantaged, largely minority students, she describes her estrangement from the progressive process-writing movement because of its inadequacy in affirming the culture of African-American children as well as the creativity engendered by and within that culture.

It has begun to dawn on me that many of the teachers of black children have roots in other communities and do not often have the opportunity to hear the full range of their students' voices. I wonder how many of (these) teachers know that their black students are prolific and "fluent" writers of rap songs. I wonder how many teachers realize the verbal creativity and fluency black kids express every day on the playgrounds of America as they devise new insults, new rope-jumping chants and new cheers. Even if they did hear them, would they relate them to language fluency?[5]

Delpit did not come to these conclusions easily. In her reflective article she emphasizes her support for and practice of process-writing activities in her early teaching and also describes her frequent clashes with other minority teachers who stressed discipline and practice in handwriting, oral and written grammar, and traditional methods of writing instruction.

I was an exception to the other black teachers. I socialized with the young white teachers and planned shared classroom experiences with them. I also taught as they did. Many people told me I was a good teacher: I had an open classroom; I had learning stations; I had children write books and stories to share; I provided games and used weaving to teach math and fine motor skills. I threw out all the desks and added carpeted open-learning areas. I was doing what I had learned.[6]

The results, however, were not what she hoped for. While Anglo-European students made exceptional progress, African-American students did not. Some did learn to read, but not as rapidly as did their Anglo-European counterparts. Others simply enjoyed the different approach, played games, and did little else. Delpit wondered why.

It was not until several years later, as a teacher educator herself, that she began to understand. From conversations with African-American teachers in the field as well as her own experiences with teacher trainees, she came to realize that the process-writing techniques, which stressed helping African-American children to "find" their voices, served instead to silence them. African-American children have "voices" but they rarely receive the message that their perspectives are valid. In fact, their uses of language, their wit, sarcasm, and way of "sounding" on each other are devalued in schools, even "explained away." This devaluation in turn results in students who lose motivation to display these talents. Thus, they receive the message that in order to be "acceptable," they must abandon their own voices for those of the majority culture. The quandary of the teacher then becomes how to establish inclusive dialogue in the classroom. How can teachers assist these students to use standard writing procedures and structures so that they can retain the flavor of their own voices while being understood by those who use language that is acceptable in school? For Delpit, the process of developing inclusive dialogue involves a reexamination of those elements of the educational system which are considered "progressive" to determine whether or not they support and involve minorities. She urges university researchers, school districts, and teachers to give more than cursory attention to the views of their minority colleagues and constituents, and reminds us that the key is to understand the variety of meanings available for any human interaction, and not to assume that the voices of the majority speak for all.

Project EXCEL:
Research into Inclusive Dialogue

The examples so far illustrate the importance of inclusive dialogue, especially in classrooms with diverse populations, as well as the profound difficulties of attaining it in educational settings. The next example represents an attempt to connect the norms of excellence and equity through inclusive dialogue. It comes from a collaborative effort between a high school English teacher, Margaret Smith, and two African-American university professors, Carolyn Hodges and me. As teacher educators and university researchers, we wanted to understand how adolescents, characterized by their ethnicity and/or socioeconomic circumstances as "disadvantaged," defined scholarship. Smith, as the classroom teacher, wants to know how she is including student dialogue in her instruction, while not trading such an equitable goal for academic excellence. Thus, Smith and other school and university colleagues became participants with us in a shared learning experience called "Project EXCEL," an enrichment program sponsored by the University of Tennessee.

In this ongoing project, we are examining the precollege experiences of African-American adolescents who are disadvantaged because of their economic status and lack of quality schooling experiences. Additionally, the participants' other experiences in their regular school classrooms are studied for comparison. Teachers and parents also help to interpret these students' classroom interactions. In these ways, my colleagues and I seek to include multiple perspectives on enrichment within which to frame conclusions. Moreover, these perspectives provide the inclusive conceptual framework for examining the data collected. Using a phenomenological approach to the perceptions of project participants, we attempt to understand how precollege enrichment is viewed by those it affects directly and indirectly. Primarily, we are all interested in how these students approach academic work (both in their regular classes and in EXCEL) and how these approaches relate to their definitions of scholarship and to themselves as scholars.

In follow-up studies of the participants, we continue to explore these issues, believing this understanding to be critical to our examination of the educational experiences of adolescents with college aspirations who are disadvantaged by inadequate schooling and socioeconomic status. Project EXCEL provides college level work in reading, writing, and foreign language skills (German and French) as well as simulated college lectures, seminars, and assignments given by university faculty in a variety of disciplines. Additionally, the program assists students to develop appropriate career paths by involving them early in personal goal setting, investigation of various career options, and participation in internship and community service experiences which they design and execute with adult mentors. Teachers, parents, and university researchers collect data on the participants prior to their entry into the program, during their involvement in the program, and after they have enrolled in colleges and universities or entered careers. These data allow us to construct academic profiles of the students who participate in the project.

Using extensive classroom observations, in-depth interviews with students, and analysis of student work—both in the project and in their regular classes—we also examine the effect of teacher-directed instruction in the program on the construction of individual definitions of scholarship.[7] In overarching findings, the data suggest the importance of understanding the hidden curriculum of public schooling which causes some disadvantaged students, particularly those from disenfranchised racial and ethnic groups, to disengage from competition with their majority counterparts. Even if they possess the abilities to compete, they are still excluded from opportunities to excel. This normative curriculum, with its unarticulated emphasis on obedience and deference to authority, docility, subordination, extrinsic motivation, external control, dependence, and fatalism, handicaps the majority of minority and low-income children and undermines their abilities to achieve either equity or academic excellence. The need for inclusive dialogue is apparent.

MARGARET SMITH'S BACKGROUND AND BELIEFS

Margaret Smith, the EXCEL English teacher who conducted teacher research with the project from its inception, was also the individual whom the students identified in follow-up interviews as "the person" who had influenced their development as "scholars." She had been teaching college preparatory high school English for fifteen years, in both city and county systems. A small, middle-aged African-American woman, she has received numerous teaching awards. As one who had demonstrated her commitment to understanding the learning process for African-American students, Smith's reflections as well as those of the students, their parents, and other university and school colleagues allowed me, as a teacher educator and researcher, to build this preliminary case for the use of inclusive dialogue in research, instruction, and teacher preparation in multicultural education.

Smith's stated philosophy of teaching is "fashioned from what I didn't get in my own education." This relates to her own educational experiences which she describes as "woefully underpreparing her for academia." Because of this, she has made it her goal to give a student "much more than he or she needs" and to "accept nothing less than the best the student has to offer." Smith sees the role of the teacher as analogous to a "walking witness . . . who gives the best she's got, teaching by example." For her, the role of teacher is to teach not only theories or principles, but more importantly, their application or use in practice. In addition to academic concepts, a teacher "helps students see the utilitarian purpose of learning, instills values, including reverence for honesty, integrity, racial pride, and diversity." Ultimately, Smith wants to contribute all she can to "ensure they [the students] have a good life."

Several times, over the course of the project, Smith was to refer to this philosophy in support of her teaching. In one conversation with me, she recounted her frustration with the students' work habits.

I would like to see some work done in trying to change the work habits and the attitudes the students expressed in terms of the way they present themselves to others and with EXCEL. . . . They have more of the regular year than they have of me. I think that is part of the problem.

In another conversation she spoke of her belief that the students possess a view of "acceptable" that is different from her view:

I find this true of all the students. They do not want to go back and look at anything unless it is "wrong." "Acceptable" is fine for them. Once they have done something, then that is it. You should be pleased that I have done it. And therein lies the reward. I did it. If I ask them to write a paper, then I am supposed to be very pleased because they wrote it; I am not to criticize, I am not to evaluate it. I should simply accept that they did it.

Smith believed that students operated in a school environment which overtly and covertly affected their perceptions of excellence and scholarship. Part of witnessing for her involved overcoming the students' misconception "that they are better (academically) than they are," without stifling the potential for academic excellence which she fully believed they possessed. This was accomplished partially by acting as a role model, teaching students more than just the content. As Smith explained:

Proper values need to be taught as well. Good work ethics, honesty and integrity, and the importance of those values in a person's life. I think the best way to do that is to model it . . . always on the job, doing the job. These students understand that and think upon it. I have students say that to me all the time. . . . I think those things are important—often more than subject matter. I got a letter from a parent at the end of last year. As well as thanking me for everything I had done for his daughter during the year, the parent stated that she had learned self-discipline and the importance of dedication to a task and seeing it out to the end. I think things like that are important.

For Smith, teaching clearly involved more than just imparting information; it demanded the kind of knowledge sharing or inclusive dialogue in which students engaged in active rather than passive roles. This was confirmed in my observations of Smith's classroom instruction as well as her own anecdotal reports in which teacher-student and student-teacher respect prevailed. Smith described her relationships with students as good, but not "buddy-buddy." She reported that she deliberately cultivated the kind of professional distance which would allow her to be both "business-like" and (still) "have fun—laugh, and even cry sometimes with students." To illustrate this, she remarked that students often "hang around" after school and share jokes with her, even though these same students refrain from telling jokes which distract others during class.

Smith rarely used praise or rewards as positive reinforcement. She described herself as satisfied only when she got the best students had to offer, and that rarely happened. In contrast, the data did not support a negative classroom climate. This teacher seldom used the word "no," or told students they had done poorly. Instead, she simply had them keep working on an assignment until it met her standard of acceptability, which was "the best they had to give."

While on the surface this kind of instruction might appear exclusionary or punitive, interviews with students revealed that they considered this one of the most important experiences they had in

EXCEL. Far from being excluded from the dialogue, they believed that Smith's refusal to permit them to "get by" with little work actually represented her insistence that they not accept mediocrity, even in themselves. Later, in follow up interviews, these same EXCEL students, now enrolled in colleges and universities, credited Ms. Smith's high standards for their own successful writing experiences as first-year college students. For them, the dialogue was both beneficial and inclusive. Here is a summary of the key techniques she used.

FACILITATING INCLUSIVE DIALOGUE IN SMITH'S CLASSROOM

Active participation. For learning tasks in the English class, Smith employed active teacher instruction/discussion, equal participation of students in questioning, and individualized and variable learning experiences. Less than 20 percent of the instructional time was spent in activities other than teacher-directed instruction, lecture, demonstration, or discussion. Smith saw her job as one of teaching during the entire class period, and making each assignment meaningful. Frequent questioning was used to evaluate student mastery of subject matter; data from classroom observations confirm that all students participated equally. Indeed, in all but two classes I observed, Smith directed nearly identical numbers of questions to each of her students during a lesson. Individualization of instruction was achieved by varying the amount and quality of the work expected from each student. Smith candidly admitted to pressing students until she got the best they had to give.

In-depth questioning. Smith reported that students must not only know a theory or practice, but be able to apply it. During my visits to her classroom, I often heard her say: "And the next question is . . . ?", with the students replying, "Why?" Smith used this method of questioning during grammar and vocabulary lessons, as well as in discussions of literature. A recurring theme in Smith's research discussions was the idea that African-American youth internalized "helplessness and passivity" because of teacher focus on rules rather than rationale. "Black students have been taught that if they can get the right answer; they will never be asked to *explain how they came by it.*" For this reason, she consciously chose in-depth questioning and response as a way to force students to state a rationale for their decisions, whether correct or incorrect.

Wait-time. Smith paused each time she asked a question to allow students to think before they responded. These pauses lasted on average from one to five seconds before the question was rephrased. The teacher encouraged students to think by verbally indicating the acceptability of "thinking time." With reluctant students, Smith probed until the students provided an answer. At no time did she permit students to "opt out" of participation, stressing that the only unacceptable answer was no answer. Further, Smith reiterated in class and in the discussions about the class, that all students had a contribution to make, and that their opinions and input were valid and important.

When probed about this seemingly "traditional" approach to questioning, Smith explained that her experiences with students, both in EXCEL and in her own classroom, suggested that they believed rapid responses connoted intelligence. "Of course, we teach them this, when we ask questions in "rapid fire" fashion, sometimes two or three at once." Smith's concerns were borne out in classroom observations of EXCEL and non-EXCEL students in which teacher "wait-time" averaged between one and two seconds.

Absence of the word "No." Students were never told they had given the wrong answer. If answers were incorrect, Smith probed for the reason a student gave a particular answer until the student corrected the answer. She stated that she considered self-correction a learning process which should be directly addressed during instruction. If answers were incomplete, she pressed for clarification by rephrasing, asking leading questions or giving clues. She also sought other students' input to improve the quality of the answers, particularly in discussions of literature. Smith indicated correct or complete answers by changing the tone and volume of her voice as she repeated or summarized answers.

Smith's approach was in direct contrast to those in non-EXCEL classrooms. A consistent finding in the regular English classrooms was that students were routinely corrected when they made errors. Rarely were they expected to self-correct or to give rationales for their answers.

Living her beliefs. Observations made by university researchers support a close congruence between Smith's stated philosophy of teaching and her practices in the classroom. The student interviews suggested that Smith's philosophy of teaching and resulting practices assisted in the academic development of the EXCEL participants. The observations further suggested that high teacher expectations and appropriate role modeling produced work from students which demonstrated abilities beyond their own expectations. In turn, the realization of their abilities had significant influence on the development of the EXCEL students as scholars. Perhaps the most interesting finding across teacher-researched and university-researched summaries, however, was the fidelity manifested in the relationships between Margaret Smith and her students.

Connecting Nested Knowing and Inclusive Dialogue

In the beginning of this chapter, I argued for the importance of taking seriously the experiences of culturally diverse students and teachers when establishing educational norms for multicultural education, rather than relying on ethnocentric and noninclusive hypotheses about how mainstream teaching should stress excellence and minority teaching should stress equity. I'd like to return to that point in arguing for inclusive dialogue, as I also add one other point. Because the educational scholars in this chapter believed themselves to be knowledgeable critics and creators of knowledge, rather than merely the recipients of others' knowledge, they were able to challenge such norms. The examples of Fine, Delpit, and Smith provide insights (from different standpoints) into how teachers view themselves, their subject matter, and their students. Indeed, these examples support the conceptual frameworks of Belenky, Tarule, Clinchy, Goldberger,[8] Gilligan,[9] and Lyons[10] which suggest that teachers' perspectives on knowing, on their views of themselves and their students as "knowers," powerfully affect the actualization of their craft and their inclusive dialogue styles.

Epistemologically, inclusive dialogue would embody, in Lyons's terms, "nested knowing,"[11] that is, a teacher's views of knowing and his or her assessment of students as knowers, on the one hand, and students' own perspectives on the other. Both teachers and students share an interdependence as "knowers" which affects the teaching and learning experiences they fashion.

Smith's enactment of inclusive dialogue was an example of nested knowing. It included the construction of learning tasks, the insistence on justification for all responses, and the refusal to accept less than what she considered "the students' best." Her means of developing an instructional program which merged excellence and equity through inclusive dialogue resulted from her own philosophical beliefs about education, her assumptions about the knowledge needed and the knowledge already possessed by the students, and her commitment to a higher standard of academic preparation than either she or the students had experienced in public schooling. In more than one discussion

of her work, she decried the lack of high academic expectations as well
as the paucity of challenging experiences offered to minority and low-
income students. She suggested that both minority and nonminority
teachers are grounded by their teacher preparation in a Eurocentric
teaching tradition which tends to characterize transmission of knowledge as unidirectional rather than as reciprocal interaction. While diverse traditions do exist, they are relegated to the periphery in debates
on educational reform, and are rarely offered as part of the mainstream
curriculum in teacher preparation programs.

The Development of Inclusive Dialogue through
Teacher Research

The experiences of these researchers from varying positions and
perspectives underscore the importance of teachers' understanding of
inclusive dialogue for educational excellence and equity. Working
within diverse populations of students and teachers, for example, both
Delpit and Smith came to reevaluate education and their own
instructional philosophies and the kind of academic preparation which
engendered them. Each, in turn, used this knowledge to influence her
own epistemological perspective on the processes of teaching and
learning.

Individual teacher reflections on practice, particularly those of
teachers of color, are too often viewed as idiosyncratic by researchers
and policymakers rather than as confirmation of some shared
perspectives in differing contexts. With resurgent interest in
qualitative methods such as case studies, ethnographies, and
phenomenological investigations, researchers have assumed that
teachers' perspectives are important in understanding the schooling
process. However, scant attention has been given to the messages
inherent in teacher voices, particularly the voices of teachers of color,
from any perspective or standpoint. Rather, it is as if each teacher's
voice represents a single data point among myriad other data points
and those who conduct quantitative research studies quickly assert
that one set of observations does not yield generalizations.
Consequently, insufficient analyses have been conducted to ascertain
the thematic structure of what teachers of color are saying. They are
talking about their conceptions of process, context, and the difficulties
of actualizing their philosophies as inclusive dialogue. However,
because their words vary there is an assumption that each teacher's
reflections are idiosyncratic rather than a confirmation of linking ideas

about the same phenomena (that is, context, how to include diverse perspectives, the creativity required in the teaching act, and their frustrations with imposed instructional models).

Viewed at one level of analysis, the illustrations of teachers' "voices" in this chapter are saying different things. Viewed at a higher level, from an assumption of common themes on inclusive dialogue, they all *mean* the same thing. It is this higher level of meaning, of nested epistemologies, which makes teachers' descriptions of their experiences such a powerful window on cultural diversity as well as an important catalyst for recasting debates on the hegemony of race, class, and gender.

Conclusion

As these varied illustrations of teacher voice suggest, educational practice with diverse populations is replete with countertensions which can serve to silence exposure and criticism as surely as they can elicit change and reform. When research by teachers on inclusive dialogue in multicultural education enters the mainstream of educational debate, then teacher practice can legitimately begin to assist the profession and those who fashion policy to understand their own complicity in perpetuating the structural problems of racism, sexism, and discrimination. Such critical debate might allow teachers in particular to uncover how certain forms of pedagogy create the dichotomies which thwart their best instructional efforts with minority students. Equally important, these inclusive dialogues offer opportunities to better understand how nested epistemologies affirming both excellence and equity can positively impact the practice of schooling. Teacher research on inclusive dialogue could be a key to educational reform.

NOTES

1. Beverly M. Gordon, "The Marginalized Discourse of Minority Intellectual Thought in Traditional Writings on Teaching," in *Research and Multicultural Education: From the Margins to the Mainstream*, edited by Carl A. Grant (London: Falmer, 1992), pp. 19-31.

2. Geneva Gay, "Designing Relevant Curriculum for Diverse Learners," *Education and Urban Society* 20, no. 4 (August, 1988): 387-398.

3. Sonia Nieto, *Affirming Diversity: The Sociopolitical Context of Multicultural Education* (New York: Longman, 1992), p. 97.

4. Michelle Fine, *Framing Dropouts* (Albany: State University of New York Press, 1991).

5. Lisa D. Delpit, "Skills and Other Dilemmas of a Progressive Black Educator," *Harvard Educational Review* 56, no. 4 (1986): 380.

6. Ibid., p. 381.

7. Olga M. Welch, Carolyn R. Hodges, and J. Henderson, "Project EXCEL: The Effects of Teacher-directed Instruction on the Development of Academic Ethos in Minority College-bound Students," *Louisiana Education Research Journal* 17, no. 1 (Fall, 1991): 35-47.

8. Mary Belenky, Blythe Clinchy, Nancy Goldberger, and Jill Tarule, *Women's Ways of Knowing: The Development of Self, Voice, and Mind* (New York: Basic Books, 1986).

9. Carol Gilligan, "In a Different Voice: Women's Conceptions of Self and Morality," *Harvard Educational Review* 47 (1977): 481-517.

10. Nona Lyons, "Two Perspectives: On Self, Relationships, and Morality," *Harvard Educational Review* 53 (1983): 125-145.

11. Nona Lyons, "Dilemmas of Knowing: Ethical and Epistemological Dimensions of Teachers' Work and Development," *Harvard Educational Review* 60, no. 2 (May, 1990): 159-180.

CHAPTER IV

Personal Renewal and Social Construction through Teacher Research

KENNETH M. ZEICHNER

In this chapter I consider the extent to which the teacher research movement has contributed to the processes of educational reform in various ways.[1] (1) What effects does it have on the control of the knowledge or theory that informs the work of teachers? (2) Is it able to promote individual teacher development and a higher quality of teaching? (3) What influence does it have on institutional change in the immediate settings in which teachers work? (4) What is its impact on the making of a more democratic and decent society for everyone?

Many people are realizing the tremendous power of teacher research and have joined the teacher research community. Although I count myself among them and spend a great deal of my professional life either engaged in research about my own educational practice or in supporting the action research of teacher educators, student teachers, and teachers, I raise these four questions partly to challenge the uncritical glorification of teacher research that is often apparent among its proponents.

For example, there are those who see teacher research and the empowerment of teachers associated with it as ends in themselves unconnected to any broader purposes. It is often asserted or implied that if teachers are further empowered, more reflective, and are researchers of their own practice, they will necessarily be better practitioners and the knowledge produced through their inquiry is necessarily worthy of our support.[2] This view ignores the fact that the greater intentionality and power exerted by teachers may help in some cases to further solidify and justify practices that are harmful to students and may undermine important connections between institutions and their communities.[3] Uncritical glorification of

Kenneth M. Zeichner is a Professor in the Department of Curriculum and Instruction, School of Education, University of Wisconsin—Madison.

knowledge generated through teacher research is, moreover, condescending toward teachers and disrespectful of the genuine contribution they can make both to the improvement of their own individual practice and to the greater social good. We need to take teacher research much more seriously and take a hard look at the purposes toward which it is directed, including the extent of the connection between the teacher research movement and the struggle for greater social, economic, and political justice.

There has been wide-ranging debate in the literature about what real teacher research is and what it is not, about the specifics of the action research spiral, about whether teacher research must be collaborative or not, about whether it can or should involve outsiders as well as insiders.[4] This discourse, although highly informative in an academic sense, is essentially irrelevant to many of those who actually engage in teacher research, for there are many different cultures of teacher research. I use the term "teacher research" in a very broad sense to refer to systematic inquiry by practitioners about their own practices.[5] I do not adopt the now familiar distinction among technical, practical, and critical or emancipatory research[6] because this classification creates a hierarchy that devalues teachers, although some may interpret my arguments as "socially critical" and based in that camp of teacher research which has sometimes been linked with critical social science. While I share many of the political commitments of those who identify themselves as oppositional to the status quo, this link with critical social science and critical theorists in universities has alienated many in the teacher research community in part by creating the perception that the "critical" is somehow out there in the macro world, above and beyond the world of practitioners, and that teachers' struggles in the micro world in which they live daily are somehow insignificant in the large scheme of things.[7] Terms such as "individual" and "classroom" take on negative meanings and teachers are criticized for focusing their research within their classrooms and for not trying to reform schools and society more directly through their research.

I will therefore argue here that these separations between technical and critical, between micro and macro, are distortions and that the critical is in reality embedded in the technical and in the micro world of the practitioner. Every classroom issue has a critical dimension. Individuals or small groups of teachers may not be able to change unjust societal structures through their research, but these teachers can and do make real and important differences in terms of affecting the life chances of their students. While it is important for at least some teachers to be engaged in efforts aimed more directly at institutional change and community action, most teachers will continue to focus on the classroom no matter how much they are inappropriately criticized for doing so by critical theorists in the universities.

The reality is that the political and the critical are right there in front of us in our classrooms and other work sites and the choices that we make everyday in our own work settings reveal our moral commitments with regard to social continuity and change. We cannot be neutral. While we should not ignore efforts to change structures beyond the classroom, the classroom is an important site for socially critical research, or teacher research that is connected to the struggle for greater educational equity and social justice.

My own links to the teacher research community will explain this concern and commitment. I was introduced to the idea of teacher research as a teacher in an inner-city elementary school in New York State in 1969. The school that I had just entered as a new teacher had undergone a great deal of racial conflict in the years just before I came. As part of the community control movement that was sweeping the United States at that time, the largely African-American parents whose children attended the school had negotiated an arrangement with the school authority that gave them an official role in the governance of the school. When I entered the school, the staff and parents were beginning a series of organizational development workshops facilitated by a professor from a local university. The workshops used an action research framework to address the numerous problems that had plagued the school. During these early years of my teaching career, I began to see the potential of action research for contributing in important ways to the remaking of the school as an institution, for improving school and community relations, and for promoting a quality educational experience for everyone's children.

Like many teachers at that time, I had been educated to believe that the answers to problems of practice resided in the research and theories that emanated from universities. I had been taught as a student teacher to believe that real research "with a capital R" was conducted by university academics and that it was my job as a teacher to implement the results of their findings. My own experiences as a participant in the action research community within my school and my growing awareness of the failure of most if not all projects that ignored the expertise of teachers while attempting to reform schools from the outside[8] inspired me to enroll in a graduate degree program which emphasized action research and organizational change in schools.

Ironically, despite all my experience as a practitioner of action research, my doctoral dissertation was not an action research study. It was a study of the social relations among children in classrooms other than mine. Although action research had become an important part of my life, it was not considered appropriate at that time (1976) to accept an action research study as a thesis for a graduate degree—still a restriction in many universities despite the broadening definition of educational research.

For the last fifteen years, I have been conducting research related to my own practice as a teacher educator and university instructor, including my practice as a facilitator of teacher research. Most of my published research and writing has involved a critical analysis of my own practice. I also spend much of my time supporting the research of students in my graduate classes who are studying their practices as teacher educators and supporting the research of student teachers and of teachers in the local schools.

I have, therefore, been an active supporter of action research and have put myself on the line many times to defend the right of teachers and teacher educators to take control over our own practices, and to take control away from the politicians, professional reformers, and school improvement entrepreneurs who still dominate the business of educational reform (see chapter 5). Why then would I criticize the practice of teacher research? My response is that, although I am committed to the values and principles associated with teacher research (e.g., its commitment to democratize the research process and to give greater voice to teachers in determining the course of policies that affect their daily work), I am also committed to the joining of teacher research with the larger issue of building a more humane and compassionate society.

Teacher research is not fulfilling its potential to play a part in the building of a more just world. When I go to a meeting of action researchers, I always expect to feel a certain sense of solidarity and a shared sense of outrage at the conditions under which many of our fellow human beings are forced to live, at the growing gap between the rich and the poor, at the erosion of democratic processes. And I expect to experience a shared contempt for that most painful of all situations that allows an enormous number of children to live in conditions of poverty. There are some thirty million of these children in the United States today.[9] Despite my expectations for connecting teacher research with the lessening of these sufferings and injustices within and beyond the school, and despite the origins of the action research movement before the middle of the century in the efforts to combat race and class prejudice and in community action work,[10] oftentimes there is today little apparent concern over these matters of educational equity and social justice in the teacher research community. Sometimes it seems as though teacher research and the empowerment of teachers are pursued in ways which are totally oblivious to the current situation for the people who, by anyone's definition, do not share equally in the rewards of our society. Sometimes teacher research seems too self-serving.

Teacher Research and the Control of Knowledge

In the last two decades, the terms "teacher research," "reflective practice," and the "reflective practitioner" have become slogans for educational reform all over the world. On the surface, this international movement in professional education can be seen as a reaction against a view of teachers as technicians who merely carry out what others outside the classroom want them to do, and a rejection of top-down forms of reform that involve teachers merely as passive participants. The movement involves a recognition that teachers must play active roles in formulating the purposes of their work as well as the means. These slogans also signify a recognition that the generation of knowledge about good practice and good institutions is not the exclusive privilege of universities and research and development centers, and that teachers also have theories that can contribute to the knowledge that informs the work of practitioner communities.[11] Although there is the danger that these sentiments can lead to unthinking rejection of university-generated knowledge, there is a clear recognition that we cannot rely on such knowledge alone for teacher development and institutional improvement. Externally produced knowledge is often important in helping us to gain perspective on a situation and to link our efforts to the work of others.[12] There are valuable things to be learned from university-generated theories, but this external discourse must feed into a process of inquiry that is initiated from the ground up. (For a more detailed discussion, see chapter 2).

From the perspective of the individual teacher this means that the process of understanding and improving one's work must start from reflecting on one's own experience, and that the sort of wisdom derived entirely from the experience of others (even other practitioners) is inadequate and sometimes even illusory.[13] The slogans of reflection and teacher research also signify a recognition that the process of learning to be a teacher continues throughout one's entire career, that no matter what teacher education programs do, and no matter how well it is done, we can at best only prepare teachers to begin practice. There is a commitment by teacher educators to help prospective teachers during their initial training to internalize the disposition and skill to study their work and to become better at it over time, in short, to take responsibility for their own professional development.

It is claimed that the teacher research movement can be subversive and make a significant contribution to change in the control of the educational knowledge that informs the work of practitioners and policymakers. Stenhouse stressed that it is essential to make public the research of teachers so that (1) other teachers can benefit from the inquiries of individuals or groups and (2) teacher educators, university researchers, and policymakers can incorporate the knowledge produced through these inquiries into courses for prospective and practicing teachers. Teacher research thereby potentially feeds the deliberations through which educational policies are formed.[14]

As a result of the continuing growth of teacher research communities and their publications, Cochran-Smith and Lytle, for example, have argued that the discourse about schools and schooling has been widened to include the knowledge and perspectives of teachers.[15] Although this has been somewhat true, particularly in the area of English and Language Arts education, there are real limits to the degree the discourse has truly been widened.

Even today, with the growth of teacher research communities and the relatively easy access to teacher-generated knowledge, we still see that the educational research establishment, in its attempt to articulate a "knowledge base" for teaching, has generally disregarded teachers' knowledge of their craft.[16] For example, in the most recent edition of the American Educational Research Association's *Handbook of Research on Teaching* there are thirty-five chapters. Over a thousand pages are devoted to such topics as teaching mathematics, social studies, classroom management, and bilingual education. Not a single chapter was written by a classroom teacher and there are few, if any, references to anything a teacher has written.[17] The same is true for *Knowledge Base for the Beginning Teacher*, a very influential publication in the United States, and for most other books of its kind under the editorial control of university academics.[18] The fact that many teachers do not have time to write is sometimes offered as an excuse for this, but that view ignores the extensive material that *has* been published by teachers and could be drawn upon. Although the purveyors of the "knowledge base" in education have become more willing to tolerate teacher research, when it comes to defining what is real educational research, teacher research does not count.

In the Special Interest Groups (SIGs) on Teacher Research and Action Research in the American Educational Research Association (AERA) there are a few classroom teachers, some of whom present papers at the AERA Annual Meeting, but their status and significance in the organization are clearly marginal. Action research has not managed to alter the balance of power between academics and practitioners when it comes to defining what counts as educational research and its influence on policy deliberations.

The picture is no brighter when it comes to the question of the degree to which the knowledge generated through teacher research is incorporated into courses offered by colleges and universities for prospective and practicing teachers, again with the possible exception of English and Language Arts education. There has been a rapid growth of practitioner research groups throughout the school systems of the United States, but the work of these groups has not noticeably affected teacher education programs in colleges and universities. Few course syllabi include readings that identify the voices of teachers and the knowledge generated through teacher research.

Several years ago at a research conference, one of my graduate students and I presented a paper about the use of action research with our student teachers. During the session Bridget Somekh, Coordinator of the Classroom Action Research Network, raised a question about the degree to which we were making use of the knowledge that was produced each semester by our student teachers. While we frequently used our students' action research studies as examples of research by student teachers, we had been doing very little to use the knowledge that was generated in these studies.

My awareness of this contradiction bothered me a great deal and I began to ask more questions about the degree to which my other graduate courses (most of which praised the value of teacher research and even engaged students in such research) incorporated the voices and practical theories of teachers. I found that readings in my courses were for the most part positively oriented toward teacher research and reflective practice and that they challenged the hegemony of the researchers on "effective teachers" and "effective schools" in the United States who have sought to impose change in schools from the outside. But the voices in these readings were mainly the voices of academics, not those of teachers. Despite my commitment to teacher research, my actual practice undermined my intended message to students. Were my student teachers really learning about the role of teachers as knowledge producers and reformers if they never were assigned to read anything written by a teacher, or another student teacher?

As I see it, in working with student teachers and teachers the task is to find a more central place for teacher-produced knowledge which incorporates the voices of teachers and students in teacher education courses. A balance between knowledge generated by practitioners and that generated by academics needs to be attained in a teacher education curriculum. This example of my personal struggle with the contradictions between my practice and my rhetoric shows that, even when there is an expressed commitment to the notion of teachers as researcher, the commitment sometimes does not go far enough.

Action Research and Individual Professional Development

Has teacher research facilitated the development of individual teachers? Here the evidence overwhelmingly indicates success. The literature in education is filled with personal accounts of how teachers feel that their classroom practices, and in some cases their professional lives, have been transformed through teacher research. They believe it has helped to boost their confidence, to narrow the gap between their aspirations and realizations, to understand their own practices and their students more deeply, to revise their personal theories of teaching, and to internalize the disposition to study their teaching practice over time.[19] This kind of evidence led Grundy and Kemmis to conclude:

The firsthand accounts of teachers and students who have been involved in these projects reveal that action research has often been a major and significant experience in their personal or professional development and often a uniquely transforming experience. In short, there is plenty of evidence in print and in people to justify a claim for action research based on performance rather than promise.[20]

In facilitating teacher research, I have often been overwhelmed by the responses of teachers and teacher educators to the opportunity to have their own issues drive their professional development. Very few of the teachers with whom I have worked or whom I have observed working with my colleagues in the Madison (Wisconsin) schools, have found teacher research to be less useful than the conventional kinds of staff development they have experienced. Importantly, most teachers I know who have experienced teacher research continue doing it beyond their initial encounter with it and they bring others on board. Teacher research groups have been multiplying in the Madison schools and it is becoming very difficult to sustain facilitative support. There is little doubt that teachers find teacher research enormously valuable intellectually and that they feel it enhances the quality of their teaching.

In the United States there is still unfortunately a dominance of staff development and school improvement programs that ignore the knowledge and expertise of teachers and that rely primarily on the distribution of prepackaged and allegedly research-based solutions to school problems, often at great expense.[21] The selling of educational solutions and gimmicks (what I have come to refer to as "snake oil" staff development) is still big business today in the United States despite all the teachers who have had the experience of action research and other grass roots forms of staff development. When teachers have the experience of action research the overwhelming majority come to the conclusion that they are on to something that matters.

Whether this sense of personal renewal has actually been accompanied by a higher quality of teaching and learning is another matter. Some claims have been made over the years that better teaching is associated with teachers who research their practice. For example, Elliott and Adelman claimed with regard to the Ford Teaching Project that "action research leads to an improved quality of work—pupils of teachers who have engaged in action research demonstrate superior performance in areas addressed in the research."[22]

Cochran-Smith and Lytle have argued that teacher research has fundamentally transformed the nature of instruction in the classrooms of teacher researchers.

When teachers redefine their own relationships to knowledge about teaching and learning, they reconstruct their classrooms and begin to offer different invitations to their students to learn and know. A view of teaching as research is connected to a view of learning as constructive, meaning-centered, and social. . . . Teachers who are actively researching their own practices provide opportunities for their students to become similarly engaged. . . . What goes on in the classrooms of teacher-researchers is qualitatively different from what typically happens in classrooms.[23]

Cochran-Smith and Lytle and their colleagues in schools in the Philadelphia area have presented us with convincing examples of this phenomenon in recent years. I have also watched this occur in the Madison schools, where some teachers use teacher research as a tool to help them change their teaching approach to one that is more meaning-centered and responsive to students.[24]

However, I have also seen teachers use their research to implement more effectively behavioral management systems and other kinds of teaching that are very unlike what Cochran-Smith and Lytle describe. Teacher research is undoubtedly satisfying for teachers and helps them do better what they want to do, but what they want to do covers a wide range of alternatives, including those outside the world of constructivism in which teachers and students construct knowledge rather than passively receiving it from others. Whether or not the changes teachers achieve through action research can be considered "improvements" is an issue that depends on the merits of what is achieved and whether it is worth achieving in the context of education within a democratic society. Cynthia Ellwood, an experienced action researcher in the Milwaukee schools, has argued that teacher research can sometimes lend greater legitimacy to practices that intensify inequities.[25]

For example, there are still at least some teachers who believe that different races have different intellectual capabilities and that certain races have a natural lower ability or are incapable of learning.[26] In his recent national study of preservice teacher education in the United States, John Goodlad concluded:

The idea of moral imperatives for teachers was virtually foreign in concept and strange in language for most of the future teachers we interviewed. Many were less than convinced that all students can learn; they voiced the view that they should be kind and considerate to all, but they accepted as fact the theory that some simply cannot learn.[27]

Are we willing to accept any changes that are produced through the research of teachers as necessarily good? Despite all the good things that have been achieved in the classrooms of teacher researchers over the years, large numbers of children continue to be left out of the rewards generated by teacher development and school improvement efforts. And they will continue to be left out until there is more explicit concern with the equitable distribution of outcomes in relation to these improvements.

Action Research and School Change

A third area in which teacher research can potentially have a transformative impact is with regard to the institution of the school (see chapter 5). It has become very common in recent years to criticize teachers for taking too narrow a view of teacher research, for emphasizing personal renewal at the expense of social reconstruction. This argument says that the emphasis by teacher researchers on classroom action research has ignored the structural conditions that shape their actions within the classroom.[28] Teacher research, which is felt to have the potential to disturb the deep structures of schooling, is criticized for failing to change institutions. For example, Kemmis has concluded that "Educational action research has been captured and domesticated in individualistic classroom research which has failed to establish links with political forces for democratic educational reform."[29] Lawn has taken a similar view and has called for "school-work research" that addresses those aspects of teachers' work which define it and create the contradictions they have to deal with, such as job definition, resources, colleague relations, and supervision.[30]

While I support the general view that at least some teacher research should focus at the institutional and community levels, there is a serious problem with the calls for schoolwork research as they are typically presented. There is a hidden text in these calls that is perceived by many teachers as denigrating: "There are bigger and more important things going on beyond your limited world of the classroom. I can see them. Why can't you? Stop wasting your time with the trivial matters of trying to improve the learning of your students. If you really want to improve that learning, take on the institution and conditions will be created that will make these improvements possible." This negative portrayal of teachers who choose to maintain a focus on classroom research is unjustified. It is possible to encourage and support schoolwork research without denigrating classroom research.

Despite all the criticisms of teachers for the narrowness of their research efforts, there are many examples of situations where groups of teachers have engaged in research that has resulted in important changes at the institutional level such as changes in policies of the school and of school authorities. In addition to the most publicized cases, such as the efforts of the Boston Women's Teachers' Group to educate other teachers about the structural contradictions in their work and about the misplacement of blame in such terms as "teacher burnout,"[31] there are many lesser known cases where teacher research has affected school policies. I am, therefore, not pessimistic about the current status and future of schoolwork research. In fact, I would argue that as teachers pursue issues within the classroom, their attention is naturally drawn to the institutional context in which the classroom is located.

For example, a group of Madison elementary school teachers recently conducted a study about the complexities of their work. The results were used in negotiations between the teachers' union and the school board to gain more released time during the school day. After the teachers developed a set of orienting categories to structure the research, faculty and students from the university followed teachers around, carefully documenting all the various activities in which the teachers were engaged.

A small group of teachers and I met to discuss the information we had gathered. They planned a presentation to members of the local school board to educate them about the nature of elementary teachers' work. The teachers eventually won their battle to secure additional released time. What they got was not tremendous—an extra hour per week—but it was important. During the process over two hundred teachers came together to support the cause, and school board members were educated about the complexities of teachers' work. Small victories matter. There are many of them throughout the teacher research community.

As Allison Kelly has argued, a focus on these small victories can enable teachers to break out from the determinism which says "It's too big for me, there's nothing I can do" and to avoid the disillusion that frequently comes from not having reformed the world all at once.[32] Teacher research can be an important link in a larger effort toward social reconstruction, and the importance of each small accomplishment along the way must be recognized.

The degree to which the teacher research movement has affected the course of educational policy making seems very limited. Despite evidence that some school authorities are allocating more institutional resources to support teacher research groups, the overall course of educational policymaking in Britain and the United States in recent years seems to have disregarded teachers and teacher educators altogether. Britain has its recent Educational Reform Acts.[33] In the United States there is a similar intensification of efforts to keep control of decision making away from those who do the work of teaching and teacher education.[34] In many countries both teachers and teacher educators have far less control over what they do today than they did a decade ago. One response in the teacher research community to the recent efforts to centralize control over school curriculum, assessment, and teacher education has been to urge teacher researchers to fight to take control of education away from the bureaucrats and politicians. But to date, in an economic climate in which many governments have sought to rationalize public spending and to integrate public policy more fully with industrial needs,[35] we have been largely ineffective.

Action Research and the Struggle for Social Justice

Some criticize the call for action researchers to intervene in the social, economic, and political processes of a society. A militant group of university academics, it is said, is attempting to hijack the teacher research movement to accomplish goals contrary to those of teacher researchers. Many regard these "agitators" as well-intentioned but naive about the complexities of practitioners' work. In a widely read polemic, Rex Gibson has compared them to Salvation Army tambourinists, and John Elliott has called them dangerous radicals.[36]

The call for social responsibility, as it has often been made to teacher researchers, can certainly be criticized. However, we cannot be neutral or indifferent to issues of social continuity and change even when we choose to focus our research within our immediate work settings such as the classroom. We cannot help but intervene.

Educators who work in societies that claim to be democratic have certain moral obligations to intervene in ways that contribute to a situation where those with whom they work can live more fully the values inherent in a democracy. For example, in a democratic society all children must be taught so that they can participate intelligently as adults in the political processes that shape their society.[37] This is not happening. It is an international problem that affects most of humankind and that has had its most visible effect on the poor and on ethnic minority and immigrant groups throughout the world.

There is currently overwhelming evidence in the United States of a growing crisis of "savage inequalities."[38] Race, gender, social class, language background, religion, sexual preference, continue to play strong roles in determining who has access to a quality education, as well as access to quality housing, health care, and rewarding work that pays a decent wage. These factors continue to affect the incidence of a whole host of "rotten outcomes" such as malnutrition, child abuse, childhood pregnancies, violent crime, and drug abuse. A black male child born in California in 1988 is three times more likely to be murdered than to be admitted to the University of California.[39]

Some government policymakers suggest that these problems have been caused by the schools. But schools did not cause these problems and school reform by itself cannot solve them. Educators need to play a conscious role in whatever spheres we choose to work, to examine the social and political implications of our own actions, and to act in ways which promote the realization of democratic values.

For teacher researchers, this means that what has frequently been sensationalized as socially critical teacher research should not be considered an exotic tangent to the teacher research movement, something that is engaged in only by those who go to graduate school and become literate in the latest critical or postmodern social science theories, or by those who pay homage to certain currently fashionable university theoreticians. All teacher researchers should consider at some point along the way the social and political implications of their practices and act on them. This does not mean that they should consider only these things every waking minute, or that doing so will make clear the way to the achievement of a more democratic situation. It means that there needs to be more public concern among teacher researchers for what we can do as educators and human beings to lessen the pain and suffering that surround us every day.

A few years ago Gabby Weiner described what she saw as two separate segments of the teacher research movement in the United Kingdom—the mainstream movement and the gender research movement (see also chapter 1). The mainstream movement, according to Weiner, concentrated on issues related to the professional development of teachers and placed emphasis on the process of reflective inquiry rather than on the outcomes of the research. In contrast, she saw the gender researchers as placing more of an emphasis on the outcomes of teacher research and as committed to increased social justice within a professional development framework. According to Weiner, both groups of researchers were concerned with the liberation and emancipation of teachers, with creating conditions where teachers, not academics and external researchers, could develop educational theory grounded in classroom practice. But only the gender researchers, in her view, connected their efforts explicitly to questions of equity and social justice. Weiner expressed the hope that in the future teacher research should embrace the dual aims of increased self-knowledge and increased social justice.[40] Weiner is right in her call for a focus in teacher research on both personal renewal and social reconstruction. Despite her pessimistic conclusions regarding the lack of attention in teacher research to issues of social justice, there have been and continue to be teachers who have acted on the social and political implications of their practice in their research, both classroom research and schoolwork research.

In addition to the more widely publicized and large-scale efforts, such as the projects on "Girls into Science and Technology" and "Sex Differentiation" in Britain in the 1980s,[41] there are many examples of teachers who by themselves, or with a small group of colleagues, have connected their research to the dual aims of personal renewal and social reconstruction. In their classroom research, student teachers and teachers in Madison and elsewhere in the United States have explored alternative forms of assessment and student grouping practices, and have pursued race and gender equity in relation to such areas as science and computers.[42]

A group of student teachers at the University of Wisconsin-Madison has been engaged in teacher research which focuses on finding out more about the communities from which their students come and about the cultural resources that their students bring to school (that is, what students already know and can do), so that their teaching can be more culturally responsive and equitable across lines of race, gender, and social class. They have been examining their classroom and school cultures in relation to the various cultures of their students and thinking about how policies and practices in their classrooms and schools affect children from various backgrounds.[43] Such research projects serve to expose the real but often hidden connections between the micro and the macro and help us see how what we do every day as teachers is necessarily related to social continuity and change.

Conclusion

The community of teacher researchers needs to connect research and the facilitation of research to the achievement of both personal renewal and social reconstruction. On one hand, the glorification of personal renewal and empowerment in teacher research as an end in itself, while neglecting our social responsibility, is too self-serving. On the other hand, the call for social reconstruction and social justice sometimes is set forth in a manner that crushes the individual and denigrates those removed from the specialized language of social theory in the university. This also is too self-serving. We need to learn how to transcend the tribal wars that continue to divide us.

Vigorous exploration of the social and political implications in classroom research does not entail withdrawal from the kind of schoolwork research and community action which directly confronts institutional policies and structures, or from the kind of work that directly challenges the gatekeepers of what is considered "real" educational research. These efforts should be encouraged and supported, but not at the expense of classroom research and the dignity of teachers. Moreover, all educators no matter where we choose to focus our research efforts—in the classroom, in the school, in the university or college, or in the larger community—need to continue to speak out against the policies that we view as educationally unsound or morally bankrupt. We also need to become and stay connected to larger social movements that are working to bring about more social, economic, and political justice on our planet. Although teacher research can only play a small part in this broader struggle, it is an important part. As a research community, we need to have a greater public social conscience and become more explicitly connected to the struggle to bring about a world where every child has access to a decent and rewarding life. Each one of us ought to ask every day, What am I doing in my involvement with teacher research to help move us closer toward this kind of world?

NOTES

1. An earlier version of this paper was presented as a keynote address at an International Conference on Action Research sponsored by the Classroom Action Research Network, Worcester College, Worcester, U.K. in September, 1992.

2. For substantiation of this assertion, see Kenneth M. Zeichner, "Connecting Genuine Teacher Development to the Struggle for Social Justice," *Journal of Education for Teaching* 19, no. 1 (1993): 5-20.

3. Kenneth M. Zeichner, "Contradictions and Tensions in the Professionalization of Teaching and the Democratization of Schools," *Teachers College Record* 92, no. 3 (1991): 363-379.

4. John Elliott, *Action Research for Educational Change* (Buckingham, U.K.: Open University Press, 1991); Jean McNiff, *Action Research: Principles and Practice* (London: Macmillan, 1988); and Stephen Kemmis and Robin McTaggart, *The Action Research Planner* (Geelong, Australia: Deakin University Press, 1988).

82   PERSONAL RENEWAL AND SOCIAL CHANGE

5. Susan Lytle and Marilyn Cochran-Smith, "Learning from Teacher Research: A Working Typology," *Teachers College Record* 92, no. 1 (1990): 83-103. The terms "action research" and "teacher research" are used synonymously in this chapter.

6. Wilfred S. Carr and Stephen Kemmis, *Becoming Critical: Education, Knowledge, and Action Research* (London: Falmer Press, 1986).

7. Jack Whitehead and Pamela Lomax, "Action Research and the Politics of Educational Knowledge," *British Educational Research Journal* 13, no. 2 (1987): 175-190.

8. John Goodlad and M. Frances Klein, *Looking Behind the Classroom Door* (Worthington, Ohio: Charles A. Jones, 1974); Seymour Sarason, *The Culture of the School and the Problem of Change* (Boston: Allyn and Bacon, 1971).

9. Clifford M. Johnson, Leticia Miranda, Sherman Arloc, and James Weill, *Child Poverty in America* (Washington, DC: Children's Defense Fund, 1991).

10. Herbert Altrichter and Peter Gstettner, "Action Research: A Closed Chapter in the History of German Social Science?" in *Participatory Action Research: Contexts and Consequences*, edited by Robin McTaggart (forthcoming); Susan Noffke, "Action Research: A Multidimensional Analysis" (Doctoral dissertation, University of Wisconsin—Madison, 1989).

11. Susan Lytle and Marilyn Cochran-Smith, "Teacher Research as a Way of Knowing," *Harvard Educational Review* 62, no. 4 (1992): 447-474.

12. Jean Ruddick, "The Improvement of Teaching through Research," *Cambridge Journal of Education* 15, no. 3 (1985): 123-127.

13. Richard Winter, *Learning from Experience: Principles and Practice in Action Research* (London: Falmer Press, 1989).

14. Lawrence Stenhouse, *An Introduction to Curriculum Research and Development* (London: Heinemann, 1975).

15. Marilyn Cochran-Smith and Susan Lytle, "Communities for Teacher Research: Fringe or Forefront?" *American Journal of Education* 100, no. 3 (1992): 298-324.

16. Peter Grimmett and Alan MacKinnon, "Craft Knowledge and the Education of Teachers," in *Review of Research in Education*, vol. 18, edited by Gerald Grant (Washington, DC: American Educational Research Association, 1992), pp. 385-486.

17. Merlin Wittrock, ed., *Handbook of Research on Teaching*, 3rd ed. (New York: Macmillan, 1986).

18. Maynard Reynolds, ed., *Knowledge Base for the Beginning Teacher* (New York: Pergamon Press, 1989).

19. Chris Day, "Teachers' Thinking, Intentions, and Practice," in *Teacher Thinking*, edited by Rob Halkes and John K. Olson (Lisse: Swets and Zeitlinger, 1984), pp. 73-84; John Elliott and Clem Adelman, "Reflecting Where the Action Is: The Design of the Ford Teaching Project," *Education for Teaching* 92 (1973): 8-20; Stephen Kemmis, "Action Research," in *International Encyclopedia of Education: Research and Studies*, edited by Torsten Husén and T. Neville Postlethwaite (Oxford, U.K.: Pergamon, 1985), pp. 35-42; Rosemary Webb, *Practitioner Research in the Primary School* (London: Falmer Press, 1990).

20. Shirley Grundy and Stephen Kemmis, "Educational Action Research in Australia: The State of the Art," in *The Action Research Reader*, edited by Stephen Kemmis and Robin McTaggart, 3rd ed. (Geelong, Australia: Deakin University Press, 1988), pp. 321-335.

21. J. Ronald Gentile, *Instructional Improvement* (Oxford, Ohio: National Staff Development Council, 1988).

ZEICHNER83

22. Elliott and Adelman, "Reflecting Where the Action Is."

23. Cochran-Smith and Lytle, "Communities for Teacher Research," p. 318.

24. Barbara Brodhagen, "Assessing and Reporting Student Progress in an Integrative Curriculum," in *Classroom Action Research Studies* (Madison, WI: Madison Metropolitan School District, 1992).

25. Cynthia Ellwood, "Teacher Research: For Whom?" (Paper presented at the Annual Meeting of the American Educational Research Association, San Francisco, 1992).

26. Sally Tomlinson, "Ethnicity and Educational Achievement in Britain," in *Ethnic Minority Children in Europe*, edited by L. Eldering and Jo Kloprogge (Amsterdam: Swets and Zeitlinger, 1989), pp. 15-37.

27. John I. Goodlad, *Teachers for Our Nation's Schools* (San Francisco: Jossey-Bass, 1990), p. 264.

28. Peter Holly, "Action Research: Cul-de-sac or Turnpike?" *Peabody Journal of Education* 64, no. 3 (1987): 71-99; Martin Lawn, "Being Caught in Schoolwork: The Possibilities of Research in Teachers' Work," in *Quality in Teaching*, edited by Wilfred Carr (London: Falmer Press, 1989), pp. 147-162.

29. Stephen Kemmis, "Of Tambourines and Tumbrils: A Response to Rex Gibson's 'Critical Times for Action Research,'" *Cambridge Journal of Education* 18 (1986): 50-52.

30. Lawn, "Being Caught in Schoolwork."

31. Boston Women's Teachers' Group, "The Other End of the Corridor," *Radical Teacher* 23 (1983): 2-23.

32. Allison Kelly, "Action Research: What Is It and What Can It Do?" in *Issues in Educational Research: Qualitative Methods*, edited by Robert Burgess (London: Falmer Press, 1985), pp. 129-151.

33. Peter Gilroy, "The Political Rape of Teacher Education in England and Wales," *Journal of Education for Teaching* 18 (1992): 5-22.

34. Michael Apple, *Teachers and Texts: A Political Economy of Class and Gender Relations in Education* (New York: Routledge, 1986).

35. Mal Hewitson, Erica McWilliam, and Clarrie Burke, "Responding to Teacher Education Imperatives for the Nineties," *Australian Journal of Education* 35, no. 3 (1991): 246-260.

36. Rex Gibson, "Critical Times for Action Research," *Cambridge Journal of Education* 15, no. 1 (1985): 59-64; Elliott, *Action Research for Educational Change*.

37. Amy Gutmann, *Democratic Education* (Princeton, NJ: Princeton University Press, 1987).

38. Jonathan Kozol, *Savage Inequalities* (New York: Crown, 1991).

39. Gloria Ladson-Billings, "Who Will Teach Our Children?: Preparing Teachers to Successfully Teach African-American Students" (Paper presented at the California State University Teleconference on Cultural Diversity, 1991).

40. Gabby Weiner, "Professional Self-Knowledge versus Social Justice: A Critical Analysis of the Teacher Researcher Movement," *British Educational Research Journal* 15, no. 1 (1985): 41-51.

41. Judith Whyte, *Getting the Girls into Science and Technology* (London: Routledge, 1985); Van Millman and Gabby Weiner, *Sex Differentiation in Schools: Is There Really a Problem?* (York: Macmillan, 1985).

42. Jennifer Gore and Kenneth M. Zeichner, "Action Research and Reflective Teaching in Preservice Teacher Education," *Teaching and Teacher Education* 7, no. 2 (1991): 119-136; Donna Cutler-Landsman, *Lego TC Logo: Bridging the Gender Gap* (Middleton, WI: Elm Lawn Elementary School, May 1991).

43. This work examining the relations between home and school cultures is similar in some respects to what Arville McCann did in a British infant school and to what Shirley Brice Heath did in the United States. See Arville McCann, "Culture and Behavior: A Study of Mirpuri Pakistani Infant Pupils," in *Practitioner Research in the Primary School*, edited by Rosemary Webb (London: Falmer Press, 1990), pp. 183-201; Shirley Brice Heath, *Ways with Words: Language, Life, and Work in Communities and Classrooms* (New York: Cambridge University Press, 1983).

Section Three
THE SOCIOPOLITICAL CONTEXT
OF TEACHER RESEARCH

Introduction

In this part of the volume the epistemological questions raised in Section One are explored through specific working examples. Assuming transformative standpoints about who can know and what can be known, the authors have taken seriously the role of relationships in research. The chapters provide examples where university researchers put themselves into equations for scientific research, raising not only the questions of the nature of power inherent in relationships but also illustrating varied attempts to reconstruct those relationships. Rather than following traditional (and presumably apolitical and objective) formulations of educational research where the relationship between researcher and researched remains unproblematic because "the researcher is taken out," leaving only the knowledge of the "researched" to be examined, these university faculty are working to overcome such a deficit approach to teachers' knowledge. They have moved educational research forward by developing both their methods and their findings from a standpoint of "we" instead of "them" and "us." The chapters suggest that it is no longer appropriate simply to appreciate different forms of research. It is now necessary to understand that social constructions of knowledge determine not only what is known but which methods are appropriate for particular uses of research. The broad differences in the examples selected for this section demonstrate the range of intersecting topics and methods which can be variously constructed in this work.

CHAPTER V

The Promise of Collaborative Research in the Political Context

F. MICHAEL CONNELLY AND D. JEAN CLANDININ

The title of this paper evokes memories and stories of working with teachers in their classrooms, of engaging in sustained conversations with groups of teachers, and of writing narratives with participants of our shared work. The title may bring forward similar stories for other readers. For us, it is these stories that ground our knowledge of the promise of collaborative research for school improvement.

As people come together in collaborative research in schools, they are engaged in a practical activity. Like other practical school activities, collaborative research creates a political context among participants. Every day evidence of the political quality of the relationship among collaborators is seen in the negotiation that occurs among participants and in the interest participants have in outside relationships established by other members of the collaborative. In addition to creating a political context, collaborative research occurs in a political context specified by cultural, social, and institutional settings in which the research is embedded. Every day evidence of the political quality of school settings is seen in the negotiation that occurs between participants and others in the school, and in the interest these others show when two or more people come together in extraordinary ways.

Not only is collaborative research enacted in these two kinds of political context, it *is* political. When we worked with teachers in Bay Street School classrooms,[1] we collaboratively constructed a particular set of relationships in which questions of mutuality, equality, and voice were important. The creation of these relationships was a

F. Michael Connelly is Director of the Joint Center for Teacher Development at the Ontario Institute for Studies in Education and the Faculty of Education, University of Toronto, Toronto, Ontario, Canada. D. Jean Clandinin is an Associate Professor and Director of the Center for Research for Teacher Education and Development, University of Alberta, Edmonton, Alberta, Canada.

political act because it grew out of a complex and extended process of negotiation which resulted in all participants doing things differently relative to each other and to others in the school, and because it (the negotiation process) altered the established theory-practice relations between our university and Bay Street School—relations based on the university being perceived as concerned with theory, whereas the schools were perceived as being concerned with practice. "Interest" was generated in our research activity and in the more general possibilities it suggested for altered school-university relations. As our work progressed, personal relationships within the collaborative research group changed. So too did relationships between participants in the collaborative group and others in the school. In these ways the political act of creating a collaborative research study set in motion a process that altered the political contexts of the project, educational relationships within the school, and the imagined relationship of the school to the university (see also chapter 5).

This sketch of the Bay Street School project contains the outlines of the promise of collaborative research in a political context. Promise resides in the potential for the political acts of collaborative research to change the political context of theory-practice relations between school and university. In the following, we shall expand on this outline by discussing how political contexts are expressions of overlapping and competing professional knowledge contexts which are learned and changed through the sharing of stories. In so doing we will develop the concept of a professional knowledge context—the context within which teachers and university faculty live and develop their own professional knowledge. The remainder of this essay is not taken up with the nature and content of professional knowledge but with the professional communal places in which teachers and university faculty live.

Promise is a useful metaphor for thinking about changing participants' professional knowledge contexts that govern theory-practice relations between universities and schools. Promise conveys a sense of imaginative possibility. Imaginative possibilities are the best we can, and should, anticipate for these altered relationships. The expressive potential of any particular collaborative inquiry is a complex function of the participating parties, their intentions, and their particular political context. Our own sense of possibility, sketched in a chapter in a recent curriculum handbook, is illustrative. We wrote:

When we stilled our researchers' voices to hear the teachers recount the stories of their lives in classrooms and schools, we sensed a need to have spaces in which both stories, those of researchers and teachers, could be heard. As we learned to listen to the teacher stories and as we became aware of the ways in which our stories were lived out in the classroom, we saw that both stories could be told. Neither voice was silenced, nor did we seek to achieve a mere compromise or consensus between the stories. A new kind of story of the teacher as curriculum maker was being constructed, one in which both the stories were told. . . . Kennard describes this collaborative relationship as "a mutual research, revisioning and restorying, a way of achieving voice within the exigencies of our narrative impulse."[2] This mutual construction of stories that arise from collaborative inquiry provides possibilities for change in the practices of teachers as curriculum makers and in the kind of research we envision. These possibilities spring from the close connection with the worlds in which teachers live out their stories.[3]

The promise of collaborative research set forth in this statement reflects our histories as collaborators with each other and with teachers and students. It also reflects the topic and its curriculum handbook context. Though we expect that our hopes will be shared by some, we know that relationships are negotiated anew with each set of collaborating participants. Each such negotiation creates its own possibilities. In effect, collaborative research sets in motion situations of expressive potential for participant relationships and for the knowledge contexts in which they live. Participants' stories are lived and told, retold and relived in ways that could not be imagined with certainty at the outset of any particular collaboration. Within each particular collaboration, the working relations, the stories, and the part participants play in each others' stories are continually renegotiated. With each negotiation come new possibilities for renegotiating participants' professional knowledge contexts.

Collaborative researchers may, of course, adopt almost any methodological form and thereby create the appearance of still more promising possibilities. But it is not research method that creates possibilities; rather, it is the existence of mutual inquiry relationships. A collaborative ethnography is still an ethnography. But the collaboration that produced it has the potential to alter the participants' understanding of each other as well as embedding the separate understandings of each in the ethnography. Two people working together change each other through the process. Thus, while a collaborative ethnography remains an ethnography, it contains elements intermixed in a different way than if the ethnography had been performed by either a teacher researcher or a university researcher. The different ways each experiences the work of the other is at the heart of the possibility of participants' changed knowledge of one another and their respective political settings. At bottom it is the political quality of collaborative research that conveys its promise to alter the political context of school-university relations.

Professional Knowledge Contexts

In this section we look more closely at the professional knowledge contexts of schools and universities (see also chapter 9). We specifically focus on the way the stories that make up professional knowledge contexts shape the stories that are lived and told in collaborative research projects. Pervasive within both professional knowledge contexts is a theory-practice story in which the university is a place of knowledge and reflection and the school is a place of action. The resistance of university faculty to becoming meaningfully involved in school-university partnerships is testimony to the living power of the story. University faculty are "comfortably couched in the security of (their) traditional roles and responsibilities, and collaboration seems to mean that the other partners will be doing the changing."[4] University faculty do not want to get involved in the messiness of school practices which they expect from the story. This story is not, however, wholly of the university's making. It is told by research funding agencies, policy makers, school practitioners, parents, and other community members. Indeed it is a story of the Western world. The universality and taken-for-grantedness of this sacred story, along with the subtle way it influences how school and university people view and act toward one another, give this story a "sacred"[5] quality. We refer to that story in this chapter as the sacred theory-practice story. It creates a pervasive moral structure governing the actions of university and school people. We will discuss the way this sacred shaping story and the more "mundane" professional stories of everyday institutional life are, themselves, potentially reshaped within collaborative research.

We are only beginning to understand schools and universities in terms of professional knowledge contexts constituted by professionally shared stories. We are trying to think through the consequences of imagining our professional lives as being lived out in knowledge contexts composed of institutional stories, myths, rituals, and symbols which define our work life.[6] One of the first noticeable consequences is that the professional knowledge contexts of schools and universities are intertwined. They are each held up by the same societal context and both partake of the same educational community and its political context. As this chapter is written, for instance, North America is in an economic recession. Government decisions are being taken which affect the entire educational system. Furthermore, specific decisions which affect schools impact on the university and vice versa. Professionals in both institutions know this and hold stories in common about education and about such matters as larger classes and their impact on student achievement and teacher satisfaction, the availability of funds and energy for research, development, and school improvement, and so on.

Noticing this consequence of thinking of our professional lives in storied knowledge contexts may seem unremarkable until it is realized that common ways of behaving belie the fact of professionally interwoven stories. For example, those of us who live in universities are central characters in the sacred theory-practice story as it affects the relationship between universities and schools. Seldom, if ever, do university researchers recognize that their own professional knowledge is embedded in and therefore under study in their research on schools. Instead of acting on this autobiographical quality they proceed, instead, as if they had, as the philosopher Mark Johnson calls it, "a God's-eye-view"[7] of schools . . . distinct, untouched by schools, able to see them for what they are, able to understand them in special ways, and with the authority to advise them on courses of action. It is inevitable that a university teacher, studying school teaching, infuses the work with his or her professional knowledge of teaching. The fiction of the God's-eye-view is that the researcher's self stands outside the object of study.

We call such sacred stories professional knowledge stories. Sacred stories define professional knowledge contexts and govern the political relations between schools and universities by shaping the specific mundane stories to which individuals adhere. "Mundane" professional stories such as "I don't do professional development days because I can't make a difference on a one-shot basis," or "Night classes are a waste of time because I spend most of my time getting teachers to stop telling war stories," or "The increasingly strong ethical guidelines for research on human subjects prevents good research from being done" are common stories told by university faculty. These mundane professional knowledge stories create character roles for individuals. Stories such as these, acted out in a myriad of ways, define the possible relations among school and university people and are, therefore, of political importance.

What we intend to convey by the term "professional knowledge context" becomes clearer perhaps if we look at aspects of professional life in universities and schools. An important aspect of the professional knowledge context of the university is the university's reward structure. One of the mundane professional knowledge stories is a story in which teaching is of secondary importance to research and publication. Rewards are given for research and publication rather than for teaching. A second aspect of the university professional knowledge context comes out of a story of university faculty as experts, the ones who know the answers. Expert knowledge comes from research and with expert knowledge comes authority. Part of the university's professional knowledge context is also composed of stories about schools and teachers. The university stories of school teachers are most often stories of people with routine practices, of people with secure, tenured positions, of people who need to be made accountable through evaluation processes, of people who have less knowledge than university teachers. These stories are ones built around a view of hierarchical relationships between schools and universities. Schools and teachers tend to be seen in a service relationship to university and university faculty. Schools provide research sites for the university, teachers and children are research subjects, schools are where universities send student teachers to apply teaching theory and to "practice teach."

Teachers, too, live in a storied professional knowledge context. Their knowledge context has much in common with the knowledge context of the university. They are both teaching institutions, there are ongoing teaching and research relations among them, and they share the sacred theory-practice story. But their mundane professional knowledge stories have their own flavor and some stories are special to the schools. Their professional knowledge context is composed of stories of cutting corners because of too much work, of personal exhaustion, of emotional splits between their personal and professional lives, of a lack of authority in a hierarchical structure, of trying one's best for children with special problems, of coping with mixed ability classes, of teaching classes that are too large and composed of children of varied interests, of rest and recuperation, of enjoyment in teaching a certain topic, and so on.

Part of school teachers' professional knowledge context is also composed of stories of the university. Their stories of university faculty are of people with little pressure, more reflective time, and more freedom to construct their own work lives. According to these stories, university faculty are knowledgeable, theoretical, and act as if they had certain answers. Though many school practitioners' stories tend to dismiss university faculty as inexperienced, impractical, and arrogant, their face-to-face relations tend often to be marked by a sense of hierarchy and teacher diffidence, qualities to be expected given the sacred theory-practice story.

There are other features of the professional knowledge context of schools and universities. For example, there are temporal rhythms which develop around the cyclic organization of time in our institutions. For instance, Stephanie, a first-grade teacher, developed a rhythmic knowledge around the cycle of school holidays and planned her units around holidays such as Thanksgiving. To understand Stephanie, her children's learning and her classroom practice, it is important to understand schooling's temporal, rhythmic nature.[8] University faculty and school teachers develop a rhythmic knowing around these cycles. The cycles and, therefore, the rhythmic knowing of teaching within each of these professional knowledge contexts are, however, quite different.

We see these professional knowledge contexts most clearly in teacher education settings. Schön describes the particular, taken-for-granted, ways of educating professionals within the universities. Schön's account is essentially an account of the sacred theory-practice story in which knowledge is applied to action and in which the source of knowledge is the university.[9] This application of the sacred story sets up certain story lines for people to live out in professional education. This story is now a taken-for-granted way of educating professionals and forms part of the professional knowledge context in which we live. The temporal, physical, and social organization of the universities is structured around the sacred story in order to facilitate these ways of educating. As we and our students live out our lives of professional education we come to know ourselves, each other, and our respective institutions in certain ways. Students who become teachers have learned to live a story in which they play a certain role vis-à-vis university faculty. University faculty live out their parts in the same sacred story. The university is, therefore, privileged with respect to the sacred story because of the teacher-student relationship which exists between the universities and the schools. Almost everyone tells the same story. But the university is most responsible for transmitting it each generation.

This illustration of what we mean by "professional knowledge context" in teacher education turns out to be more than a mere example. The promise of collaborative research to alter the political context and to reconstruct the sacred story rests on a foundation of new relationships among school practitioners and university faculty during the act of collaborative research. But research is a comparatively small enterprise at the university-school interface. If all research were collaborative, the ratio of coparticipants to all teachers and university faculty would still be comparatively low. But teaching relationships between schools and universities are experienced by almost everyone on both sides. We believe that the promise of collaborative research is, therefore, best thought of in terms of the relationship of research to teaching. No doubt the conceptual pathway to a new sacred story may be smoothed by ameliorating other impediments in the political context. But if the sacred story of the relationship of schools to universities is not transformed in teaching, a retold story emanating from collaborative research will be swallowed and digested as a version of the existing sacred story. One of our agendas, therefore, is to reimagine the relationship of research to teaching.

Learning to Construct Collaborative Relations: Difficult Conditions for Collaborative Research

The sacred theory-practice story is so deeply embedded in the narrative histories of schools and universities that new collaborative forms of research struggle against taken-for-granted mundane stories of what to value in research and how it is to be conducted. Procedures, processes, and rules in teachers' professional knowledge contexts work against their involvement in collaborative research. Too often teachers are told that they should not spend time engaging in shared work with university faculty. Teachers who do so spend personal time and money on their involvement. They are often kept on the margins of professional groups. When they begin to speak of their involvement in such projects they are sometimes dismissed as trying to "get ahead" in the system rather than being seen as engaged in a process of personal and professional growth and as trying to effect change in schools.

Something similar happens when university researchers begin to work against the grain (see chapter 9) and begin to live and tell a story of engaging in collaborative work with teachers. Part of the university's knowledge context is that collaborative research is less readily funded and the research results more difficult to publish. Research procedures, processes, and rules in the university are built around stories of research in which university faculty do research on teachers as subjects. For example, ethical guidelines are set up to require university faculty to protect school personnel as subjects rather than to support them as collaborators. Merit and promotion committees are accustomed to assessing research productivity on noncollaborative research. In such projects, there is no need to establish collaborative working relationships based on enormously time-consuming processes of building trust. Administrators and university merit and tenure committees have difficulty understanding the crucial necessity of the time required to work together in collaborative research.

Our sketchy account of the professional knowledge contexts of schools and universities cast in the form of sacred and mundane stories frames the promise of collaborative research in the political context. Conceptualizing schools and universities in terms of knowledge contexts allows us to understand the possibility of transformation and educational growth in ourselves and in our institutions. The promise of collaborative research is that, through learning to live and tell new stories, the professional knowledge contexts in both universities and schools may change.

Bringing Research to Teaching and Teaching to Research

We made the point above that the fulfillment of the promise of collaborative research depends heavily on the influence of research on teaching. Without this connection research is too minor an enterprise in the overall scheme of education to make a significant difference to the professional knowledge contexts in schools and universities (see chapter 5). There are, of course, ongoing attempts to have research influence practice via teaching. Professors in graduate schools of education expect their teacher-students to become familiar with relevant research. To a lesser extent this applies as well in preservice teacher education, though here there is considerable ambivalence toward the value of research findings for improving the preparation of teachers. Though this ambivalence is extended to the ongoing professional development of teachers, research results are imported into the professional knowledge context of schools through selected policy initiatives and through programs for curriculum development and professional development. Most research which enters the professional knowledge context this way has a strong ideological basis and is often connected to current fancies. Consider for instance, elementary school programs which are often developed around one or another currently well-known theory of child development. It tends to be the ideological outlook of the theory that enters the professional knowledge context and not the specifics of research studies. Documents are prepared and workshops given which are essentially designed to complete the phrase "research shows that . . . ." Thus, it tends to be what Joseph Schwab called a rhetoric of conclusions that enters the professional knowledge context of schools rather than the spirit and content of inquiry.[10]

But even if research results were satisfactorily fed into the professional knowledge context of schools and universities, the relationship of the universities to schools would essentially remain unchanged. It might even be argued that the successful adoption of research results would simply strengthen the theory-practice split between universities and schools and eventually lead to the strengthening of the sacred story.

Research is also brought to teaching through the study of teaching. Research on teaching accounts for a significant proportion of North American educational research. The American Educational Research Association has produced three handbooks of research on teaching[11] and only recently has turned to the production of handbooks in such other areas as curriculum.[12] It is ironic, however, that while university faculty have devoted considerable attention to injecting the results of this research into the professional knowledge context of schools, it has not become part of the professional knowledge context of universities. It is well known that there are comparatively few studies of university teaching and that university teachers do not use, in their own teaching, the findings they so heartily wish teachers in elementary and secondary schools would use. They simply do not practice what they preach.[13] Again, even if the universities practiced what they preached, the central sacred theory-practice story would either be unaffected or strengthened. The plot would remain the same.

It will be clear by now that we do not believe much is to be gained by efforts to better utilize research on teaching in schools and universities. Too many development and implementation resources have already gone unproductively to this effort without a recognition that the potential for the improvement of education was low in the first place. Changing the professional knowledge context of schools and universities by adding results of research on teaching has small payoff. Instead we believe that energy should be devoted to reimagining the relationship of research and teaching to one another. We need to imagine ways to bring research to teaching and infuse it with a spirit of inquiry; and we need to imagine ways of bringing teaching to research and infusing it with a spirit of educational growth. We believe that teaching needs to be seen as a form of inquiry and that research needs to be seen as a form of teaching for those who do research.

The separation of research from teaching is so entrenched in the professional knowledge context of educators that it could justifiably be said to constitute another sacred story. Research is research and teaching is teaching and the two should not be confused. This sharp separation of research from teaching helps account for the fact that research is mostly seen as a prerogative of the universities. It also helps account for university teachers' attitude toward not using research results to improve their own teaching practice while promoting such use for school teachers.

Teaching, of course, is a central mission of universities but its status within the universities is low compared to research. Faculty members frequently "buy out" of teaching with research funds and, as noted above in our comment on the university reward structure, it is commonly acknowledged that the most prestigious and easy route to promotion and tenure is publication of research. Conversely, research is commonly conducted by school people in large school districts which sometimes have research offices. In such cases, the notion of research tends to mimic the most valued research forms in the university community. Surveys, summaries of school reports, program evaluations, and statistical data are in evidence.

One of our own amusing research stories is that of making application for a narrative research study to a local school board's research department and eventually having our application rejected because we were not doing research according to the criteria for research formulated by the board's research committee. At the same time and for the same reason we were told to go ahead with our work because the committee's only concern was to evaluate research and, since ours did not qualify, we were granted access to the schools. Thus, while teaching and research do coexist in the professional knowledge contexts of both universities and schools, it is a coexistence born out of the separation of theory and practice. We are trying to imagine, instead, a sacred story which would conceptualize and define research in terms of teaching, and teaching in terms of research.

The Promise for Change

So far, we have expanded the notion of the political context for collaborative research by exploring the sacred theory-practice story of the relationship of universities and schools. Arrayed against such a political context, collaborative research may seem to have little promise. The record confirms this pessimistic impression. Individuals in schools and universities learn and enact existing professional knowledge stories. But the link between individuals' stories and professional knowledge stories is the same link that, turned around, holds promise for magnifying the possibility that individual stories may change the sacred one. The possibility depends on understanding collaborative research as a political act consisting of specific people. To enter into a collaborative relationship is to create a new story outside of or aside from the sacred one. The collaborative research relationship changes the character a school teacher or a university faculty member lives in his or her story of research. And if these people talk and write about their work, thereby creating new professional knowledge stories, there is the possibility for change in the sacred story.

For us, therefore, the promise of collaborative research is in the possibility of changing the professional knowledge contexts of schools and universities. We see this happening in two related ways: teachers are increasingly claiming ownership of research, and collaborative research between university faculty and school teachers is being undertaken.

There is a developing literature and tradition of teacher research. Some of this research is closer in spirit to the plot line of the sacred story than is other teacher research. For example, Lieberman and Miller write about the conditions that need to be in place to encourage teachers to engage in research (see also chapter 11). They write that:

The research sensibility must be infused into the dailiness of the school. Such an infusion takes time and commitment. It begins with an acknowledgment of the importance of norms of collegiality and experimentation; it builds on shared problem identification and a mutual search for solutions; it depends on taking a risk in the classroom; it requires the support of colleagues.[14]

By themselves these sentiments may be mainly an expression of the sacred theory-practice story. If that view were taken to the extreme, teachers would do both research and teaching in much the same way as researchers do both.

Another example of teacher research comes out of a narrative research tradition in which teachers write their own stories of practice. Because these stories, written as teacher research, focus on a teacher's teaching they tend to express an intimate connection between research and teaching. They are, therefore, less likely to be an expression of the sacred theory-practice story. Teacher research is now finding its way into university classrooms. For the most part, it is mostly used in an illustrative way as university teachers use it to show prospective teachers insights into the lived world of teaching.[15] But as these teacher research accounts are heard there is pressure for the university's professional knowledge context to change. Increasingly there is a story of teachers as producers of research rather than as consumers of it.

Teacher researchers are also beginning to change the professional knowledge contexts in schools. They are questioning traditional university stories of ownership of research. They are now occasionally asked to talk about their research at conferences and on professional development days. Furthermore, there is some movement toward teachers asking to work with other teachers in teacher research. Evidence of this movement is found in such organizations as the Among Teachers Community,[16] and the Teacher Research Special Interest Group of the American Educational Research Association. Funding through teachers' federations and other groups is becoming available for teacher research.

A second related way in which the professional knowledge contexts of schools and universities are changing is through collaborative research. Some teachers and university faculty are beginning to meet in a middle ground of connection in research projects. Such projects are marked by the negotiation of purpose in which both university faculty and school teachers share responsibility. On this middle ground special attention is paid to issues of trust, voice, equality, ownership, and mutuality. Each one of these issues can be more time-consuming and difficult to negotiate for a group of collaborating researchers than for a single researcher. When collaboration is between individuals from different professional knowledge contexts (school and university) the problems of negotiation are magnified. In many ways collaborative research is the most difficult kind of research given what we have written about the professional knowledge contexts of both institutions. For individuals to move outside their institutions, to try to stay open to individuals from other institutions in which there is a radically different professional knowledge context, has the greatest risk but also the greatest potential for educational reform. The risks for university faculty and for school teachers are different in kind and degree.

University faculty who break from the sacred theory-practice story by living and telling stories of themselves outside the stories of expert, of knowledge production, of certainty, and of hierarchy are taking professional risks. They give up a familiar privileged story for the uncertainties of a new story of equality that is constructed as they engage in a conversation about collaborative research. There is much to give up and much to change in the ways university faculty live their lives. Hollingsworth describes what she gave up as a university teacher moving into a collaborative research project:

> I had to change my interactions so that I was no longer telling teachers what I knew (as the group's "expert" on the topic of reading instruction) and checking to see if they learned it, to a process of working with them as a co-learner and creator of evolving expertise through nonevaluative conversation. To accomplish that shift, I had to get still and listen; I also had to struggle publicly with what I was learning. Because the new format required that I form an ongoing relationship with these teachers, transformation in my own learning as a researcher and a teacher educator became an equally important measure of determining the success of teachers' knowledge transformations.[17]

When we have negotiated that middle ground in our collaborative projects, we have often talked about our new insights, our awakenings, and transformations as we learn to tell and live new stories. Teachers have also expressed similar insights about their transformed practices. The collaborative conversations of the projects in which all participants tell and retell their stories foster the possibility that participants will have changed practices. As participants share their stories of collaboration and transformed practices with friends and colleagues a ripple effect is created.

There is also promise for change when teachers and university faculty write and publish their accounts of collaborative research. These accounts become the nucleus of new stories to be told in the professional knowledge contexts of both institutions. As these stories begin to be read in the two institutions there is the possibility of reshaping the professional knowledge contexts in both school and university.

Summary

Is this a good time to be thinking about changing the professional knowledge contexts of schools and universities? Some might think not, given the current economic climate and the popular labeling of schools as places of crisis. But we are optimistic. Many teachers, at least in Canada, are beginning to feel angry about their lack of voice in influencing education decisions, policy prescriptions, and research. But while some of this anger is unimaginatively expressed as an anger of resistance much of it is channeled imaginatively. Teachers have begun to form support groups and research groups and some are beginning, tentatively, to reach out to universities. At the same time, some university faculty, inspired by feminist and qualitative research methodologies and alternative conceptions of knowledge, are reaching out to engage teachers in collaborative research settings.

These efforts are, however, up against a more formidable political adversary than that generated by a poor economic climate and an attitude of mistrust of schools. The adversary is the unseen, unfelt, ever present sacred theory-practice story which separates universities and schools along hierarchical theory-practice lines. The sacred theory-practice story, transmitted through university-practitioner relationships in situations involving teaching-learning and research is essentially reproduced in school administration, school structures, and, of the utmost importance, in the teaching-learning relationships between school teachers and students. Parents and others in the educational community also tell the sacred story. This telling is often unsubtle and direct as political pressure groups demand higher levels of student achievement in the knowledge and skills that teachers are expected to hold and transmit to them.

Teachers' professional knowledge is created out of a professional life lived at a double boundary, one with the university and one with the parental community. On the one side, the sacred story specifies a hierarchical teaching and research relationship between faculty and practitioners with practitioners at the bottom. On the other side, the sacred story specifies a similar relationship between teachers and students with teachers at the top. At the latter boundary, teachers become life theoreticians and students the practitioners of life as the sacred story played out in university teaching and research relationships is replayed at the school level.

The sacred story is maintained by the mundane professional stories that define university and school professional life and which specify forms of relationships between universities and schools. Collaborative research can alter the political quality of life in universities and schools for participants because the sacred theory-practice story must give way if successful collaboration is to occur.

But, on balance, there is so little research that even if all research were collaborative its positive effects would tend to be swamped. For this reason we believe that the promise of collaborative research lies in a revived commitment to bringing research to teaching and teaching to research, both in universities and in schools, and in their teaching and research relationships.

The reason it is desirable to change these hierarchical relationships is essentially the same reason given for preferring collaborative research relationships: people are treated equally rather than hierarchically; authority is shared; respect and reciprocity of response equally confirms collaborating partners. Lives are brought to relationships and lives are enhanced in educational relationship. There is no imposition of one life on another. Instead, educational communities of value to university faculty and school teachers, and to school teachers and students are created.

The justification for changing the stories that shape the lives of practitioners and academics in the professional knowledge contexts is not that doing so will improve their lives—though this is a significant objective in itself—but, rather, that it has the potential for school improvement, better education for individuals, and positive social development. We believe that this is the ultimate promise of collaborative research.

In its idealized form, then, collaborative research is a political act which alters its immediate political context. It fosters different teaching relationships in the universities and in the schools according to a retold sacred story and is potentially regenerative of itself as new teachers enter the schools and as school students become part of society and give social voice to a new sacred story. The political context with which we began this essay is ultimately the community at large. As the Deweyan philosopher John McDermott said, "Experience grows at its edges."[18] Bit by bit this is how we imagine that the creation of new professional knowledge stories will change educational experience personally and societally.

NOTES

1. See F. Michael Connelly and D. Jean Clandinin, "Personal Practical Knowledge at Bay Street School: Ritual, Personal Philosophy, and Image," in *Teacher Thinking: A New Perspective on Persisting Problems in Education*, Proceedings of the first symposium of the International Study Association of Teacher Thinking, edited by Rob Halkes and John K. Olson (Lisse: Swets and Zeitlinger, 1984), pp. 134-149. D. Jean Clandinin, *Classroom Practice: Teacher Images in Action* (London: Falmer Press, 1986).

2. Barbara Kennard, "Moments of Seeing: Parallel Stories of Narrative Change in Collaborative Relationships" (Unpublished paper, University of Calgary, 1988).

3. D. Jean Clandinin and F. Michael Connelly. "The Teacher as Curriculum Maker," in *Handbook of Research on Curriculum: A Project of the American Educational Research Association*, edited by Philip W. Jackson (New York: Macmillan, 1992), pp. 363-401.

4. Robert L. Sinclair and Anne E. Harrison, "A Partnership for Increasing Student Learning: The Massachusetts Coalition for School Improvement," in *School-University Partnerships in Action: Concepts, Cases, and Concerns*, edited by Kenneth A. Sirotnik and John I. Goodlad (New York: Teachers College Press, 1988), pp. 87-105.

5. Stephen Crites, "The Narrative Quality of Experience," *Journal of the American Academy of Religion* 39, no. 3 (1971): 291-311.

6. F. Michael Connelly, D. Jean Clandinin, and Michael Fullan, *Teacher Education: Links between Professional and Personal Knowledge*, Sponsored Research Proposal no. 0904 (Ottawa: Social Sciences and Humanities Research Council of Canada, 1990).

7. Mark Johnson, *The Body in the Mind: The Bodily Basis of Meaning, Imagination, and Reason* (Chicago: University of Chicago Press, 1987).

8. D. Jean Clandinin and F. Michael Connelly, "Rhythms in Teaching: The Narrative Study of Teachers' Personal Practical Knowledge of Classrooms," *Teaching and Teacher Education* 2, no. 4 (1986): 377-387.

9. Donald A. Schön, *Educating the Reflective Practitioner* (San Francisco: Jossey-Bass, 1987).

10. Joseph J. Schwab, "What Do Scientists Do?" in *Science, Curriculum and Liberal Education: Selected Essays*, edited by Ian Westbury and Neal J. Wilkof (Chicago: University of Chicago Press, 1978), pp. 184-228.

11. N. L. Gage, ed., *Handbook of Research on Teaching* (Chicago: Rand McNally, 1963); Robert M. W. Travers, ed., *Second Handbook of Research on Teaching* (Chicago: Rand McNally, 1973); Merlin C. Wittrock, ed., *Handbook of Research on Teaching*, 3rd ed. (New York: Macmillan, 1986).

12. Philip W. Jackson, ed., *Handbook of Research on Curriculum* (New York: Macmillan, 1992).

13. Larry Cuban, *How Teachers Taught: Constancy and Change in American Classrooms, 1890-1980* (New York: Longman, 1984).

14. Ann Lieberman and Lynne Miller, "Teacher Development and Professional Practice Schools," *Teachers College Record* 92, no. 1 (1990): 105-122.

15. Kathy Carter, "The Place of Story in Research on Teaching" (Invited address at the Annual Meeting of the American Educational Research Association, San Francisco, 1992).

16. The Among Teachers Community (A$_c$T) is a community of teachers sponsored by the Joint Center for Teacher Development at the Ontario Institute for Studies of Education and the Faculty of Education, University of Toronto and the Center for Research for Teacher Education and Development at the University of Alberta. A$_c$T publishes *Among Teachers*, a teachers journal alternately published at the University of Alberta and the Ontario Institute for Studies in Education with the University of Toronto.

17. Sandra Hollingsworth, "Learning to Teach through Collaborative Conversation: A Feminist Approach," *American Journal of Educational Research* 29, no. 2 (1992): 375.

18. John J. McDermott, "Experience Grows by Its Edges: A Phenomenology of Relations in an American Philosophical Vein," in *Streams of Experience: Reflections on the History and Philosophy of American Culture*, edited by John J. McDermott (Amherst, MA: University of Massachusetts Press, 1986).

CHAPTER VI

Teacher Research to Change Policy: An Illustration

J. MYRON ATKIN

What happens when a small group of California teachers who have been designated by their school districts to serve as mentors for other teachers sets out independently to change policy with respect to the program of which they are a part? And what are the results when they conduct a systematic study of the issues that concern them, publish that study, and then follow up with a plan to use their research and the resulting monograph as instruments to bring about the policy changes they wish to see?

A group of seven mentor teachers embarked in 1988 on such an enterprise. I was one of two people from a university who assisted them. This chapter is anchored in that particular effort. The study in which the teachers engaged is used here as a vehicle for highlighting questions that seem to be associated with teachers engaging in research that has a policy focus. The study and the circumstances surrounding it are also used to illustrate how research of this type by teachers is different from (and usefully supplements) the kinds of studies that engage more conventionally oriented educational researchers when they try to illuminate and affect policy.

While research by teachers gradually is becoming more prominent on the education scene, as this volume demonstrates, it usually is conceived and conducted as a method whereby teachers undertake an investigation to improve their own classroom practice. Teacher-initiated research is employed less often to alter the setting within which teachers work and the factors that govern their professional activities—in short, to change key elements of the policy system itself (see chapter 2).

Some disclaimers are in order. First, the underlying perspective here, inescapably in view of the authorship, is that of a professor—a person who essentially is an outsider in the world of mentor teaching

J. Myron Atkin is a Professor in the School of Education, Stanford University.

and one, therefore, who is relatively uninformed about the subject of the actual research that was taken up by the group. I attempted (and am still attempting) to facilitate the work of the seven mentors (now nine) as they conducted their research. In that role, I learned about issues that seem important to them. But whatever special competencies and contributions I may have brought to the group stem from my own professional concerns and interests, which were always tangential to the matter of improving the State of California's mentor-teacher program.

In relating part of the story of what came to be called by those who participated "The Mentor Teacher Study Group," I refer to some of the group's more finely focused insights about mentor teaching and its dilemmas. They are included to provide the reader with the grounding necessary to comprehend the observations about influence on policy that are the main topic of the chapter. Therefore, a second disclaimer is necessary: The richness of an insider's view of mentor teaching and how it might be improved, its challenges and problems, best come from the mentors themselves, not from this author. Several of their insights are reported here, but much deeper comprehension of the substance of the research is best obtained from the written report of the mentors themselves. My aim is to present some observations from the vantage point of one actively involved in the process from the beginning, but as a facilitator with his own interests and agenda, not as an expert on the intricacies and challenges of mentor teaching.

Universities and Practical Research

So why was a professor involved in the first place? My own motivation for helping to launch the Study Group centers on concerns developed over several decades as a faculty member (and Dean of the School of Education) at two major research-oriented universities, the University of Illinois at Champaign-Urbana and Stanford. I have come to believe that educational research as we view it today is not an enterprise that makes much of a difference on actual educational events, either in classrooms or in forums where decisions are made about the directions and workings of the educational enterprise itself. Moreover, practical impact often is not even its primary goal. Educational research is an undertaking with its own rhythms and objectives that only sometimes corresponds with the professional concerns of teachers and those charged with the actual responsibility of creating the conditions under which classroom teachers try to meet their responsibilities (see also chapter 3).

It is true many educational researchers harbor the view that their work can affect schools. They believe that if the findings of their research were to be carefully and wisely applied, certain practices would improve. They assume that practice will change for the better if they successfully pursue the delineation of principles that are broadly applicable. Their job is to identify those principles. Other people have the job of applying them.

The quest for universals and the methods that have been developed to identify them, however, comport poorly with the kinds of practical knowledge teachers and policymakers need. Furthermore, teachers and policymakers usually ask questions and cope with dilemmas that are seldom posed by university-based researchers. As a teacher in the midst of a carefully crafted lesson, should I go off on what seems a tangent in responding to a particular student's important question? Not to do so fails to capitalize on a responsive chord that seems to interest many students in the class; the discussion could also lead to some important ideas. To respond to the student in detail, however, risks losing one of the main points of the planned lesson.

Teachers must cope with such dilemmas dozens of times every day. They ask questions quite different from the sorts of generalized and decontextualized inquiries that absorb most researchers. Researchers want to know how most people behave, for example, when faced with new opportunities to learn certain concepts, or at least when identifiable classes of people try to learn those concepts. They aim to generate knowledge that pertains to as wide a set of people and situations as possible. Those with practical responsibilities in actual classrooms, on the other hand, want and require knowledge that is concrete, timely, prudent, and particular to their own circumstances and students.

Policymakers face similar choices. Should a career ladder for teachers be established that includes differential pay on the basis of some measure of merit? How might a new curriculum in science that emphasizes cross-disciplinary themes best be promoted in a school district or state? There are many studies and much useful information that relate to each of these questions. Educational researchers have surveyed certain districts that have instituted merit pay, and they have reported on recruitment and retention rates of teachers that may be associated with various plans. They have looked at different methods of identifying teachers for the merit track. Other researchers have studied strategies for curriculum innovation. What happens when programs have been introduced from the state level? How do teachers develop a stake in successful introduction of the new program?

These studies, at least many of them, are rigorous and useful, but they cannot possibly be attentive to many of the relevant factors in a particular situation where they might be applied. What has been the stance of the governor (or chief state school officer, or district superintendent, or chair of the relevant legislative committee)? How much can the state pay for the new plan in a tight budgetary climate? Who is supporting the plan, and who is opposing it? What trade-offs are possible? In the last analysis, political choices must be made in the light of some constraints and deeply held values, the influence of key figures and how much they might be willing to alter their views, the timeliness of the proposed change in the light of other items on the education agenda—and much more (see chapter 6).

Almost always, the view of those most likely to be affected by the decisions that are made is a missing ingredient in the information collected to support, modify, or resist a given initiative. How do the teachers react to the prospect of a cross-disciplinary curriculum? At what levels does it have appeal, to what people, and what is the nature of reservations they may have? What light might be shed on the merits of the matter by those most closely involved in its possible implementation? Might the new approach have to replace something that seems valuable? Can teachers themselves do justice to the new program in view of their own strengths and interests?

Teachers' views, when they are sought, are usually factored into the deliberations through their officially designated representatives. Sometimes school principals are assumed to reflect the views of teachers adequately. Often it is the union leadership. Even when teachers' ideas and suggestions are requested, however, the frame of reference is usually that of people in the state or district office. Questions to teachers tend to center more on implementation, for example, than on worth. It is rare that teachers' views are sought early about the desirability of a particular initiative. These days, much of the policy focus is on student achievement and how it might be improved and assessed. Teachers' concerns, however, often go beyond such matters and relate, for example, to the classroom dynamics. How might they be changed as a result of the innovation? How would my own teaching style be affected by the proposed change, and how would it affect my own students? In the case of merit pay, the effects on the teacher and the immediate school community are likely to be more prominent in the opinions of teachers than in those of school-board members—and much more prominent than in legislators' opinions.

Of even deeper significance, rarely do teachers have an opportunity of *initiating* a systematic study of something that they themselves believe would be an educational improvement. They seldom have the opportunity to identify a focus for educational improvement, then bring their own experience and insights to bear in forging a new method of working or a new approach. Teachers only very rarely define the issues that have greatest influence on their own practice. "Reforms," almost always, are generated from outside the school or school district by people in distant places who have only minimal knowledge of concrete and local circumstances. Almost always, teachers are reacting to the initiatives of others.

Many educational researchers, including those who specialize in policy-related matters, have never taught in elementary or secondary school classrooms, nor have they had operational responsibilities in the policy arena. They have only an indistinct view of the capabilities, motivation, priorities, and wisdom of teachers and others faced with the necessity of taking action. The typical researcher's perspectives usually are derived from observation and reading, not from having engaged personally in the activity. They are spectators, not insiders. And they are judged in their own professional activities by different criteria than are those whose responsibilities are more directly related to providing actual educational services.

What Knowledge Do Teachers Seek?

So how do teachers get wiser about their professional responsibilities, and in what ways is the knowledge they seek and obtain different from that secured in the course of conventional educational research?

California created a mentor-teacher program in 1983 (SB813, the Hughes-Hart Educational Reform Act). The language of the act stipulates (or the legislative history suggests) that the major reasons for the initiative were to recognize excellent teachers, to enable them to have an impact beyond their own classrooms, and to provide a method of advancing their careers without requiring that they leave teaching and take up posts as administrators. A closely related purpose, mentioned in the legislation, was to retain excellent teachers in the public school system. The mentor-teacher program enables each district in the state to designate up to 5 percent of its experienced teaching force as mentors. Each participating district must develop its own plan for selecting mentors. For the period they serve, which is limited to three years (though appointments may be renewed in many districts), mentors receive a salary supplement of $4,000. An additional $2,000 is made available to the district to support the work of each mentor. One of the primary purposes of the act was to create a system whereby those designated as mentors assist other teachers, particularly but not exclusively the new ones.

The study began in the fall of 1988 when the seven mentor teachers started voluntarily to meet under the auspices of the Stanford/Schools Collaborative, an organization that had been in operation for several years to strengthen relations between Stanford University and schools in neighboring communities. The Collaborative had received a $15,000 grant from the Walter S. Johnson Foundation to support research by mentor teachers. Beverly Carter, the Collaborative's director, thereupon invited mentors affiliated with the University in an existing program to come to an orientation session to consider the possibility of a research effort.

The seven mentors were those who remained after an initial meeting of about twenty, at which I had discussed my interest in research by teachers and indicated my willingness to meet regularly with any of the mentors who might want to pursue the matter. For these seven, the Collaborative then created a setting wherein meetings could be held on a regular basis. The newly named Mentor Teacher Study Group included mentor teachers from four school districts on the San Francisco Peninsula. Beverly Carter and I served as conveners, facilitators, and, initially, note-takers.

The first few meetings of the group were devoted largely to the participants getting acquainted. Common interests were identified, professional and personal. There was also considerable discussion, naturally enough, of the state's mentor-teacher program. Gradually a pattern of monthly meetings evolved during which the group would open up some issues regarding mentor teaching for a couple of hours, then continue the discussion over dinner. (Grant funds were used to pay for the dinners. There were no stipends for the teachers, initially, or additional financial compensation for Beverly Carter or me.) Despite the purpose of the meetings, to plan and then conduct research, Beverly Carter and I could detect little effort during the first four or five sessions that seemed directed toward identifying a particular focus for the group's activities—nor did we try to encourage the group to move quickly toward defining a specific topic.

Much of the initial conversation was about what each of the seven was doing in her professional role and how each person's assignment was different in important ways from everyone else's. Each clearly was interested in what the others were doing, and each mentor, before long, spoke freely about dilemmas and problems that were being faced. Such topics, in fact, captured more time than any others in the first few meetings. Embedded in the stories that were being told, however, was a strong and unmistakable undercurrent of immense satisfaction about the work they were doing, in fact a tone that the group itself later came to consider celebratory. It was clear, also, that members of the group liked one another.

It was perhaps this sense of accomplishment and pride that caused the members of the group to become concerned about what they saw as possible threats to the program as they had come to know and work in it. As they spoke, they began to pick up indications in the stories they shared that the mentor-teacher program was being modified in ways that they believed ran counter to the purposes for which it was created. For example, some of them were being asked to assume certain administrative responsibilities. The school districts in which they served were experiencing severe financial problems. Administrators were asked to take on more responsibility, or, in some cases, return to the classroom. As a result, central offices of school districts were placing responsibilities on mentors that this group believed compromised their role as fellow teachers and colleagues of those whom they were trying to assist.

Additionally, again in view of financial pressures, there was even the possibility that the mentor program might be cut back at the state level (though that possibility did not become an actual threat until much later). Because of the celebratory nature of the mentors' view of their program and the growing sense that it might be in the process of being altered in undesirable ways, the Study Group gradually turned its attention to the matter of trying to understand more about the mentor program itself. They wanted to find out about its origins and evolution. It began to appear that they most wanted to spend their time together to figure out how they might protect and improve the entire mentor program, rather than concentrating solely on how they might enhance their professional activities within the confines of their immediate jobs, which seemed to have been the initial motivation for getting together.

Research to Change Policy: Collecting Stories
and Other Data

The foundation grant had stipulated that the group of mentors would conduct collaborative research; so as conversation began to turn more deliberately to questions of what the group might study systematically, the members began seriously to consider a study of how the program itself was changing. This development was something of a surprise to members of the group since they had assumed that they would be studying ways to improve their own practice in a more immediate sense. However, since they were troubled by what they thought they saw happening to weaken the program, they decided relatively quickly to examine more global issues about the program.

One way to solidify the program, they believed, would be to point out how it affects the lives of teachers, how it is organized and administered, and its results. First, however, they wanted to focus on issues that to them were more personal, and, perhaps, perplexing. In particular, they began to get interested in why teachers choose to apply for the position of mentor in the first place. Here was a group of committed professionals who had made the choice themselves to become part of the program. Perhaps to confirm their own professional decisions, they wanted to find out what might have motivated others who had been attracted to the same role.

Better to understand the matter, they reflected on their reasons for wanting to be mentors. Ann Rounds, a high school English teacher in the Study Group, and her colleague, Ruthe Tyson, a chemistry teacher, had created an opportunity to observe in each other's classrooms. Each had admired the other, but they had had no chance to watch each other teach and little opportunity to discuss professional matters. They launched a program whereby they would meet to discuss teaching plans; then they observed one another.

The result was stimulating and helpful enough for the two of them to propose to the district that they become mentors and gradually introduce other teachers to the potential of pairing off to observe and discuss one another's work. The state's mentor-teacher program is organized such that districts have considerable latitude about how they use the funds provided for the program. Some mentors work with new teachers on the full range of challenges faced by newcomers. Others work with all teachers within a school on whatever issues are identified as important at that site. Some have a particular curriculum or instructional focus—the more effective employment of cooperative learning techniques in the classroom, for example.

Tyson and Rounds were designated as mentors by their district to promote the kind of peer observation and support program they had developed independently. The two of them then designed a program of paired peer observation that eventually included an additional twenty or so teachers. Some were experienced in the district; others not. To facilitate the work, Rounds and Tyson used some of the support funds provided by the state ($2,000 for each mentor teacher) to pay stipends to the other teachers participating in the program.

One way to gain greater insight into the overall mentor program was to start interviewing mentors outside the Study Group. The Study Group soon found that different kinds of motivation seemed to be present. For some teachers, there was a special interest they wanted to pursue, like cooperative learning. Others said that they wanted to be people who "make things happen" in the schools. In general, they learned through interviews with mentors themselves and with others in the schools that mentors are optimistic and energetic people who like to get involved deeply in what captures their imagination. They want to stay close to the classroom, however, and for that reason are not attracted to formal administrative positions (although some mentors eventually move into administration). Almost always, they are people recognized in their districts as among the most outstanding teachers, although it also became clear during the interviews that many teachers considered just as outstanding as those designated as mentors had no wish to take on the job. One of the most common reasons proffered for lack of interest in applying for the position was that it was seen as entailing a considerable amount of extra work.

Some of those who became mentors had been involved in the role in an unofficial capacity for many years. The statewide program afforded an opportunity to make the work part of the regular assignment. Another theme that surfaced in the interviews was that experienced teachers as well as novices often benefited from the work of the mentors. This result seemed a particular source of satisfaction to members of the group because the veteran teachers are seen as peers, and peer approval is a particularly gratifying feature of working with colleagues.

Since those who want to become mentors submit an application and outline what they want to do during the period of the mentorship, the program offers an opportunity to pursue in depth some independently conceived professional interest. "It's almost like starting your own business," said one mentor who was interviewed, with all the uncertainties at the outset about whether or not anyone would want the services that are being offered. At one workshop she offered during her first year as a mentor, she planned for eight people who had said they intended to participate. She planned carefully, reserved the library, and brought cookies and juice. One person came. "Now," said the same teacher, "I have the contacts and know what to do. I began to make contacts in a different way." In view of the difficulty of scheduling so that many teachers could come for the same after-school session, she used more one-on-one contacts.

One of the difficulties the Study Group identified through their interviews and through a questionnaire survey of several score mentors in the San Francisco Bay Area was that mentors in some districts felt isolated. They had little opportunity to share ideas and experiences with other mentors. Since they were not part of the administration, they did not participate in those discussions, either.

Shaping a Report

At about this time, members of the group decided to write a report of their research. They believed that what they were learning might be of broad interest. Publication would also enhance the credibility of their work and enable them to promulgate their views in places where they might not otherwise have influence. For several meetings, they turned their attention to outlining the kind of report they might write.

It was at this stage that Beverly Carter and I may have had our strongest influence on the Study Group's deliberations. Information had been collected through interviews and questionnaires. It was clear that important perspectives were surfacing and that the mentors had something to say that probably would be of considerable interest to others. Their picture of a research report, however, based on what they had seen, was that of a rather formal document. Statistical tables and analyses, hypothesis testing, and a dispassionate voice, for example, were features they had come to associate with educational research. They weren't sure they could do it, or if they wanted to.

The two of us from the University made a plea for the Study Group to try to put aside the goal of producing a report that would look like standard education research. Whatever credibility and influence the Study Group might have, we said, stems from who they are: people with intimate knowledge of the program and how it does or does not work. The report would have its greatest influence if it projects their own voices about mentoring—the perspectives, opinions, and recommendations of perceptive people who speak from the wisdom of their own experience. They are teachers, not trained researchers. To try to shape their insights to fit a form used by university-based researchers would result in a publication that would mask their own vision and muffle their own voice.

Perhaps with some apprehension, but certainly with relief about not attempting a task beyond their interest and capability, the group developed an outline for their report. It would start with a bit of information about the statewide program, but then move quickly to a description of themselves, why they decided to become mentors, and what attracted them to the Study Group. They then would move on to describing other mentors and their jobs, information they had obtained from the interviews and questionnaires.

They decided further context for their activities would be informative, and so they described something of the variety among mentor programs found in the area, how they are organized, how mentors are selected in some of the districts, and what the programs are like. In almost all cases, those wishing to serve as mentors submit an application with a description of the program they want to pursue. This procedure assures considerable variation from district to district, and the Study Group considered it important to accent the diversity.

The next section of the report emphasized what the Group saw as benefits of the mentor program, using anecdotes gleaned from the questionnaires and follow-up interviews. Most of the mentors worked with other teachers on projects like making mathematics instruction less abstract through the use of manipulatives, and teaching reading through subject fields like social studies and science. One teacher embarked on a study of Advanced Placement (AP) courses. Her focus was on policies and practices with respect to these courses in her own school. Some classes labeled "AP," for example, did not require students to take the Advanced Placement test. The children were encouraged to take the courses because they would "make their transcripts look good." The course loads exhausted many of the students, apparently to no other purpose than to fortify their résumés. Her work led to elevation of districtwide concern about the issue and the establishment of a committee to study the matter and make recommendations. This part of the report was highly personalized and accented the satisfactions derived by the mentors from their work, liberally quoting from the interviews they had conducted.

Having described key elements of the program, the next part of the report identified issues that the group believed needed attention. These included the fact that many teachers (and others) had come to see the mentor program as "extra work for extra pay" rather than as a vehicle for expanding the influence of excellent teachers and keeping them in the profession. Some teachers, in fact, likened serving as a mentor to moonlighting. Another issue that received attention was the time limitation on a mentor appointment that some districts had instituted. The legislation provides for appointments for up to three years, but in some districts mentors are not eligible for reappointment. (The state is silent on the matter.) Another issue that was highlighted is the project approach to mentoring that is fairly widespread in the area. Such a conception of the program tends to minimize the mentoring element to achieve special short-term goals.

A few other problematic elements of the mentor-teacher program were identified, including the lack of a supportive organizational structure for mentors and the fact that in many cases the mentor program exacerbated the disengagement of the school principal from matters of curriculum and instruction. Some principals who were interviewed believed mentors ofen worked at cross-purposes with the school administration. The report concluded with a section titled, "What Are Our Worries, Hopes, and Dreams for the Mentor Program?"

Writing the Report

Different sections of the report were written separately in initial draft by each of the mentors. They relied on information secured from the interviews and questionnaires, plus facts and insights generated during the group discussions. The main lines of argument and all matters of interpretation were thoroughly examined in meetings of the Study Group as a whole. One person, however, Sue Krumbein, wrote the final draft for publication.[1] A readable report, the group decided, is best communicated with a single voice. They wanted a clear and coherent picture presented in the printed document. Krumbein therefore provided transitions between sections, and also extensively rewrote much of the submitted material. All the mentors had the opportunity to react to Krumbein's drafts, almost always during a meeting of the entire group.

The process worked fairly smoothly, though it was fraught with possible pitfalls. Few people like to see their writing revised. Apart from pride of authorship, it is not always easy to preserve the original meanings in the revisions. Nevertheless, the work went well, and most of the actual writing and revising was done over a single summer—a sharp contrast with the protracted discussions and interviewing that had gone on during the preceding months. Funds from the foundation grant were used to pay $800 stipends to each of the seven members of the group for the summer's work on the report. This sum was the only financial compensation associated with the Study Group's activities.

Printing of the work was supported through the grant, enabling the group to produce an attractive, inexpensive monograph (including a two-color cover). It was distributed to some persons in the state education department, a few members of the legislature, all mentors affiliated with the Collaborative, administrators in neighboring school districts, and a list of people who had requested copies. The monograph was also made available at cost ($2.50) to anyone who expressed interest. News of the report got out quickly, and the first printing was soon exhausted. Orders and inquiries came mostly from within California, but eventually from many other states with mentor programs. It turned out that the Study Group's publication was one of the few to that date (1990) on mentor teaching, and the topic was rapidly receiving broad attention. There was a reprinting that brought the total number of copies in circulation to 4,000. (That run was soon exhausted, too.)

Making a Difference

Soon after the publication was released, alarmingly and coincidentally, the possibility arose in Sacramento that the mentor teacher program might be eliminated! California was sinking deeper into its financial crisis. As a way of meeting budget cuts, discussions were initiated that many people believed might lead to suspension or eradication of the statewide mentor-teacher program. Word of such a possibility spread through the state.

This prospect galvanized the Study Group. They devoted a meeting to the subject and decided to target key policymakers in statewide education to lobby for continuation of the program: in the governor's office, in the legislature, in the state department of education, as well as in local districts. They sent personal letters to these people, along with copies of the report. Follow-up phone calls and personal visits were made to several of them. Study Group members drew liberally from their research as they pointed out the benefits of the mentor-teacher program and how the state would be adversely affected by its elimination. They had facts, stories, insight, and conviction.

Though the dynamics of political decisions are inevitably murky, it is now widely believed throughout the state that the actions of the Collaborative's Mentor-Teacher Study Group had a significant effect in rescuing the program from elimination. The decision to retain the mentor program was, in fact, remarkable. It is freestanding as a legislative initiative. As such, it is a relatively simple matter to identify the program in the state budget as a line item and eliminate it. Savings would have been considerable since the mentor program costs about $60 million a year. From a political standpoint, it could perhaps have been abolished more easily than forcing education cuts across the board. A relatively small number of people, well under 5 percent of the state's teaching force (since not all districts participate in the program), would be affected directly. Though indirect effects of cutting this program might be extensive, they are more diffuse and sometimes easier to deal with politically. For example, all the mentors would retain regular teaching positions if the program were to be eliminated; so no jobs would be lost.

Unsolicited comments about the power of the report stimulated members of the Study Group to speculate about the reasons for their possible influence in helping to save the program. Some thought that the report and the related follow-up activities provided a coherent picture to the interested reader of how the program actually works, not just what some people say about it. And the Study Group had special knowledge that they believed was conveyed to legislators and others. To know the program, to really know it, is to love it, they said.

Individual teachers usually are not high enough on the policymaking ladder to be taken seriously when new directions for education are to be identified and pursued. But here was an instance in which seven articulate teachers, people who work directly with children and with other teachers, were able to provide those who decide on budgets with detailed and personal information about what would happen if the program were curtailed. True, such testimony is not unusual when programs are threatened, but in this case the advocates had produced a well-written, research-based, and information-filled document that they could point to in trying to argue for and legitimate a decision to save the program. And the document could be used in a similar fashion by a politician or state education department official if she or he were so inclined.

The Power of the Personal

What more might there have been about the report that gave it special credibility and impact? I believe that it was partly the mentors' status as insiders that led those faced with the budgetary decision to take seriously what the report claimed and recommended. The clear and personal voice with which the mentors spoke—unfiltered through the lenses and prose of school administrators, academics, policy experts, or anyone else—conveyed a refreshing, credible, and direct message. It almost certainly was also the case that the novelty of a written document produced by such a group, jointly prepared in an effort that linked teachers with staff from the University and carrying the University's imprimatur (but written solely by the teachers), commanded respect and attention. Such a report had never been seen before.

Furthermore, standard policy-oriented research tends to stress the view from the top. And it almost always is based on a systemwide perspective. How is education in the state as a whole operating? What is the evidence of progress or lack of it? Do benefits correspond with costs? Such a set of questions typically leads to examination of such matters as average class size, teacher salaries, incremental changes in costs per pupil, teacher retention rates, student test scores, and hundreds of similar "indicators" (a term taken from the world of economic reports and forecasts, and familiar to legislators and their analysts).

With respect to decisions about mentor programs, policymakers would expect to consider such matters as the number of teachers who apply and the percentage who are designated as mentors, the average length of time they stay in the position, the attitudes of administrators and others about the program, the number of teachers reached by mentors, how mentors' careers might be affected by the program in terms of formal positions that are sought and secured, organizational factors that relate to mentoring, and the effects mentoring has on teacher retention or student achievement.

In fact, the Mentor Teacher Study Group itself initially considered directing its own efforts toward research on such issues and questions. It is not without interest to teachers to know about teacher-retention rates or cost-benefit analyses or changes in average class size.

Furthermore, their concept of research had been formed largely by reading reports of investigations that had been designed to obtain information of this type.

On the other hand, teachers have no special window on such matters, nor do they have unusual competence to collect such data. One factor that may have been responsible for the long time it took for the Mentor Teacher Study Group to decide on their research focus was their implicit assumption that they were to engage in a certain type of "research," the kind that they all had seen from time to time and that fills journals devoted to research. Such a prospect may not have seemed particularly attractive. It would have required them to use techniques with which they had only passing familiarity and to adopt perspectives—those of researchers or policymakers—that they did not find natural or congenial.

Looking back, one can be struck anew with how much of the conversation of the members of the Study Group, not only at the outset but throughout the deliberations, centered one way or another on personal satisfaction in their professional roles: on how much they enjoyed working with other teachers, on the pleasure they derived from pursuing classroom approaches they believed made a difference in the lives of children, on the gratification associated with being a person who inspires others to try to achieve their potential. A tone of fulfillment was embedded in much of their conversation, and this is what they as mentors wanted to perpetuate. They had become distressed that their impact might be blunted by the fact that some districts were tending to shift administrative duties to mentors as a result of administrative cut-backs. They were detecting a weakening of the program where some districts routinely rotated the mentorships. Extra pay for extra work seemed a destructive concept that had entered into the minds of many teachers. These developments caused them concern. They cared, both personally (because of the effects on their own levels of satisfaction) and professionally (because of the consequences for children and for other teachers).

It is not necessarily that policymakers would find the factors that interested the mentors unimportant, though it is difficult to relate "pleasure," "gratification," "fulfillment," and "enjoyment," even of some of the most productive teachers in the state, to legislative and administrative action. However, such considerations do not readily relate to the kind of "systemic" issues with which policymakers usually deal. Furthermore, those who do policy research have little firsthand understanding of the absolute centrality of such matters in the lives of mentor teachers. At some level, legislators and their aides, for example, realize that schools are only as good as the people who teach there. They know that it is important to examine motivation of teachers, particularly of those who are the best. But policy discourse at the present time seems inhospitable to such considerations, since the "data" teachers report seem soft and ephemeral. Confounding the matter, those who try to assemble such information usually do not have the deep knowledge of mentoring that is required to ask the right questions, look for the most relevant influences, and convey the kind of compelling stories that persuade other people. They do not have an insider's view.

This is the main reason, I believe, why the research of the Mentor Teacher Study Group was consequential in the state and beyond. The group identified issues that are important to people who work inside the system. By conducting their research, then publishing it, they made perspectives visible that clearly are important but that are seldom illuminated by the kind of studies done for or by those in the traditional decision-making roles, by those who spend their professional lives nearer the "top" of the education system than in the classroom itself. The perspectives in the report clearly were those of intelligent and knowledgeable people who spoke from deep personal experience at the level where educational services are actually provided—where the children are. Their views had a kind of specificity and verisimilitude that is rare in policy studies. And it was supported by a reasoned passion in support of the main lines of argument that is almost never seen in the kinds of studies usually prepared for policy purposes.

Teacher inquiry into a range of emerging policy issues would be similarly revealing. National assessment, national curriculum, voucher plans, transitions from school to work, and methods of improving teacher education are just a few of the topics that are seldom illuminated by systematic inquiry conceptualized and conducted by the teachers themselves. For every one of these issues, teachers would bring to bear some perspectives available from no other source.

It is difficult to speculate with any confidence about the prospects for teacher-conducted policy-oriented research in the years ahead. One could reasonably argue that the Mentor Teacher Study Group was a special case. The conditions for its creation—a small grant, supportive yet unintrusive participation by the University, the inclination to prepare a written report—are unlikely to be replicated elsewhere. Few models exist to suggest what is possible. Therefore, it may be unrealistic to expect research of this sort by teachers to become a regular feature of the policy scene.

The need for a teacher perspective on policy issues, however, is great. And it does not diminish as controversial educational matters claim an ever larger share of national attention. While it may not be realistic to expect much teacher research on policy matters, even in a professional climate that increasingly values teacher research generally, the prospects are not completely discouraging. It may be of more than passing interest to note that the Mentor Teacher Study Group, several years after its first publication (and after spending all the foundation grant), is still meeting and conducting research. Their membership even has expanded a bit. They have identified a new set of issues that concern them, and they expect to prepare another publication.

Perhaps activity of this sort carries its own rewards. It seems to be stimulating and satisfying. In this one case, at least, it had consequences. While there is no particular reason to expect policy research by teachers suddenly to become a major feature of decision making in education, the fact that it exists and, more important, seems self-sustaining, suggests that this type of venture may grow. Any activity undertaken voluntarily by capable people—any activity that they enjoy and that seems to have the promise of being influential—has the potential of claiming increased attention, respect, and influence. The challenge lies in creating the circumstances for such activity to get started.

Note

1. Dawne Ashton, Lynette Dowling, Suzanne Krumbein, Doris Rausch, Ann Rounds, Viola Sullivan, Lora Traveller, *Where Do We Go from Here in the California Mentor Teacher Program? Recommendations by Seven Mentors* (Stanford, CA: Stanford/Schools Collaborative, School of Education, Stanford University, March, 1990).

CHAPTER VII

Rewriting "Gender Equity" in Teacher Research

SANDRA HOLLINGSWORTH AND JANET L. MILLER

Sandra Hollingsworth and Janet Miller are middle-class, white, women professors and teacher educators in their forties who also have been engaged in separate six-year-long teacher-researcher collaboratives. They agreed to co-create this chapter as a series of conversational letters which would both explore the issue of "gender equity" in teacher research and help them get to know each other personally and professionally. Drawing upon the histories that ground their personal experiences, the authors reflect in their writings about teacher research from various feminist perspectives on achieving gender equity and social change in schools. In particular, the authors speak personally about the complexities of social positions, values, relations, and political imperatives in accomplishing such a charge. Janet Miller begins the conversation by writing to Sandra (Sam) Hollingsworth.

Dear Sam:

Thanks so much for asking me to consider issues of gender equity within contexts of teacher research. I think that the topic has great implications for both how and why we do our work as teacher-researchers. However, I can't really write or talk easily about "teacher research and gender equity" as a topic per se, because I don't see or feel my work as a teacher-researcher and with other teacher-researchers in that framing alone. I do agree that gender has become *one* important basis for discussions and analyses of possibilities for school change and for both students' and teachers' enhanced educational opportunities.[1] And certainly I agree that gender equity must be considered in discussions of the political contexts of teacher research. But if seen as an end in itself, "gender equity" becomes a

---

Sandra Hollingsworth is Associate Professor in the Department of Teacher Education, Michigan State University. Janet L. Miller is Professor of Education at the Beloit (WI) campus of National-Louis University.

framing that, for me, obscures the intersections of gender, race, class, age, sexual preference—and any of the other multiple social constructions and positionings that collide within my various and shifting contexts and identities.

For example, my contexts include university classrooms where I teach and national conference arenas where I present versions of the intertwined nature of my teaching and research. These contexts also include K-12 classrooms, where I often go to work with teachers and to teach students as part of ongoing in-service programs. They also include my participation, with five K-12 teachers, in a six-year teacher-researcher collaborative. In all of these contexts, I struggle with an expectation of myself, shared often by my students, by classroom teachers, and by my fellow teacher-researchers, to be identified as an "expert," to be the one who will provide the answers or who will at least point the way. That expectation, of course, comes with the traditional academic and hierarchical positioning of professor as creator and conveyer of knowledge.

But the expectation to be the "expert" also emerges from and gets complicated by my internalizations of social expectations for females to be caring, nurturing, helpful. I often have manifested that internalization of "good girl" by expecting myself not only to be helpful to others, but also to look for, and provide answers for others, if that indeed is what they express as their need. With that particular "good girl" identity, I often have posited myself as helper, as one who attempted to please others by meeting their needs and expectations, oftentimes to the detriment of my own. Because that identity was reinforced consistently in my white middle-class background, I have had to struggle with its persistent eruptions, particularly in my work as a female academic.[2]

And so, as a long-time "good girl," I continue in my attempts to understand larger social, cultural, economic, and political sources of that "good girl" construct, and to identify ways in which I am complicit in its manifestations.[3] Given my particular enactments of "good girl" behavior over the years, influenced as they were by my class and race, it would be very easy for me to slip into the role of "expert" or authority, all in the guise of "helping" or attending to others' needs and interests. Thus, for example, I continue to work against my internalizations and enactments of socially constructed versions of women who, because of their "essential" characteristics of nurturer and caregiver, are deemed most suited to work in the "helping professions" such as teaching. At the same time, even as I work against such stereotypic representations of women, of myself, I also do not want to negate those aspects of nurturance and attentiveness that I do wish to preserve in my teaching and research.

So this complex mixture of identities gets particularly sticky in university classrooms or teacher-researcher collaboratives, where students and teachers often bring both expectations and lived realities of hierarchical and gendered relationships into our work together. For, of course, they too have received similar messages about the roles of women and men, of professors and students, from the institutions in which we do our work. And, depending also on their varied positions with respect to gender, race, age, and class, I may well be not only the one who "should" know, who "should" impart knowledges and determine research agendas for them, but also the one who "should" do these things in a nurturing and supportive way.

What has happened for me in the past few years, especially in the context of my six-year collaborative work with five other teacher-researchers who work in K-12 settings,[4] is that I have been able to allow those various expectations to collide. Our teacher-researcher collaborative has enabled me to express my doubts, frustrations, and puzzlements about how to collaborate with classroom teachers when I am in a traditional role of greater power in terms of research agendas, processes, and evaluations. I have felt and heard the ambiguities that these teachers have expressed about their initial expectations that I should "know" how we would do our collaborative research. I have been confronted with their suspicions that I "knew" and just wasn't telling them (one teacher suggested that maybe I was doing sort of an "inquiry" or "discovery" approach to teacher research with them). And I have had to deal even with anger that I, in fact, didn't "know" how to go about this whole thing of constructing a critically oriented teacher-researcher collaborative. And I have struggled with my "good girl" tendencies to try to comply with their expectations so that they would still want to work with me, would still, in fact, like me.

Thus, for me, hierarchical structures of the institution oftentimes indicate that I should posit myself as "expert," particularly in relation to my work with students and with K-12 teachers. These institutional expectations have collided with my own and others' internalizations of versions based on race, age, gender, or class, for example, of how I should be in the world in relation to others' needs and interests. Those collisions shattered any unitary version that I might have had of myself in the role of professor. And those collisions have created some momentarily cleared spaces in which I could examine the ways in which any unitary category of analysis, such as "gender," must be considered in relationship to myriad other categories that describe my positions in the world.

And so I still struggle, within attempts to effect reciprocal and collaborative interactions and relationships in my teaching, researching, and consulting, to claim neither "expert" nor "good girl" as my total identity. So to talk only about "gender equity" as a guiding construct in these struggles would be to reduce some complex intersections of social positionings and identities in my life to a one-dimensional version. I could be constructed, within the confines of "gender equity" framing, for example, as a woman academic who is struggling to be listened to, respected, and acknowledged as a creator of knowledge *in the same ways* that a male academic would be in particular educational situations and contexts. But given the examples I've offered above, that version would reduce the ways in which my gender, my class, my race, my sexual identities, my academic roles, and my internalizations of others' expectations for those positionings make my particular identities and contexts as a woman academic mean something different than those of male academics.

So how do we get to the undersides of framings such as "gender equity" within political contexts of teacher research? What might we do to address, rather than avoid, the messy intersections and collisions of identities and social positionings within teacher research? How do we look for ways in which the framing of issues of choice, of opportunity, of equal access, of "equity" can limit our visions of what teacher research might address and enact within agendas for school reform and change by defining those issues *only in relation to* already established male hierarchies, forms, structures, or practices?

I debated such questions as a member of our teacher-researcher group that formally met from 1986 through 1992. And yes, the women in our group, the five out of six members, struggled over gendered notions of ourselves as teachers, as administrators, and we worried that we didn't have all the right answers all the time, as we thought we were supposed to if we were doing our jobs well. In particular, two of the women, Beth and Marjory,[5] who moved after twenty years in classroom teaching positions into administrative roles during our last three years together, also talked about feeling added pressure to perform well just because they were women in the still predominantly male field of educational administration. And we all worried that our caring about others was seen only as a "woman's attribute" rather than as a way of being in the world that we thought would be good for everyone to try. We struggled with issues about being "good girls" who have become "good teachers," and we also saw how being "good girls" was, in fact, very different for each of us.

And yes, Kevin, the male school psychologist in our group, worried about how he was constructed as "the leader" as well as the "problem solver" in the elementary school where he did much of his counseling. He told us about playing golf with the high school principal and sometimes even the district superintendent, and about how he knew that we wouldn't have the same access to those men, even though they often don't talk about school at all as they make their way around the course. "It's just the access that sets me apart, I know," Kevin said to us on more than one occasion. And he noted that Beth and Marjory, although they were now administrators, would not be invited to play golf with these particular male administrators.

So, in many ways, some of these struggles are over issues of "equity." Who has access to the powers that often structure the form and content of our daily lives as educators? How much of that power in school is still male-dominated, and what can women, as teachers, as researchers, and as students, do to gain access? Those are important questions if one wants to move up and into the existing power structures, to "gain power" in ways that still form hierarchies and still exclude or push others to the margins of decision making, curriculum construction, textbook selection, or determining of research agendas. And that's my trouble with the notion of "gender equity" here—it could construct teacher research as a way of reinforcing existing structures that ultimately are predicated on exclusion—or at least on the notion of "insiders and outsiders" as a "natural" part of any organizational structure. If one "does" teacher research, does that mean that one could have more access to the powers that be, to the people who control the what and where and how of schooling?

That's how some versions of teacher research might be constructed—as ways of "having a say" in the reforming and restructuring of schools. And yes, of course, I want to have a say, but in ways that allow me to disrupt the boundaries of what is "sayable." And I want teachers who work in K-12 classrooms to be able to say what they want in terms of creating curriculum, of determining goals, of constructing equitable forms and arenas in which they and their students can learn together. But I also want us to be able to question the very power relations that characterize efforts at school reform and that set boundaries for what is sayable and unsayable within those efforts as they are being constructed. I want us to be able to question how our roles as teachers, as students, as parents, as administrators are socially constructed in multiple ways. Those constructions rewrite the category "gender" each time they intersect and even collide when we begin to consider ourselves within framings of our gender, race, class, age, physical and mental abilities and disabilities, sexual preferences— within the various and myriad identities that we inevitably bring to our educational intentions, processes, and forms. And I want us to be able to research those kinds of questions within the contexts of "teacher research."

For it is within contexts that include teachers' and students' participation in school reform that I think we can truly begin to engage in work that interrupts, questions, and challenges all notions of equity that isolate gender from other positionings and that maintain men as the standard up to which women are to be brought.

Teacher-researchers claim to situate our questions and dilemmas within the daily struggles of teachers and students. And those struggles are much more complex than any isolating notion of gender or any comparative notion of equity can address. I think that placing teacher research within political contexts thus requires us to attend to the complexities of power relations and identities that differently intersect and collide in the hallways and classrooms where we meet. Obviously, I feel strongly that these interactions and collisions can expand and enhance our feminist commitments to "gender equities," both as topics for and objects of teacher research. I look forward to hearing your responses to my concerns about the ways in which we frame our work.

Best regards,

Janet

Dear Janet:

You have raised many complex and provocative issues about discussing teacher research in terms of gender equity. I am personally empathetic with your views since I have shared similar experiences, feelings, and confusions, and also because I share your thoughtful enthusiasm about the possibility for this work. Opening to the potential of full generative participation in our lives and work—not just contributing to the hierarchical power of school structures as they presently exist—educators now have the opportunity to challenge, deconstruct, selectively integrate, and/or rewrite some of our gender-designated roles as "experts" and "caregivers." In the introspection of our multiply backgrounded lives, we are all each and more. In the power-driven frames which organize the lives of teachers and students in "a woman's profession,"[6] however, we might be less able to recognize those possibilities. Without addressing head-on the subtle gendered positioning and expectations for teacher (e.g., "technician" and "caregiver") and researcher/policymaker/administrator (e.g., "power broker" and "evaluator"), then tolerance of, compliance with, or resistance to the existing structures of schooling, which are predicated on such exclusionary divisions, might appear to be our only reasonable options.

As you bring to my consciousness many problematic issues in the framing of teacher research and gender equity, Janet, you also underscore ways that multiple and shifting identities too often are lost within the confines of the existing political structures of schooling. You remind me, also, of the recent report of the American Association of University Women, *How Schools Shortchange Girls*,[7] which speaks to the complexity of the equity issues that emerged from the study, even with an investigative focus on gender. The report details, for example, how girls (in general) receive significantly less attention from classroom teachers than boys, but African-American girls have fewer interactions with teachers than do white girls, despite evidence that they attempt to initiate interactions more frequently than white girls do. The authors of the report recommend more support and released time for teacher-initiated research on the many curricular and classroom variables that affect student learning, paying particular attention to gender.

In response to these and other provocative challenges that you brought to mind, I want to attempt to address the question of equity as an achieved integration and expansion of multiply grounded values. Rather than speak of "gender equity" in terms of women's attaining equality with men's standards, I want to address the continuous transformation in both male and female life roles with respect to rewriting the occupations of "teacher" and "researcher." I want to begin the discussion of integration by writing about the surprises in my life and work which have come with new ways of seeing and appreciating the values and modes traditionally associated with and devalued as "women's ways." I begin with an emphasis on gender not to the exclusion of the other important and interconnected identities of myself, but to honor its position as the first facet to catch my attention about my own differences—an awareness, pointed out to me by courageous women, which led me to see the interconnectedness of other differences that you also have so gently and persuasively explicated. I have become open not only to the differences but the links between the multiple identities of gender, race, class, age, and sexual identities, for example. Thus I have been fortunate enough to integrate the previously silenced, unintegrated, and unremembered ways of being which were part of my girlhood and womanhood. These links include such bonds as care, reverence, listening, gentle questioning, hope, storying and restorying, as well as specialized expertise, attentiveness, rage, and political positionings and possibilities. I've been able to use these links as center ground, from which I could open up my teaching, my research methods, my writing, and attempt—as you argue, Janet—to disrupt the boundaries of the known by creating intricate connections between them.

Over the years, for example, I have come to look upon my teaching as research. I've learned the benefit of joining research and practice into a single concept which does not accord higher status to "researcher" (and to the stereotypical qualities that accompany the term) than to "teacher." In the integrative transformation of praxis, questioning has replaced certainty; my role as a teacher "expert" has become integrated with my many other teaching, learning, and living roles. This multifaceted view of my work was not always present. As a graduate student, my early teaching stance with preservice teachers involved passing along what I knew in a well-socialized hierarchy from expert to novice. The perspective was one of a professional duty or obligation—backed by positivistic arguments for information processing and the culture of my graduate education in educational psychology. I then "researched" other teachers' learnings objectively and dispassionately in terms of how well they understood the knowledge that I presented to them in class. As long as my teaching context remained within the confines of university coursework, my own role or instructional stance also seemed to remain intact. I had no external stimulus for change. And the internal stimulus—a sense of discomfort in my judgmental, authoritarian, and nonconnective stance as an educator—was too deeply buried under school- and society-molded expectations of what successful adults and scholars ought to look like. The heart of my girl-child who loved Alice in Wonderland games where *everyone shall win and all shall have prizes* went unremembered.

The next chapter of my story to embrace teaching as research began as I graduated and took a job as an assistant professor at the

University of California, Berkeley. With a little more academic freedom and permission from the California climate to examine my soul, I was now interested in the longitudinal effect of teachers' learning on *my* teaching: the boundaries of my classroom walls expanded. I collaborated with research assistants to study systematically my teaching as an influence on twenty-eight new teachers' learning in two literacy courses and as applied to practicum settings.[8] Like any teacher who has difficulty attending both to the flow of the lesson and the sense students make of it, I found this sort of pulling back to be very useful. Systematically analyzing these longitudinal data allowed me to become more precise in my understanding of preservice teachers' content learning. I began to see where the new teachers' attention rested and what personal and institutional features (including my teaching) seemed to be blocking their learning and transfer of curricular and pedagogical theories of literacy to classroom settings.

To learn more, I continued to follow, observe, and interview seven teachers, roughly representative of the full sample of twenty-eight, into their fourth and fifth years of teaching. We formed a collaborative group of six women and one man, meeting every month socially to talk about their literacy practices. At that point the earlier and formal boundaries of teacher and researcher turned into a relationship of friends. I began to know these teachers as full, complex, knowing, and caring people, to listen to their own senses of expertise, to their own ways of researching their teaching. I learned that, as their instructor, I had omitted attention to the inclusive concept of curriculum which they saw as necessary for learning to teach: the urban environments to which most of them were assigned; the school-based socialized or normative beliefs about teaching and learning which countered their own senses of educating; and the means of seeking continued education and support in those difficult beginning years. Conversational analyses of their learning in this teacher-researcher collaborative taught me—among other things— that until these new teachers had an opportunity to talk about their basic concerns with social interaction and relationship issues—issues which were personally important to them—they could not attend well to the content and curriculum of literacy.[9] These teachers had awakened in me a sense of caring for them in relationship to me and all of our remembered, unremembered, and potential identities; I wanted to change my stance as an educator—to free both them and myself to the full potential of teaching and learning that we might create together.

Simultaneously, changes in my personal and professional life made me look inward and name the particular features about me—woman, author, Southern-born, single parent, child-abuse survivor, professor, artist—as if they mattered to my way of representing myself in the world and required voice. As if they were not variables which could be neutralized and devalued. I wanted to reclaim my many-faceted selves into the adult being of my teaching, writing, and research.

The result of such a collision between my roles of expert, learner, researcher, critic, friend, and caregiver in the collaborative teacher-research setting led me to a new chapter in my understanding of teaching as research. To overcome both my own limitations within the boundaries of university coursework and the power of gender, class, and other factors that silence expectations of teachers in schools, I saw that I would have to change radically my epistemological approach to practice. My new sense of my role as teacher educator moved into the philosophical, moral, and political realms. I no longer saw value in encouraging teachers to make cognitive changes by learning what worked within the same theoretical paradigm. I wanted to move outside of the known into other worlds of possibility. I hoped we could expand our epistemological boundaries and bondages by first identifying the *public* and *private* paradigms for teaching and learning we used, then critiquing our own and others' ways of knowing. To begin this process, I asked teachers to own and articulate their practical, critical, and imagined experience as valid knowledge.[10] By achieving a sense of equity in their own realities as teachers in "a woman's profession" with all of its problematic inequities, they began to make their classrooms truly equitable places to learn—in the sense of integration, transformation, and reimagination of the multiple identities emerging within their classrooms.

To encourage teachers to develop a critical perspective of teaching as research through which they could contain, evaluate, and create a responsive and equitable curriculum for themselves in relationship with particular children and overcome the problematic and limiting structures of schooling, I began to use principles of feminist pedagogies and methodologies in my teaching-research.[11] From my learning in the teacher-researcher collaborative group, I brought into my courses features such as connected conversation, self-evaluation, continuous critique, shared agendas, a commitment to social change, and a valuing of specialized knowledge each of us brought to our relationships. In other words, *I* still had expert knowledge about literacy and each of the teachers I taught had valuable forms of knowledge that I had shut out when I considered myself and my university colleagues the only experts. It was also clear that teachers had questions but that I had not been able to work with them on their questions because of the institutional structure of separating coursework from fieldwork, of separating my teaching from research, of separating the teachers from me. Thus, I invited their practice-based and biographical experiences into our course, and asked all of us to ask questions about our teaching and our lives. I then facilitated collective work on methods for analyzing or understanding them. I learned some amazing things about school inequities and injustices. In story after story of their own schooling, teachers wrote about the loss of self-esteem and self-knowledge. They wrote of trying hard to measure up to someone else's standards, but never really succeeding. Their own questions, imaginings, and ways of knowing were never good enough.

In an effort to shift attention away from the research questions or procedures *I* might favorably evaluate in our classrooms, and to achieve instead the desired outcomes of teachers' ownership of their own potentials for the creation of knowledge, I encouraged teachers to evaluate their own learnings. Courses now developed through group consensus. We suspended attention to established solutions or methodological procedures until we were clear about our own projects and questions, how those questions came from our own personal or private theories of teaching and learning, how they varied from public or external theories, and how teaching could be viewed as research.

The dialogical relationships between my teaching, research, and relational involvement with the ongoing teacher-research collaborative group led to continual changes in all three. As the boundaries of my teaching broadened to experiences in relationship to the teachers and a commitment to social change, the most recent chapters of my story as teacher educator have become less those of transmitting knowledge and measuring outcomes, and more those of cooperative and critical creation of knowledge, with identified ways of knowing, critique, and shift as outcomes.

It is important to note again that the changes I made were more than intellectual exercises; they came about because of a quest for meaning in my own life. For example, only when I fully embraced my own need for connections and responsiveness in my personal life as a feminist scholar and opened myself to intimate involvement with the teacher-research collaborative group was I able to engage in a transformation that valued my many positions in the world, beginning with a new construction of "woman."

As I came to know myself as a feminist educator, I not only questioned but explicitly made room for values and perspectives often associated with women's socialized experiences in my teaching and research. No longer accepting the socialized forces to reject "soft" modes of analysis and writing that was required of me in a graduate school experience dominated by cognitive psychology, I could now joyfully reclaim and celebrate the poetry and story which were part of my pregraduate school life. Narrative modes of inquiry and reporting, for example, appealed to me because narrative requires analysis in terms of connection and response, and because it is an intimate rather than objective analysis of justice and productivity, right and wrong. Outcomes from narrative inquiries led me to understandings and new directions rather than explanations and prescriptions.[12] Viewed through one reading of feminist theory, I saw the narrative voice as a critically compassionate and relational one, where the researcher was placed in as critical a perspective as the researched. It was a position where I felt honest, honorable, equitable, and whole internally, and from which I could let go of the external critique of my academic colleagues who were skeptical about the value of such research.

Reclaiming my girlhood preference for narrative over formal logic, I found that the experiential wholeness of teaching-research could be caringly juxtaposed rather than forced into fragmented and decontextualized parts. It is partially because of that wholeness (explained by many different aspects of background including gender, race, and class) that narrative became a familiar format against which the teachers in our collaborative group and I could begin to tell and understand our different stories, raise questions about our own perspectives and practices, break our silences, reclaim our unremembered voices, rewrite the present, and reenvision our futures. As stories from our and others' teaching questions are interwoven, the full fabric of our story might suggest ways to build an equitable narrative unity which comes from the freedom of inclusion: the opportunity to find out how individual methods and voices are validated by other perspectives, even those which appear contradictory. The restoried whole, with its beginnings not only in gender equity but in many different groundings, could become a catalyst for a deep understanding of our common work, for moving forward beyond the existing frameworks together.

With hope,

Sam

Dear Sam:

I truly think that the detailings of the shifts in your identities as teacher-researcher-feminist-learner are important in illuminating the ways in which our subjectivities are never fixed. The changes that you have described, especially within the contexts of your teacher-researcher collaborative, are similar in so many ways to mine. And yet, even though we are of the same gender, class, and race, for example, I am curious about the different ways in which we have internalized, enacted, and worked to confront the implications of those particular identities within our work as teacher-researchers.

For example, I have used the phrase "narrative of community"[13] to describe the work of our teacher-researcher collaborative. At first glance, this seems somewhat similar to what you have described as a possibility of teacher research: "to build an equitable narrative unity which comes from the freedom of inclusion. . . ."

And yet, I still worry about the easy ways in which both our experiences as teacher-researchers and our intensified turnings toward feminist perspectives might be read as seamless, unitary, almost incessantly cheerful narratives of equitable and inclusive relationships with our fellow teacher-researchers and of concurrent growth and development. Instead, I want to call attention to the complexities of collaboration as a form as well as a vessel for teacher research. Those complexities include the myriad ways in which notions of unity within community get complicated by individuals' multiple and often changing subjectivities.[14] Individuals' needs and desires shift, sometimes ever so subtly, within the context of collaboration, and those shifts necessarily affect working relationships as well as the direction and intentions of the research projects. To assume an achieved equity within collaboration for such relationships or research intentions, whether it be with an emphasis on gender, race, or class, for example, is to ignore the ways in which those varying identities often collide or collude within ourselves.

For example, when the two female teachers turned administrators in our group started to talk about added pressures that they felt in assuming traditionally male-dominated positions, tensions emerged in our teacher-researcher collaborative. In particular, the first-grade teacher, Katherine, and the elementary special education teacher, Cheryl, were upset when both Beth and Marjory started to talk about teachers as "they." As we began a heated discussion about the still often standard teacher-administrator dichotomy, Katherine challenged both women's assertions that it was easier to be a classroom teacher. "It's not easier!" she exclaimed. "And I can't believe that you could forget so quickly what it's like to be in a room with kids all day."

Cheryl added, "Yes, it sounds as though you have forgotten already what it's like to have kids hanging on you, you've forgotten what they smell like, what it feels like to be responsible for these children."

And Kevin interjected, "And you surely don't forget what it's like to be walking down the hall and be told by your principal that you can't be carrying that cup of coffee."

This encounter, and many others since this particular episode, exemplify, I think, the complexities of shifting roles within a teacher-researcher collaborative. Further, they exemplify the ways those roles are constructed by social and cultural expectations and norms, not only within the structures of schooling in which we teach and research, but also within our collaborative. As a collaborative, we researched with Beth and Marjory as they themselves researched and struggled with their decisions to leave the classroom and to enter educational administration. We talked about their assumption of these administrative roles in terms of gender equity within the profession, and we discussed the gendered inequities of the ways in which they, as women, felt pressure to perform in a superior manner, just so they might be considered adequate for their new roles. What we had not anticipated, but what we have had to deal with in many intense meetings, was the way in which those shifting roles and expectations created momentary rifts in the apparent unity of our collaborative. And those rifts had to do, in particular, with expectations, assumptions, and preconceptions based especially on gender about the relationships among teaching, administration, power, control, authority, and voice. Those rifts challenged as well notions of collaboration that imply constant unity or total agreement. As Katherine noted, "just because you get to see the bigger picture now as administrators, that doesn't mean that we classroom teachers don't have anything to say about that picture."

Thus, identities that emerge within the often protective circle of collaboration also often shift within the ever changing and sometimes contradictory dynamics of collaborative teacher-researcher work. And those identities are ones which often change even more dramatically outside the collaborative context. Outside that context, struggles to be heard, to be seen, to be taken seriously as educators who regard teaching and researching as conjoined aspects of educational processes are more pronounced, given the still dominant technical-rational orientation in the field of education. So a danger of collaboration as a framing for equitable forms of teacher research is that we may assume an easy association among our collaborative peers. But that association also may obscure acknowledgment that our positionings based on gender, age, sexual preference, or any other factor could indicate ways in which we still might be silencing one another, or ignoring another's particular positioning within the group at a particular moment, or directing the nature of the group's investigations.

Thus, in order to question issues of gender equity, say, not only within the contexts of our collaboration or our teacher-research emphases, but also within the very power relations that characterize efforts at school reform, I think that we must pay attention to the work of feminist researchers who call into question the ways in which such categories as "voice," "subjectivity," "democracy," "validity," or "gender" are socially constructed in multiple ways that rewrite those categories each time they appear or interact or collide within particular social and cultural situations.

If we intend to incorporate the category of "gender equity" as part of our intentional work within the political contexts of teacher research, we need to acknowledge not only the scholarship that has deconstructed teaching as "women's work,"[15] but also feminist perspectives that call into question the ways in which teaching, research, and curriculum have often been constructed as exclusionary. Women, people of color, people with disabilities who are also educators have been excluded not only from educational decision making or curriculum creation, but also from the very contents and constructions of those contents that they teach and research.

Further, we also need to question, to challenge, and to change the oppressive aspects of structures of institutions, of the disciplines and conceptions of research within which we work, because it is not sufficient, in the name of "gender equity," to simply "add" us into those existing structures.[16]

So before we can be "free" to include not only multiple perspectives but also our own multiple social and cultural identities and positionings in relation to others and to the work in our field, we need extended inquiry into those identities and positionings and into the very concept of freedom as relational.

Of course, I agree that work such as the Wellesley report gives us continued and substantial challenge to research areas of inequity within schooling contexts as part of our work as teacher-researchers. And yet, as you pointed out earlier, Sam, that very report demonstrates that "gender equity" cannot be separated from issues of race and class. Thus, the political contexts in which we engage as teacher-researchers, within or without collaborative framings, encourage us to attend to the complexities of inequity, for example. And that focus also requires that we acknowledge and *research* the ways in which our own voices are implicated in the silencing of others, the ways in which our own understandings of teacher research harbor gaps, silences, exclusions, erasures of others' experiences and understandings. Only then might I feel that we can begin to talk and act with the "freedom of inclusion."

Yours,

Janet

Dear Janet:

I sat outside on my porch swing to read your response to my last letter on teacher research and gender equity. Except for the natural rocking of the swing and a gentle breeze moving the leaves through the morning sun around me, the scene in which I sat was so still that a cardinal almost joined me—thinking perhaps that I was also a natural and unthreatening part of the landscape. He reconsidered at the last moment and flew off into the brush. His movement at once brought to mind the complexities of perception and intention and compelled my own movement inside the house to write to you.

The ways in which we see our connections and differences around the topic of this chapter seem not only interesting but instructive. Perhaps an artifact of my "nice girl" past, but one which I currently choose to retain, is that I am optimistic about both the possibility and challenge of this work. Even as we write to each other, I have a sense that our common passion for understanding, deconstructing, and reimagining both teaching and research, our respect for our evolving friendship and colleagueship help us both articulate and hold our various and shifting meanings into the topic of gender equity, and lead us to be curious about how our views have been shaped by the different configurations of our lives.

Your story describes how your teacher-research group faced and worked through a major challenge to its identity when two women teachers became administrators. Even though our group has not shared that experience, I was reminded that we also have confronted many challenges and clashes of identity in our six years of work together involving issues of equity around "teacher" and "researcher." In the beginning of our conversational meetings, I was the group's "author." I felt free to use *my* real name, since I primarily told *their* stories, using pseudonyms to protect them from political harm. As designated researcher and reporter, I was privileged in that I was both safe from risk and gained all of the credit. As our relationship developed, the teachers began to challenge my interpretations of their stories, implored me to include more of my own, and wanted to take both the political credit and the risk of claiming their own stories using their own names. Our shared stories have been written and rewritten developed around implicit and explicit themes of equity, understanding, inclusion, and vulnerability within our group, but, as you might expect, have had much more political influence in my world of the university than in the teachers' world of the public schools. Even when teachers pointed out their researched contributions to school officials, few really bothered to read or comment on their work.

Response from university faculty is often similarly unconfirming. Mary Dybdahl is still furious that she was "patted" on the head by a university researcher after a brilliant presentation at a national conference. At another state-level conference she was asked to sit down, so that the real expert in our group (me) could speak. The "we and they" of many such relationships is unconscionable but not unspeakable. Leslie Minarik and Jennifer Smallwood (women teachers of different colors in our group) recently challenged both the language and the patronization of university folk at a regional meeting on teacher research as exclusionary.

Recently our group met on retreat in the Sierra Nevada mountains to work on a forthcoming book about our collaborative lives. One of our tasks was to work through many tensions about the perceived framework for our stories. Of central importance was the way in which we have brought to consciousness, deconstructed, and reconstructed our work as teacher researchers without our group and within the problematic stereotype of teaching as "women's work"— and as institutionally separate from research. That theme, plus other discussions, confrontations, and reinterpretations of what we mean by class differences, differences which might also have been shaped by sexual orientation, race, family dynamics, and economic positionings, gave a depth to our work which would have been overlooked had we elected to write from our "good girl" and "well-mannered boy" writing stances to present a cheerful, seamless story of a unitary framing.

Your comments, Janet, reminded me that it is important to include these tensions in our stories: that we have rarely come to an honest consensus on any issue, yet we can talk about our similarities. We never feel the same from the time our talk is uttered, to the time it is transcribed, to the time it is discussed as it gets ready for print. Yet we honor our differences as part of our process, as we work to bring to equity our many-situated positions. Anthony Cody, the only male teacher in our group and father of two babies, uses "feminist" as one framing for his teaching-research. Karen Teel, a teacher, doctoral student, and mother of three teenagers, sees her work differently, placing emphasis on the dynamics of parenting as much more important to her work. So we talk to each other about our views, argue, take walks to soothe damaged feelings, write to each other, hug, try to understand, love, allow our clarified understandings to collide, see old situations from new perspectives, reconstruct our views and write again. We feel increasingly free to present some of our framings to the outside world in public print, while others will remain within our group. The frames which kept recurring over and over again across the multiple writings of our experiences—and those which we chose to make public from all of our varying perspectives— were our relationships to each other, our work and our world, and our attempts to dismantle, reorder, and reinvent the strong but subtle gender-socialized perceptions of our life roles.[17]

Janet, you have clearly and importantly pointed out the danger of using *any* unidimensional framing to achieve equitable forms of teacher research. Your point is well taken, yet leaves problematic the figure/ground perspectives of gendered-socializations, given the current realities of our positions as teachers and as teacher educators. Some of my other colleagues feel that our group's attention to gender in this work is an indication of our emerging feminism, our evolutionary nature, and even our lack of sophistication. Perhaps those critiques have merit, but they feel unnecessarily judgmental. They remind us of the correct forms of "school" to which we can never quite measure up. What we have clearly come to know and accept is that we are all at different points of understanding how the nature of our work as teacher-researchers is identified by gender, class, race, and other considerations. Those points—like the sunlight on the leaves this morning—never really become fixed, or even still. I see them all in dynamic relationship to each other, to our changing frameworks for our careers and our lives, and to our journey toward the "freedom of inclusion."

In a similar way, I sense that the inclusion of my reading of teacher research and gender equity with yours, with the teachers and administrators in our groups, and with others who read this chapter, will provide a stimulus to rethink and challenge all of our framings, including those of "gender," "relations," "freedom," and "equity." As for the process of writing and rewriting this chapter together, I am delighted in our newly discovered connections and differences and am excited about the possibilities that our combined voices might envision.

Love,

Sam

NOTES

1. Susan S. Klein, *Sex Equity and Sexuality in Education* (Albany, NY: State University of New York Press, 1992); Marilyn Sadker, David Sadker, and Susan S. Klein, "The Issue of Gender in Elementary and Secondary Education," in *Review of Research in Education*, edited by Gerald Grant, pp. 269-334 (Washington, DC: American Educational Research Association, 1991); Kathleen Weiler, "You've Got to Stay There and Fight: Sex Equity, Schooling, and Work," in *Changing Education: Women as Radicals and Conservators*, edited by Janet Antler and Sari K. Biklen, pp. 217-236 (Albany, NY: State University of New York Press, 1990).

2. Janet L. Miller, "The Resistance of Women Academics: An Autobiographical Account," *Journal of Educational Equity and Leadership* 3, no. 2 (1983): 101-109; idem, "Women as Teachers: Enlarging Conversations on Issues of Gender and Self-concept," *Journal of Curriculum and Supervision* 1 (1986): 111-121.

3. Janet L. Miller, "Women and Education: In What Ways Does Gender Affect the Educational Process?" in *Thirteen Questions: Reframing Education's Conversation*, edited by Joseph L. Kincheloe and Shirley R. Steinberg, pp. 151-158 (New York: Peter Lang, 1992).

4. Janet L. Miller, *Creating Spaces and Finding Voices: Teachers Collaborating for Empowerment* (Albany, NY: State University of New York Press, 1990).

5. The names I mention here are pseudonyms that the teachers chose to use in the book describing our first two and one-half years together. They chose not to use their own names because much of what they researched in our work together involved others who also could be implicated in the political nature of much of these teachers' inquiries. This issue of naming, of course, constitutes another aspect of the political context of teacher research, just as does the issue of authorship. These teachers chose not to participate in the writing of the book, because writing most often is not valued or rewarded in K-12 schooling contexts. They saw writing as work that I "do" as an academic. They did, however, participate in the framing and in the selection of the vignettes that comprised the collective narrative for the published version of our teacher-researcher collaborative.

6. Susan Laird, "Reforming 'Women's True Profession': A Case for 'Feminist Pedagogy' in Teacher Education," *Harvard Educational Review* 58, no. 4 (1988): 449-463.

7. Wellesley College Center for Research on Women, *How Schools Shortchange Girls* (Annapolis Junction, MD: American Association of University Women, 1992). ,

8. Sandra Hollingsworth, "Prior Beliefs and Cognitive Change in Learning to Teach," *American Educational Research Journal* 26, no. 2 (1989): 60-189.

9. Sandra Hollingsworth, "Learning to Teach through Collaborative Conversation: A Feminist Approach," *American Educational Research Journal* 22, no. 2 (1992): 373-404.

10. Mary F. Belenky, Blythe M. Clinchy, Nancy R. Goldberger, and Jill M. Tarule, *Women's Ways of Knowing: The Development of Self, Voice, and Mind* (New York: Basic Books, Inc., 1986).

11. Sandra Harding, *Whose Science? Whose Knowledge? Thinking from Women's Lives* (Ithaca, NY: Cornell University Press, 1990); Kathleen Weiler, *Women Teaching for Change: Gender, Class, and Power* (South Hadley, MA: Bergin and Garvey, 1988).

12. F. Michael Connelly and D. Jean Clandinin, "Stories of Experience and Narrative Inquiry," *Educational Researcher* 19, no. 4 (1990): 2-13.

13. Sandra Zagarell, "Narrative of Community: The Identification of a Genre," *Signs: Journal of Women in Culture and Society* 13 (1988): 498-527.

14. Biddy Martin and Chandra Palpade Mohanty, "Feminist Politics: What's Home Got to Do with It?" in *Feminist Studies, Critical Studies*, edited by Teresa deLauretis, pp. 191-212 (Bloomington, IN: Indiana University Press, 1986).

15. Michael Apple, *Teachers and Texts: A Political Economy of Class and Gender Relations in Education* (London: Routledge and Kegan Paul, 1986); Nancy Hoffman, *Women's "True" Profession: Voices from the History of Teaching* (New York: Feminist Press, 1981); Madeleine Grumet, *Bitter Milk: Women and Teaching* (Amherst: University of Massachusetts Press, 1986).

16. For examples of such feminist work in education, see Deborah P. Britzman, *Practice Makes Practice: A Critical Study of Learning to Teach* (Albany, NY: State University of New York Press, 1991); Elizabeth Ellsworth, "Why Doesn't This Feel Empowering?: Working through the Repressive Myths of Critical Pedagogy," *Harvard Educational Review* 59 (1989): 297-324; Elizabeth Ellsworth and Marilyn Orner, *Present but Not Here: Power and (Re)presentation in Education* (Albany, NY: State University of New York Press, forthcoming); Michelle Fine, *Disruptive Voices: The Possibilities of Feminist Research* (Ann Arbor: University of Michigan Press, 1992); Madeleine Grumet, "The Politics of Personal Knowledge," *Curriculum Inquiry* 17, no. 3 (1987): 319-329; Patti Lather, *Getting Smart: Feminist Research and Pedagogy With/ In the Postmodern* (New York: Routledge, 1991); Magda Lewis, "Interrupting Patriarchy: Politics, Resistance, and Transformation in the Feminist Classroom," *Harvard Educational Review* 56 (1990): 457-472; Carmen Luke and Jennifer Gore, eds., *Feminism and Critical Pedagogy* (New York: Routledge, 1992); JoAnne Pagano, *Exiles and Communities: Teaching in the Patriarchal Wilderness* (Albany, NY: State University of New York Press, 1990); Lois Weis and Michelle Fine, eds., *Beyond Silenced Voices: Class, Race, and Gender in United States Schools* (Albany, NY: State University of New York Press, 1993).

17. Sandra Hollingsworth, Anthony Cody, Mary Dybdahl, Leslie Turner Minarik, Lisa Raffel, Jennifer Davis Smallwood, and Karen Manheim Teel, *Sometimes I'd Rather Show Them Some Love: Relations, Conversations, and Feminist Research on Urban Literacy Education* (New York: Teachers College Press, forthcoming.)

Section Four
PROSPECTS FOR THE PROFESSION
THROUGH TEACHER RESEARCH

Introduction

Section Four illustrates the professional applications of the arguments presented in Sections Two and Three. The authors here make problematic the traditional structures in which educational knowledge is applied. Two chapters investigate the structures of preservice education and staff development programs which would encourage teacher researchers in self-directed or codirected inquiry. Another chapter suggests a way that curriculum and instruction might be examined and rewritten by professional teachers, using the processes of teacher research. The final chapter considers appropriate institutional structures that would support teacher research as an important professional activity.

CHAPTER VIII

The Power of Teacher Research
in Teacher Education

MARILYN COCHRAN-SMITH

Teacher research, action research, and other inquiry-based processes are now becoming commonplace in the preservice teacher education curriculum. A teacher research project is often included as an assignment prospective teachers are required to complete during student teaching or as one of a series of strategies they are exposed to in a methods course. At the same time that teacher research has gained currency as a strategy for preservice teacher education, however, it also has been vigorously criticized.[1] Critics have argued that we cannot simply advocate research by preservice teachers as a good thing to do in and of itself, but instead we must interrogate what student teachers are doing research about, toward what social and political ends, and in relation to what larger frames of interpretation and analysis.

In fact, various versions of teacher research and other inquiry processes are based on widely disparate traditions of reform, and they have multiple social meanings that are worlds apart from one another. Even when they use a common language, there are quite distinct sociological views of knowledge about teaching implicit in such processes as inquiry, collaboration, and teacher research. At one extreme is a relatively narrow view of teaching and a "scientist" or "technical" view of knowledge for teaching as codified facts and generalizations which, when applied to particular classroom situations through thoughtful inquiry, permit considerable prediction and control.[2] At the other extreme is a critical or constructivist perspective on knowledge for teaching in which practitioners themselves are among those who formulate theories to understand and alter the world of schooling through systematic inquiry and reflection about their schools and classrooms.[3] That a given preservice curriculum claims

---

Marilyn Cochran-Smith is an Associate Professor in the Graduate School of Education, University of Pennsylvania.

teacher research as a central characteristic may tell us very little about its underlying epistemology, which may derive almost exclusively from a university-certified "knowledge base,"[4] or may include practitioners' ways of knowing about teaching, learning, and schooling.

I argue in this chapter that assessments of the power of teacher research in preservice education ought to be located within networks of school-university relations,[5] particularly in the assumptions about knowledge, language, and power that are implicit in the ways teacher educators regard and work with school-based teachers. I first provide a framework for locating teacher research in the context of three types of school-university relationships—consonance, critical dissonance, collaborative resonance—that underlie many of the programs that now include teacher research as one of the learning opportunities available to student teachers. Teacher research, I claim, ought to be evaluated as a vehicle for developing the stance, implicit or explicit, that a given teacher education program takes toward the existing contexts and relationships of schooling. I then analyze the value of teacher research when it is embedded in the school-university relationship of collaborating resonance, and when it is intended as a vehicle for developing an activist stance on the current arrangements of schooling. I do this by examining the contexts in which prospective teachers are initiated into the written and spoken discourses of teaching. I argue that the real power of teacher research lies in its challenge to the traditional discourse of learning to teach—a discourse that commonly emphasizes the primacy of teaching methods, mastery of skills, and outside expertise—and its support instead of an alternative discourse that centers on the construction of knowledge, teachers' ways of knowing, and critical pedagogy.

Teacher Research in the Context of Teacher Education: Knowledge, Language, and Power

Among the most useful conceptual and historical frameworks that have been developed to make distinctions among approaches to preservice teacher education programs are the following:

(1) Tom's suggestion that inquiry-oriented programs vary along the dimensions of problematics, models of inquiry, and ontology, and his analysis of the assumptions typically underlying programs and the barriers to reforms that invert those assumptions;

(2) Grimmett's categorization of the contents and purposes of reflection on teaching—thoughtfulness about the appropriate application of research to practice, deliberation and choice among competing versions of good teaching, and reflection as a process of reconstructing experience and educational ends;

(3) Liston and Zeichner's argument that current teacher education reforms are located in their historical antecedents—academic, social efficiency, developmentalist, and social reconstructionist traditions; and

(4) Feiman-Nemser's proposal that attempts to change teacher education can be understood in terms of academic, practical, technological, personal, and critical/social orientations.[6]

Taken together these authors provide a persuasive argument that it is impossible to regard as monolithic either the current state of teacher preparation or any of the activities and processes (inquiry-based or otherwise) that occur within it. These processes do not arise in isolation, as if disembodied from their historical, political, or social contexts. The contexts in which teacher research is located include the network of relations that obtain between the university and the school, such as the structures of power implicit in the ways teacher educators regard and work with school-based teachers: how they assign teacher research projects, arrange for school observations, organize field placements, appoint adjunct and regular staff, and supervise student teachers.

Every preservice program is the product of a set of assumptions about the knowledge, language, and expertise of school-based teachers relative to the knowledge, language, and expertise of university-based teacher educators and researchers. These assumptions, and the ways they are played out in various versions of teacher research, convey potent messages to prospective members of the teaching profession about the work lives of teachers and about the parts teachers can expect to play in establishing and altering the social worlds of school. Three school-university relationships—consonance, critical dissonance, and collaborative resonance—underlie many of the preservice programs that now include teacher research, action research, or some kind of self-inquiry among the learning opportunities available to student teachers.[7]

CONSONANCE

One widespread approach to preservice preparation is to ensure that the university-based and school-based portions of preservice preparation are consistent with, and affirming of, one another. Borrowing a term used in music to describe the agreement or unison of sounds, I refer to this kind of school-university relationship as *consonance*, or accord based on common application of the results of research on effective teaching. Although school-university relationships can be consonant in a variety of other ways, those based on the premises of the research on teacher effectiveness represent the major group in this category.

With innovations designed to foster consonance, the problem with student teaching is generally identified as its failure to prepare prospective teachers to make sound professional decisions by knowing how to apply the results of educational research to classroom situations using the language and concepts of effective teaching. The goal of teacher educators is to prepare students who are both skilled "situational decision makers" and "reflective" classroom practitioners who make what other professionals would recognize as "justifiable" educational judgments. In many programs, these goals are achieved by creating a high degree of consonance between theory and practice and by providing systematic articulation between the language and messages conveyed by the university and the school. Typically this means that student teachers are trained in research-based teaching competencies, and their school-based and university-based mentors are trained to provide systematic feedback and instruction in those same competencies.[8]

Many of the large-scale teacher training partnerships of universities, state departments of education, and school districts aim for consonance between the university and the school. In some cases, they dovetail with statewide efforts to build a common curriculum for all teachers. In programs of this sort, preservice and in-service teachers are encouraged to "speak the same language, that is, to draw on the results of research on effective teaching and to concentrate on common problems they can be expected to face in their classrooms."[9] Accordingly, student teachers are trained to observe and make decisions about how to apply professional knowledge correctly. Cooperating teachers, often called "clinical instructors," also receive instruction in classroom observation and in strategies for evaluating student teachers using the language and concepts of effective teaching. Common strategies in programs based on consonance include reflection on micro-teaching incidents, reflective teaching, analysis of video- or audio-recorded classroom data, classroom-based observations and journals, training of fieldwork supervisors and cooperating teachers in systematic observation (scripting) and feedback via the strategies and language of effective teaching, and computer-simulated teaching modules.

Most student teaching innovations that aim for consonance between university and school seek to improve the status of teaching as a profession and to make student teaching more systematic and rigorous by the application of research-based knowledge on effective teaching. Few educators would disagree that the professionalization of teaching is an essential aspect of educational reform, and one which prospective teachers ought to know about and support early in their careers. Although this is a worthy goal, programs that aim for school-university consonance are based on problematic notions about the power and knowledge of schools and universities. Although these programs supposedly combine "knowledge-based empirical research" with "knowledge that comes from practical experience,"[10] in reality they train experienced teachers by constructing for them both their knowledge (that is, what they ought to see when they look at and think about the classroom) and the language used to describe it (that is, the words and conceptual categories they ought to use to talk about teaching). There is little indication in program descriptions that either experienced teachers or student teachers are encouraged to examine their own knowledge and language from multiple perspectives, draw upon their own resources to pose problems and generate theories, question the curriculum and its underlying assumptions, and challenge either the construction of a generic knowledge base for teaching or the institutional arrangements and consequences of schooling.

Significant messages about power, knowledge, and learning to teach are implicit in programs based on consonance:

(1). Teaching should be guided by an empirically certified knowledge base.

(2). The knowledge base is generated almost exclusively by university-based researchers and teacher educators; neither experienced teachers nor student teachers are regarded as potential contributors.

(3). The role of the university in preservice education is to train students to control teaching by accurately predicting which research-based knowledge applies to which classroom situations.

(4). Universities can train student teachers most effectively when the perspectives and language of their school-based mentors are the same as those of their university-based teachers and supervisors.

(5). Teacher educators, therefore, should train experienced teachers to reframe and rename the wisdom of their own experience according to the linguistic and conceptual categories constructed by the university.

In effect, then, many student teaching programs may achieve consonance between university and school by ignoring or preempting teachers' knowledge and limiting the realm of discussion and reflection on teaching to consideration of which university-certified strategies apply to which classroom problems. Implicit in both the stated rationales and the structural arrangements of programs based on consonance is the hegemony of university-based knowledge, expertise, and language. This sends a potent message to prospective school-based teachers that their own chances to be generators of knowledge, agents for change, and genuine decision makers are circumscribed by outside-of-school expertise on teaching and learning.

CRITICAL DISSONANCE

A second approach to preservice preparation in which teacher research may be embedded is to make the university-based portions of preparation sufficiently incongruous with the school-based portions to interrupt the influence of the school and prompt challenges to that which is usually taken for granted. Borrowing a term used to describe discord or disagreement among sounds, I refer to this school-university relationship as *critical dissonance*, or incongruity based on a radical critique of teaching and schooling.

In reforms based on critical dissonance, the problem with student teaching is generally identified as its tendency to bolster utilitarian and vocational perspectives on teaching and ultimately to reproduce existing practice. This conceptualization of the problem is based on several interrelated arguments:

(1). The liberalizing effects that university experiences may have on student teachers are diluted by the conservative press of school life and by teachers and administrators who emphasize management and trial-and-error learning rather than inquiry or critical reflection.

(2). Student teachers have had a powerful socialization into teaching from their own twelve years of schooling before they even begin formal preparation, and student teaching does little to alter their views. Instead, it may bolster their ability to articulate the perspectives they already have and hence contribute to the perpetuation of conservative school practice.

(3). The "liberalizing" influence of the university is largely a myth. Rather than liberalizing, many aspects of university-based preparation are themselves conservative influences that emphasize relevance over critique and encourage reflection and research on factual or technical rather than critical aspects of teaching.[11]

Each of these arguments suggests that the problem with student teaching, whether actively or by default, is its conservative effect and its tendency to perpetuate existing instructional and institutional arrangements. Perceived in this way, the goal of teacher educators is to help student teachers develop stronger, more critical perspectives that confront issues of race, class, power, and gender, and call into question the social and political implications of standard policy and practice. What makes this possible is the high degree of dissonance that emerges between what student teachers typically observe and practice in traditional schools, on the one hand, and their developing critical perspectives about the social, political, historical, and economic issues of schooling and instruction, on the other.

Although there are far fewer programs based on critical dissonance than on consonance,[12] the goal is for students to become "reflective teachers" who question and assess the origins, purposes, and consequences of schooling and work for more democratic participation in the governance of educational institutions.[13] Common strategies in programs based on dissonance include action research and teacher research projects, ethnographic studies of schooling and curriculum, student-teaching journals, curriculum study based on critical theory, alternative methods courses, university-led seminars to critique common school practices, and the construction and use of cases of practice. As the Wisconsin studies show, however, a difficulty of these programs is that critical perspectives learned at the university are not necessarily used to critique student teaching experiences, particularly in the interactions of students and their university supervisors.[14]

Programs that aim to create critical dissonance are intended to be transformative, to overcome what Katz has called the "excessive realism" of student teachers[15] by enabling them to develop the analytical skills to critique and reinvent their own perspectives. Although these are essential goals, there are a number of implicit messages about the power and knowledge of school-based teachers relative to those of university-based teacher educators and researchers, which, when taken together, are problematic in some ways:

(1). The way to link theory and practice is to bring a critical perspective to bear upon the institutional and instructional arrangements of schooling.

(2). Those outside of the institutions of schooling are the agents who have developed these perspectives and thus can liberalize and reform those inside.

(3). The wisdom of practice associated with many teachers' views of teaching and curriculum is conservative with respect to issues of class, race, and gender and needs to be gotten around, exposed, or changed.

(4). The language and conceptual frameworks useful for describing and critiquing teachers' work and work lives need not be familiar to teachers or articulated in their own voices.

The assumptions underlying programs based on critical dissonance are unlike the assumptions underlying programs based on consonance in most fundamental respects. Like programs based on consonance, however, those based on dissonance also reflect the hegemony of university-based knowledge, expertise, and language for teaching. Despite the fact that they argue for the construction of an informed "counter-hegemony" within a "language of possibility,"[16] programs based on dissonance may convey intimidating mixed messages about the ability of teachers to develop their own school-based critiques of the knowledge base for teaching and to function as active agents in transforming the educational system and thus may contribute to what Feiman-Nemser and Buchmann call the "two worlds pitfall" that separates the worlds of practice/school and theory/university.[17]

COLLABORATIVE RESONANCE

A third approach to preservice education in which teacher research may be located is to link what students learn about teaching from their field-based school experiences with what they learn from their university experiences through mutually constructed learning communities. Appropriating a term used to describe increasing intensity among echoing sounds, I refer to this school-university relationship as *collaborative resonance*, or intensification based on the collaboration of learning communities.

Underlying innovative programs based on collaborative resonance is the assumption that conjoined efforts to prepare new teachers create learning opportunities that are both different from and richer than the opportunities either the school or the university can provide alone. In these programs, the problem with student teaching is commonly thought of as its failure to provide student teachers with not only the skills needed to critique standard procedures and link theory and practice, but also the resources needed to learn from and reform teaching throughout their careers. The goal of teacher educators, then, is not simply to teach students how to teach, but to teach them how to continue learning within diverse school contexts by prolonging and intensifying the influences of university and school experiences, both of which are viewed as potentially liberalizing.

Programs based on resonance share with programs intended to stimulate dissonance the view that in and of themselves the formal aspects of preservice preparation are largely impotent to alter students' perspectives while the less formal, experiential aspects of student teaching are potentially more powerful.[18] Both recognize that an important part of what happens during the student teaching period is "occupational socialization" or learning the culture of the profession, including how to behave, talk, and think like experienced members.[19] Both recognize the difficulty of field experiences where the culture does not support ongoing learning with mentor teachers who are actively involved in professional growth and school reform. Consequently both aim to interrupt the socialization that typically occurs. But unlike programs intended to provoke dissonance, programs based on resonance simultaneously aim to capitalize on the potency of the teaching culture to alter students' perspectives by creating or tapping into contexts that support ongoing learning of student teachers in the company of experienced teachers who are themselves actively engaged in efforts to reform, research, or transform teaching.[20]

Although there are powerful norms in most schools against collegiality and in favor of the notion that one learns to teach through trial-and-error experience rather than observation and analysis, programs based on resonance seek to develop felicitous contexts for students within a broader professional culture that supports teachers' learning. What makes this possible is the collaboration of school-based teachers, university-based educators, and student teachers. A growing number of preservice programs are designed to support the collaborative efforts of school and university to help students learn from teaching. Common strategies in programs of this sort include teacher research and action research, dialogue journals with school-based supervising teachers, school-site professional development activities, placement of students in sites for school-wide reform and restructuring or with small groups engaged in reform efforts, collaborative inquiry in school-site meetings and university-site seminars, joint program planning and assessment by supervisors, teacher educators, and cooperating teachers, theory and research-based curriculum, and foundations and methods courses with assignments critiqued in school and university settings.

Taken as a whole, the messages embedded in programs based on collaborative resonance are significantly different from those in programs based on either consonance or critical dissonance:

(1). The way to link theory and practice is through a process of self-critical and systematic inquiry about teaching, learning, and schooling.[21]

(2). Inquiry of this kind occurs within a culture of collaboration wherein novices, veterans, and teacher educators alike are continually learning to teach and research their own teaching (see chapter 7).

(3). Power is shared, and knowledge about teaching is fluid and socially constructed.

(4). The wisdom, language, critiques, and theoretical frameworks of school-based teachers are as essential to a knowledge base for teaching as are those of university-based teacher educators and researchers.

(5). In the end, the power to reinvent teaching and schooling is located in neither the university nor the school, but in the collaborative work of the two.

Student teaching programs that aim for collaborative resonance are rooted in a tradition of participatory democracy. They recognize that there are many people who have developed incisive and articulate critiques of teaching and schooling based on years of professional work inside schools. When it comes to reform-minded teaching, these emic perspectives are regarded as different from, but as important as, the etic critiques developed by people who have devoted their professional lives to work about, but outside of, schools. Programs based on collaborative resonance attempt to bring together people with inside and outside perspectives on teaching against the grain—not in order to homogenize ideas or create consensus in language and thought, but in order to intensify through collaboration the opportunities student teachers have to learn to teach against the grain.[22]

Teacher preparation is thus embedded within the complex historical, political, and cultural contexts of educational reform. Teacher research is doubly embedded—within the ideologies and philosophies of particular programs, and within the larger contexts of reform. Doing research in and of itself can therefore never be regarded as one among many "techniques" or "strategies" of teaching without political and epistemological roots, or as an endpoint and goal of preservice teacher education. Rather, the power of teacher research can only be regarded in terms of its value as a vehicle to help student teachers develop a stance—that is, a way of positioning themselves as prospective teachers (and eventually across the professional lifespan) in relation to (a) knowledge (i.e., their positions as generators as well as users of knowledge for and about teaching), (b) agency (i.e., their positions as activists and agents for school and social change), and (c) in terms of collaboration (i.e., their positions as professional colleagues in relation to other teachers, to administrators and policymakers, and to their own students). What it means for new teachers to use research as a basis for teaching, then, is a question that can only be answered in particular local contexts.

Learning the Discourse of Teaching: A Case of Teacher Research-Based Teacher Education

Project START (Student Teachers as Researching Teachers) is an example of the use of teacher research in preservice teacher education.[23] In this case, teacher research is embedded in the school-university relationship of collaborative resonance and is intended as a means for developing the stance of teaching against the grain of much of what is taken for granted in the elementary school curriculum, as well as in the social interactions of adults and children, and in the social and political contexts in which the arrangements of schools and schooling are played out.

TEACHING AGAINST THE GRAIN AS STANCE ON TEACHING

Project START encourages prospective teachers to "teach against the grain," or think of themselves as decision makers and collaborators working to reclaim their roles in the shaping of practice by taking a stand as both educators and activists. This means regarding teaching as a fundamentally political activity in which every teacher plays a part by design or by default and regarding the role of teacher as part of larger school reform and social change efforts.[24]

Teaching against the grain is challenging and sometimes discouraging work for experienced teachers and for student teachers. In most of their placements, there are few opportunities for student teachers to participate in thoughtful inquiry, reflect on their daily decisions, or collaborate with others.[25] In most of their encounters with school and university supervisors, student teachers are encouraged to talk about relevant and technical rather than critical or epistemological aspects of teaching.[26] Finally, in most preservice programs, the role of the teacher as an agent for change is not emphasized, and students are not deliberately socialized into assuming responsibility for school reform and renewal.[27] This means, then, that the hidden curriculum of preservice education programs is primarily functionalist and relatively narrow.[28] Almost by definition, student teaching is intended to help beginners ease as smoothly as possible into the prevailing system. Almost by definition, school- and university-based supervising teachers are selected for their past records of successful work within the constraints of the system.

The situation may be different, however, when student teachers are researchers, when they regard their classrooms as sites of inquiry about teaching and learning as well as issues of social justice writ large and small, and when they collaborate with experienced teachers who are also learners and who are themselves struggling to teach against the grain. In these contexts, prospective teachers may have opportunities to see that larger and grander school and social reform efforts are deeply entangled in their own biographies as educators and in the decisions they make and permit others to make about the curriculum and the children in their classrooms. In these contexts it may be possible for the interactions of beginners and mentors to have a critical rather than a functional orientation to the existing social and institutional arrangements of schooling wherein the realities of schooling are regarded as socially constructed and maintained and wherein the goal of teaching is thought of as "social transformation" and "increasing justice, equality, freedom, and human dignity."[29]

PLANNING, CURRICULUM MAKING, AND SOCIAL RECONSTRUCTION: LEARNING THE WRITTEN DISCOURSE OF TEACHING

A nearly universal tradition in preservice education is to introduce the written discourse of teaching by having students design and carry out "the lesson plan." The most widely recommended model of lesson planning has a series of steps: explicitly stating objectives and goals, choosing appropriate learning activities, organizing and sequencing those activities, and specifying evaluation procedures. A growing body of research on teacher planning and teacher thinking suggests that experienced teachers do not proceed in a linear fashion when planning for teaching; in fact, the process is significantly more cyclical and recursive, more learner-centered, and structured by larger units of time and content than the single lesson,[30] and lesson planning actually plays a "modest to insignificant" role in the range of planning strategies that experienced teachers use over the course of a school year. Nevertheless, lessons endure as the major unit for planning and improving teaching in preservice education and lesson plans endure as the single form of planning taught explicitly in programs across the country.[31] Hence they continue to represent what is arguably the most visible way that student teachers are initiated into the written discourse of teaching.

Even more troubling than the mismatch between lesson plan assignments and teachers' actual ways of preparing for and thinking about teaching, however, is the image of teaching that lesson plans perpetuate. Taken as artifacts of the cultures of teaching and teacher education, the versions of lesson plans common in popular texts and prepackaged training programs suggest that both planning for teaching and teaching itself are linear activities that proceed from a preplanned opening move to a known and predetermined endpoint. Further they suggest that even though, with experience, a teacher may need to write down less of the sequence of objectives and steps, the linear process of planning and instructing is essentially the same. Most importantly, designing and conducting lessons of the sort described here endorses and perpetuates the primacy of mastery, scripture, and method. Implicit in the lesson plan is the notion that mastery is the goal of every lesson—mastery by students of pieces of knowledge that the teacher transmits to them through a carefully selected sequence of questions or activities and then tests to ensure that mastery is complete. In elementary school teaching both the pieces of knowledge to be conveyed and the sequence of steps for getting there are spelled out in detail in the teacher's manuals that accompany textbooks in many curricular areas. The tyranny of the teacher's manual is most apparent, however, in basal reading programs, which provide carefully scripted plans for every single lesson and which account for some 90 percent of reading instruction in this country.[32] Basal scripts not only tell the teacher exactly when and what to say but also control the children's part in the script by stipulating precisely which responses are to be elicited and accepted. Notwithstanding occasional directives to the teacher to "accept any reasonable answer," it is clear that both teacher and children are expected to honor the authority of scripture and stick to the script. In the end, then, since both the content and sequence of events are established at the outset of a lesson plan and more often than not provided for in prepackaged materials, the major task for the prospective teacher is to develop a repertoire of methods for getting through lessons with a reasonable amount of decorum—methods for establishing order, keeping children on the task at hand, pacing questions and activities, occupying those who finish more quickly than others, and maintaining control.

The image of teaching underlying a teacher-research-centered approach to the written discourse of teaching directly challenges the primacy of mastery, scripture, and method. When teacher research plays a central role, student teachers are invited to treat their schools, classrooms, and even their reading groups as research sites, to understand their work by raising questions and collecting data, and to discover meanings in children's behaviors and in the interpretations they actively construct for classroom events and interactions. The written discourse of teacher research is based on the notion that teachers and children together construct knowledge and curriculum through their ongoing classroom interactions. It is not intended to implement or translate theory into plans for practice, but is instead intended to uncover and help develop what Edelsky, Altwerger, and Flores describe as "theories of practice" or "theories in practice"— that is, neither theories divorced from practice nor practice unaware of its own implicit theories.[33] Implicit in the written discourse of teacher research is the image of teachers as among those who have the authority to know about teaching, learning, and schooling, and to regard knowledge from the academy as generative frameworks for understanding and constructing practice[34] rather than scripture for reproducing practice.

There are several important perspectives about teaching that are developed when students are initiated into the written discourse of teaching through teacher research rather than traditional lesson plans, perspectives that may be thought of as *analysis of learning opportunities, understanding children's understanding*, and *constructing reconstructionist pedagogy*. By doing their own research, student teachers have the opportunity to *analyze the learning opportunities* that are or are not available to children in various kinds of instruction, particularly in scripted and unscripted programs, and to consider the impact on learning opportunities when control of understanding is shifted from text and teacher to children themselves and the interactions of children, teachers, and texts. For example, through teacher research student teachers can compare and analyze (a) children's responses to unabridged literature and to abridged and vocabulary-controlled stories; (b) the interaction patterns and knowledge that are constructed from open-ended questions, from questions with one right answer, and from children's own questions and connections; and (c) the quality of comprehension when children read complete connected text as opposed to parceled-out segments of texts frequently interrupted by text-stipulated teacher questions. Analysis of data from contrasting lesson structures—including children's written work, group discussions and other verbal interactions, observations of groups and of individual children, and the textbooks and teachers' materials themselves—permits prospective teachers to critique dominant instructional programs by treating lessons as sites for inquiry and by analyzing the ways particular materials, instructional practices, and structures of social participation constrain or support children's learning opportunities.

A second perspective that is central to the written discourse of teacher research is *understanding children's understanding*, or doing what Duckworth calls "giving reason to" the ways the individual child constructs meanings and interpretations both inside and outside the classroom.[35] This is accomplished through analysis of multiple data sources collected to describe the child from various perspectives. The image of the teacher implicit in this kind of research is not one who simply applies other people's principles or accepts outside experts' placements, groupings, labels, expectations, and limits for a particular child. Rather the teacher is taken to be a builder of knowledge and theory to "interpret, understand, and eventually transform the social life of schools."[36] Similarly, the child is not regarded as receiver or object of others' actions, but as active knower and agent—always learning, always "on task,"[37] and always involved in the business of making sense of what is going on around him or her. Student teachers work to understand individual children by analyzing classroom data, drawing on the theories of practice that they construct with other teachers in their local communities as well as on the frameworks developed by other school- and university-based researchers. Through the written discourse of inquiries about individual children, prospective teachers recognize that their efforts to respond to diversity in their classrooms are located not only in the nested contexts of families, communities, and institutions but also in their own preconceptions, experiences, and assumptions about learning and teaching.

Finally, teacher research is a vehicle for helping student teachers *construct reconstructionist pedagogy*, that is, pedagogy intended to help children of all ages understand and then prepare to take social action against the social and institutional inequities that are embedded in our society.[38] One site for inquiry of this kind is the study group of children and their teacher who collaboratively explore a particular piece of children's literature or a multidisciplinary theme or topic over the course of several sessions. The study group social structure challenges many of the norms of classroom interaction and control and invites student teachers to locate and draw on alternative texts and materials to alter both the social participation and the academic task structures of conventional instruction. What is significant about these inquiries is that student teachers set out both to alter the curriculum and to alter their children's perceptions of themselves as white or African or Hispanic Americans by making issues of language, culture, dialect, history, and power an examined part of the curriculum and of their lives. Although the content of every study group is not inequity and social justice, every study group inquiry is based on a belief in the efficacy rather than the efficiency of teachers, individually and collectively, to change their own teaching lives and the course of the world of schooling (see chapter 2). Each group is also based on the premise that children are active knowers with the ability to think critically, to pose and solve real problems, to construct interpretations of texts, and to move beyond what have been shown to be the narrow limits of reading groups, homogeneous tracking systems, and diminished curriculum. Hence, these study groups help prepare children to participate in a democratic society, and the inquiries that student teachers conduct about them support the development of reconstructionist or transformative pedagogy that challenges the dominant system.

COLLABORATION, INTELLECTUAL WORK, AND THE CULTURE OF REFORM: LEARNING THE ORAL DISCOURSE OF TEACHING

A second nearly universal tradition is to initiate student teachers into the oral discourse of teaching through regular face-to-face consultations with school- and university-based supervisors or supervising teachers. Early approaches to the supervision of teaching were intended to apply uniform objective criteria to the rating of individual teachers' efficiency and effectiveness.[39] Recent renewed emphasis on the supervision of teaching has taken two paths that appear on the surface to be contradictory: one focuses on the development of deliberative and reflective conversations about teaching that are context-specific and sensitive to the felt needs of individuals, and the other focuses on the production of specific empirically certified teaching behaviors that produce standard learning outcomes.[40] Interestingly, however, the two paths appear to crisscross rather than diverge in many instances, and some innovative approaches to supervision may not be so innovative after all. Lytle and Fecho point out, for example, that although a professional development strategy called "peer coaching" emphasizes collaborative work, it continues to assume that teachers need to be "trained" (perhaps by other teachers) in order to carry back and implement in their classrooms knowledge and skills that have been generated by outside experts.[41]

Evidence that supervision continues to assume a knowledge-transmission model of training teachers is embedded within some of the innovative student teaching programs of the last decade and in recent discussions in the professional literature. In one of the two articles on preservice education included in the ASCD 1992 yearbook on supervision, for example, it is proposed that the goal of preservice supervision is to prepare reflective and internally guided teachers through collaboration and interactive discourse.[42] The language of the chapter makes clear, however, that most of the traditional premises of supervision remain unaltered, and the "cognitive coaching" approach to supervision also includes pre- and post-observation conferences about lessons (wherein the supervisor chooses between a direct and a less direct mediating style of conveying information), videotaped lessons of the student teacher with analysis based on Madeline Hunter and mastery learning, and journal writing.

Notwithstanding innovations in teacher education that really do controvert the traditional model, many current approaches to supervision at the preservice level continue to emphasize individuality, skills acquisition, and outside expertise. Even in preservice programs intended to encourage reflection or critical inquiry, much of the oral discourse continues to revolve around teaching methods and procedures as opposed to questions of substance or the means-ends relationships of the contexts of schooling. Even when beginners are invited by supervisors to reflect on their practices and even when they are "coached" rather than supervised, the oral discourse perpetuates the primacy of method and skills—with "reflection" and "deliberation" reduced in an unfortunate sense to the "new skills" of the 1990s.

When teacher research groups function as one of the major contexts in which prospective teachers learn the oral discourse of teaching, however, the primacy of method, technique, and problem solving as individual skills is challenged. This does not mean that more experienced mentors never suggest strategies for effective instruction and management. But it does mean that the discourse about teaching is rich and substantive, and it does *not* look like oral discourse based on the transmission of a knowledge base. Nor, however, does the discourse of teacher research look like supervisory interactions that many would consider more enlightened—a more experienced teacher offering moral support to a less experienced one, helping her define problem areas for further observation, or coaching her to reflect on and interpret classroom episodes in particular ways. Rather than focusing on the interactions of two teachers, one transmitting knowledge and one receiving it, and centering on "the lesson" as the unit of analysis, discourse that is teacher-research-centered is often located within the context of an intellectual community wherein everybody is a teacher-researcher engaged in the real (and endless) work of learning about teaching—raising real questions, drawing on instances of experience involving particular children, and connecting diverse experiences and themes. The unit of analysis may at times be the lesson, but when it is, it is the lesson viewed as a particular incident or case in relation to other cases that relate conceptually and thematically to more abstract principles and theories being constructed through joint work.

Several kinds of intellectual work are accomplished through the oral discourse of teacher research: *giving reason to cases, constructing the dilemmas of schooling, rethinking the language of schooling, posing problems of practice,* and *constructing curriculum. Giving reason to cases* is a way of teachers' connecting specific instances to more general ideas and linking concrete particulars to abstract explanations through shared talk. Teachers' knowledge rather than only a university-certified knowledge base is privileged in oral discourse of this kind: teachers draw on their experiences over the course of many years spent observing a variety of children who struggle to construct and express their understandings; they describe children's learning from rich historical perspectives; and they mention their uncertainties about which practices are most helpful and how their practices change over time. They weigh their explanations at the same time that they weigh the usefulness of various practices. The product of this kind of discourse is not the translation of theory to practice, much less the correct application of general procedures to specific classroom situations. Rather, the product is conjoined understanding—the joint building of explanations based on closely observed children across classrooms and time periods that no one in the group had prior to the discussion.

The oral discourse of teacher research (see chapter 3) also provides a context in which more and less experienced teachers question the normal arrangements of schools and classrooms by *constructing dilemmas,* particularly those created by the race, class, and gender inequities embedded in our educational system. Although teachers wrestle to reconcile irreconcilable issues, there is no consensus in this sort of oral discourse wherein many comments are both contradictory and critical. But the point is to name the dilemmas of teaching and wrestle with the fact that there are no answers within the current structures of schooling and society. Fenstermacher points out that in current controversies over the professionalization of schooling, the moral dimensions of teaching, although primary, are often either ignored or forgotten, and the rhetoric of teacher professionalization is located primarily in the knowledge base.[43] When teacher research groups are one of the major contexts in which student teachers are initiated into the discourse of teaching, they have opportunities to identify and confront some of the moral dilemmas of teaching. Participants in teacher research groups also raise questions about the assumptions underlying school policies and the consequences of their language and their labeling practices.

Rethinking the language of teaching[44] is a collaborative process of uncovering the values and assumptions implicit in language and then thinking through the nature of the relationships it legitimates, an activity which Tom emphasizes as a "conscious attempt on the part of the teacher to suspend judgment about some aspect of the teaching situation and, instead, to consider alternatives to established practice."[45] What is especially important about the intellectual work of rethinking language is that participants regard the teacher herself as one of the agents who has the right and indeed the obligation to make certain aspects of teaching problematic, interrogate her own knowledge and experiences, and then begin to take responsible and reasoned action within the local context.

A fourth form of intellectual work achieved in the oral discourse of teacher research is the development of questions, or what Schön describes as *problem setting*. Schön reminds us that problems of professional practice do not present themselves ready-made. Rather "the [practice] situation is complex and uncertain, and there is a problem in finding the problem."[46] In the discourse of teacher research, teachers work together to pose problems from which they can learn how to teach the individual child as well as other children: the emphasis is on understanding the generalities of teaching by exploring its particulars. Experienced teachers help student teachers frame and reframe questions, repeatedly directing them to return to observations from the classroom, uncover the prior questions that were embedded in present ones, and develop generative structures of inquiry.

Finally, the intellectual work of *constructing curriculum* also occurs in the oral discourse of teacher research. This discourse is more than deciding how to teach the material predetermined in a teacher's guide or a pupil's text. It requires that teachers consider the long-range consequences of what and why they teach as well as the daily decisions about how they teach it. Zumwalt argues that a "curricular vision of teaching" is essential for all beginning teachers if they are going to be prepared to function as professional decision makers in their field. Without it, she cautions, the beginning teacher tends to settle for "what works" in the classroom rather than what could be.[47] Often what underlies discussions of this sort are the conflicts that may exist between teachers and administrators (and among teachers themselves) about their roles as curriculum implementors and tinkerers on the one hand, or as critics and creators on the other hand. Conflicts may also arise as teachers try to sort out the possible meanings of "curriculum" itself.

Teacher Research:
Interrupting the Discourse of Learning to Teach

When we consider teacher research and its value in preservice teacher education, we must know what particular versions of teacher research we are talking about, where those versions fit into the history and traditions of teacher research and of reform in teacher education, and in what theories of knowledge and social change they are embedded. We can begin with the view that it is neither possible nor desirable to avoid ideological or topical bias in teacher research because no research is value-free or without bias and no research is without a stance (either by intention or by default) on the current arrangements of schooling. This means that treating teacher research as a more or less atheoretical and apolitical activity, as is often done in current discussions of teacher education, is not a virtue but a way to reduce teacher research to the level of technique and method separable from content, topic, and social agenda.

Teacher research has enormous potential in preservice teacher education, but not if considered as one among many (often incongruent) techniques or strategies for teaching. Its power lies in its potential to interrupt the conventional ways student teachers are initiated into the oral and written discourse of teaching, and the powerful images of teaching and learning implicit in that discourse. With the discourse of teacher research as the base, the written and oral interactions of student teachers and their school- and university-based mentors take on a critical rather than a functional orientation to the existing social and institutional arrangements of schooling. Beginners and more experienced teachers thus work together to construct and reconstruct their understandings of teaching, learning, and schooling. They endeavor to understand children's understanding; reconsider school and classroom labels, categories, and policies; examine the stereotypes and assumptions underlying their own practices and the organizational contexts of schooling; and make visible and then grapple with the interests served by the structures of schooling. Implicit in the discourse of teacher research is the image of the teacher as active agent in schooling where the prevailing realities are neither inevitable nor unchangeable. These images may well be among the most potent informal influences on beginners. Embedded in the discourse of teacher research itself is not only what more experienced teachers and teacher educators say to beginners about the kinds of teachers they should become but also the stance on efficacy, knowledge, and leadership that is implicit in the ways students learn to talk and write about teaching. That is a powerful subtext about the profession and about the horizons and borders of teacher agency in schools and larger educational systems.

NOTES

1. The critique related to "inquiry" and "reflection" as teacher education strategies is particularly relevant. See Peter Grimmett, "The Nature of Reflection in Schön's Conception," in *Reflection in Teacher Education*, edited by Peter Grimmett and Gaalen L. Erikson (New York: Pacific Educational Press and Teachers College Press, 1988), and Alan R. Tom, "Inquiring into Inquiry-Oriented Teacher Education," *Journal of Teacher Education* 36, no. 5 (1985): 35-44.

2. Both Smyth and Apple make this point. See W. John Smyth, *A Rationale for Teachers' Critical Pedagogy: A Handbook* (Victoria, Australia: Deakin University Press, 1987), and Michael Apple, *Teachers and Texts: A Political Economy of Class and Gender Relations in Education* (New York: Routledge and Kegan Paul, 1986).

3. Marilyn Cochran-Smith and Susan L. Lytle, "Research on Teaching and Teacher Research: The Issues that Divide," *Educational Researcher* 19, no. 2 (1990): 2-11.

4. See, for example, David D. Dill, ed., *What Teachers Need to Know: The Knowledge, Skills, and Values Essential to Good Teaching* (San Francisco, CA: Bass Publishers, 1990), and Maynard C. Reynolds, ed., *Knowledge Base for the Beginning Teacher* (Oxford: Pergamon Press, 1989).

5. The term "university" is used throughout this chapter to refer to schools, colleges, and universities with preservice teacher education programs that include fieldwork experiences in school settings.

6. Tom, "Inquiring into Inquiry-Oriented Teacher Education"; idem, "Stirring the Embers: Reconsidering the Structure of Teacher Education Programs" (Paper

presented at the Conference on Teacher Development: The Key to Educational Change, Vancouver, B.C., Canada, February 1991); Grimmett, "The Nature of Reflection in Schön's Conception"; Daniel P. Liston and Kenneth M. Zeichner, *Teacher Education and the Social Conditions of Schooling* (New York: Routledge, 1991); Sharon Feiman-Nemser, "Teacher Preparation: Structural and Conceptual Alternatives," in *Handbook of Research on Teacher Education*, edited by W. Robert Houston (New York: Macmillan, 1990).

7. These three relationships are described in more detail with examples of programs in Marilyn Cochran-Smith, "Learning to Teach against the Grain," *Harvard Educational Review* 61, no. 3 (1991): 279-310, and idem, "Reinventing Student Teaching," *Journal of Teacher Education* 42 (1991): 104-118.

8. See, for example, the program descriptions and conceptual discussions in Robert McNergney et al., "Training for Pedagogical Decision Making," *Journal of Teacher Education* 39, no. 5 (1988): 37-43; Marlowe Berg, Diane S. Murphy, Anne Nagel, and Ida Malian, "The Effects of Preservice Clinical Supervision on Beginning Teachers" (Paper presented at the Annual Meeting of the American Educational Research Association, San Francisco, April, 1989); and Nancy Winitzky and Richard Arends, "Translating Research into Practice: The Effects of Various Forms of Training and Clinical Experiences on Preservice Students' Knowledge, Skills, and Reflectiveness,"*Journal of Teacher Education* 42, no. 1 (1991): 52-65.

9. McNergney et al., "Training for Pedagogical Decision Making," p. 37.

10. Ibid., p. 42.

11. See the discussions by Jesse Goodman, "Making Early Field Experience Meaningful: A Critical Approach," *Journal of Teacher Education* 12, no. 2 (1986): 109-125; Sharon Feiman-Nemser, "Learning to Teach," in *Handbook of Teaching and Policy*, edited by Lee S. Shulman and Gary Sykes (New York: Longman, 1983); B. Robert Tabachnick and Kenneth Zeichner, "The Impact of the Student Teaching Experience on the Development of Teacher Perspectives," *Journal of Teacher Education* 35 (1984): 28-36.

12. Feiman-Nemser, "Teacher Preparation."

13. Kenneth Zeichner and Daniel Liston, "Teaching Student Teachers to Reflect," *Harvard Educational Review* 57 (1987): 1-22.

14. Kenneth Zeichner, Daniel Liston, M. Mahlios and M. Gomez, "The Structure and Goals of a Student Teaching Program and the Character and Quality of Supervisory Discourse," *Teaching and Teacher Education* 4 (1986): 349-362.

15. Lilian Katz, "Issues and Problems in Teacher Education," in *Teacher Education of the Teacher, by the Teacher, for the Child*, edited by Bernard Spodek (Washington, DC: National Association for the Education of Young Children, 1974).

16. Henry Giroux and Peter MacLaren, "Teacher Education as a Counter Public Sphere: Notes towards a Redefinition," in *Critical Studies in Teacher Education*, edited by Thomas Popkewitz (London: Falmer, 1987), p. 272.

17. Sharon Feiman-Nemser and Margaret Buchmann, "Pitfalls of Experience in Teacher Preparation," *Teachers College Record* 87, no. 1 (1985): 53-65.

18. Kenneth Zeichner, B. Robert Tabachnick, and Kathleen Densmore, "Individual, Institutional, and Cultural Influences on the Development of Teachers' Craft Knowledge," in *Exploring Teachers' Thinking*, edited by James Calderhead (London: Cassell, 1987); Feiman-Nemser, "Learning to Teach."

19. Richard D. Corbett, "Using Occupational Socialization Research to Explain Patterns of Influence during Student Teaching," *Journal of Teacher Education* 31, no. 6 (1980): 11-13; Carolyn M. Evertson, "Bridging Knowledge and Action through Clinical Experiences," in *What Teachers Need to Know*, edited by David D. Dill and Associates (San Francisco, CA: Jossey-Bass, 1990).

20. Virginia Richardson-Koehler, "Barriers to the Effective Supervision of Student Teachers," *Journal of Teacher Education* 30, no. 2 (1988): 28-34.

21. Cochran-Smith and Lytle, "Research on Teaching and Teacher Research: The Issues that Divide."

22. Cochran-Smith, "Learning to Teach against the Grain."

23. See Susan L. Lytle and Marilyn Cochran-Smith, chapter 2 in this volume, for further information about Project START.

24. A number of scholars make the argument about teaching as a political act. See Stanley Aronowitz and Henry Giroux, *Education under Siege* (New York: New World Foundation, 1985); Kenneth Zeichner, "Preparing Reflective Teachers: An Overview of Instructional Strategies Which Have Been Employed in Preservice Teacher Education," *International Journal of Educational Research* 7, no. 5 (1986): 565-575; P. E. Willis, *Learning to Labour* (Hampshire, Eng.: Gower, 1978); Wilfred Carr and Stephen Kemmis, *Becoming Critical* (London: Falmer Press, 1986).

25. See especially John I. Goodlad, *A Place Called School* (New York: McGraw-Hill, 1984); Ann Lieberman and Lynne Miller, *Teachers, Their World, and Their Work* (Washington, DC: Association for Supervision and Curriculum Development, 1984).

26. Zeichner, Liston, Mahlios, and Gomez, "The Structure and Goals of a Student Teaching Program and the Character and Quality of Supervisory Discourse."

27. John I. Goodlad, "Studying the Education of Educators: From Conception to Findings," *Phi Delta Kappan* 71, no. 9 (1990): 698-701.

28. Kenneth M. Zeichner and Jennifer M. Gore, "Teacher Socialization," in *Handbook of Research on Teacher Education*, edited by W. Robert Houston (New York: Macmillan, 1990).

29. Ibid., p. 331.

30. See especially the research of Christopher Clark and Penelope Peterson, "Teachers' Thought Processes," in *Handbook of Research on Teaching*, 3rd ed., edited by Merlin C. Wittrock (New York: Macmillan, 1986).

31. Ibid.

32. Kenneth S. Goodman, Patrick Shannon, Yvonne S. Freeman, and Sharon Murphy, *Report Card on Basal Readers* (Katonah, NY: Richard C. Owen Publishers, 1988).

33. Carole Edelsky, Bess Altwerger, and Barbara Flores, *Whole Language: What's the Difference?* (Portsmouth, NH: Heinemann, 1991).

34. Marilyn Cochran-Smith and Susan L. Lytle, eds., *Inside/Outside: Teacher Research and Knowledge* (New York: Teachers College Press, 1993).

35. Eleanor Duckworth, *The Having of Wonderful Ideas* (New York: Teachers College Press, 1987); Patricia Carini, *Prospect's Documentary Processes* (Bennington, VT: Prospect School Center, 1985).

36. Smyth, *A Rationale for Teachers' Critical Pedagogy: A Handbook*, p. 12.

37. Frederick Erickson, "Tasks in Time: Objects of Study in a Natural History of Teaching," in *Improving Teaching*, edited by Karen K. Zumwalt (Alexandria, VA: Association for Supervision and Curriculum Development, 1986).

38. Aronowitz and Giroux, *Education under Siege*; Ira Shor, *Critical Teaching in Everyday Life* (Boston, MA: South End Press, 1980).

39. David B. Tyack and Elizabeth Hansot, *Managers of Virtue: Public School Leadership in America, 1800-1980* (New York: Basic Books, 1982).

40. Linda Darling-Hammond and Eileen Sclan, "Policy and Supervision," in *Supervision in Transition*, edited by Clark D. Glickman, 1992 Yearbook of the Association for Supervision and Curriculum Development (Alexandria, VA: Association for Supervision and Curriculum Development, 1992).

41. Susan L. Lytle and Robert Fecho, "Meeting Strangers in Familiar Places: Teacher Collaboration by Cross-Visitation," *English Education* 23 (1991): 5-28.

42. Amy Bernstein Colton and Georgia Sparks-Langer, "Restructuring Student Teaching Experiences," in *Supervision in Transition*, edited by Clark D. Glickman, 1992 Yearbook of the Association for Supervision and Curriculum Development (Alexandria, VA: Association for Supervision and Curriculum Development, 1992).

43. Gary D Fenstermacher, "Some Moral Considerations on Teaching as a Profession," in *The Moral Dimensions of Teaching*, edited by John I. Goodlad, Robert Soder, and Kenneth A. Sirotnik (San Francisco, CA: Jossey-Bass, 1990).

44. This term is borrowed from an article by Henry Giroux, "Rethinking the Language of Schooling," *Language Arts* 61, no. 1 (1984): 33-40.

45. Tom, "Inquiring into Inquiry-Oriented Teacher Education," p. 37.

46. Donald A. Schön, *The Reflective Practitioner* (San Francisco: Jossey-Bass, 1983), p. 129.

47. Karen K. Zumwalt, "Beginning Professional Teachers: The Need for a Curricular Vision of Teaching," in *Knowledge Base for the Beginning Teacher*, edited by Maynard C. Reynolds (New York: Pergamon Press, 1989).

CHAPTER IX

Curriculum Research Together: Writing Our Work

SUSAN NOFFKE,   LINDA MOSHER,
AND CHRISTINE MARICLE

> If you don't know the kind of person I am
> and I don't know the kind of person you are
> a pattern that others made may prevail in the world
> and following the wrong god home we may miss our star.
>
> . . .
>
> For it is important that awake people be awake,
> or a breaking line may discourage them back to sleep;
> the signals we give—yes or no, maybe—
> should be clear: the darkness around us is deep.
>
> > "A ritual to read to each other"
> > William Stafford

The picture painted of the curriculum in high school classrooms over the past decade is not a very cheery one. Yet it is also a picture painted by artists who do not, for the most part, live in the world of teachers, children, and schools. Only recently has there been a rebirth of efforts to involve practitioners in the study of their own practice. While a whole range of collaborative efforts involving university-based researchers and educational practitioners is beginning to be noticeable in scholarly journals and professional meetings, very little has been done to involve teachers in the critical and collaborative analysis of the knowledge they make available to students—the ways

---

Linda Mosher and Christine Maricle are teachers of English in a secondary school in Buffalo, N.Y. While doing the work reported in this chapter, Susan Noffke was an Assistant Professor in the Graduate School of Education, State University of New York (Buffalo) and was also a Faculty Associate with the Buffalo Research Institute on Education for Teaching. She is presently an Assistant Professor of Curriculum and Instruction at the University of Illinois (Urbana-Champaign).

An earlier version of this chapter was presented at the Annual Meeting of the American Educational Research Association in San Francisco, April 1992.

they select, organize, and treat that knowledge, and the factors which may influence their actions. While the teacher's voice is increasingly heard through forms of research such as narrative inquiry, action research, and life history, the focus is often on pedagogical technique and not on the nature and form of knowledge in classrooms. In an era in the United States where questions are continually raised about what "Johnny" (and presumably "Jane") knows, the voices of teachers examining curricular issues in their own practice are increasingly absent from the public debate over "whose knowledge is of most worth." If attempts are to be made to expand the community of educational researchers beyond the academy to include teachers, then ways to involve teachers, not only in the consumption of educational research or in the development of educational technologies, but also in the production of knowledge about curriculum, must be more fully explored.

This chapter focuses on both the results and processes of three years of curriculum study by the authors—two secondary English teachers (Chris and Linda) from an inner-city "magnet" school, each with more than twenty-five years of public school teaching experience, and a university researcher (Sue)—of the knowledge that is made available in the teachers' classrooms, that is, their "knowledge-in-use."[1] By curriculum we mean that which actually takes place in the classroom, rather than curriculum as state policy, curriculum guides, or texts. Our focus was, therefore, on the selections the teachers chose to include in their classes, the ways in which they organized and treated knowledge, and the factors which affected these choices. Our purpose here is to explore not only substantive issues arising from the analysis of the teachers' knowledge-in-use but also the process by which the analysis of curriculum took place.

The theoretical framework for the study had its origins in the researcher's understanding of two traditions in educational inquiry. The first is that of critical studies, where issues of knowledge in classrooms and in the research process are seen as directly tied to issues of power and authority in institutions and in the larger social context.[2] The second tradition is that of feminist writings on the nature of science, in which the identities and interests of all parties involved in the research process move toward being on the "same plane."[3] Some attention is paid here to how that framework affected the initial stages of this project;[4] however, the overall focus is on both the process of learning to research together and on what we found out about the teachers' knowledge-in-use.

The first section provides an overview of the background of the project and describes the process by which the participants came to work together on the analysis of data drawn from the teachers' work. It is written in the third person—as what "they" did. In the second section, what "we" have "found" is outlined; yet each of the participants has a separate voice, an "I", reflecting on the process and outcomes of the study. Finally, "we" examine issues and implications of the study for curriculum research. The change in person represents the changing dynamics as we approached a more collaborative relationship.

Learning Our Work

The patterns for data collection and particularly data analysis in this work were not predetermined in a linear fashion, but rather have emerged and changed over time. The work described here began as part of a larger study of teachers' knowledge-in-use and employed standard qualitative research methods.[5] These included initial autobiographical interviews, a series of three classroom observation cycles followed by structured interviews about the teachers' reasons for selecting particular topics and handling them in particular ways, and concluding interviews.

While the *methods* for data collection were standard for field studies in education, there were significant differences between the *methodology*, the "theory and analysis of how research does or should proceed," employed in this study and those of many other qualitative studies.[6] First, Chris and Linda received assurances that all field notes and transcriptions of tapes along with any analysis would be shared with them for their comments prior to their inclusion in the data for the larger project. Any questions about the accuracy of the data, or about their inclusion or exclusion, were to be negotiated. To Sue, this meant that there would always be the possibility that Chris and Linda could at any point decide to end the research. Because traditional research has always left power ultimately in the hands of the university researcher, Sue felt this to be a necessary risk to complement the clear risks classroom teachers take in opening their doors to researchers.

The concern with power relations in educational research was grounded in Sue's own experience as a "teacher subject" in a research project, and also in the works of critical and feminist scholars. Her reading of Basil Bernstein, for example, led her to question research methods which intrude deeply into peoples' lives, expose them to close scrutiny, and yet award them no voice either in the analysis of the data or in the representation of their world in the resultant written text.[7] Because the teachers involved were women in a predominantly patriarchal society, she also felt that the danger of misrepresenting their realities through research needed to be addressed in ways that went beyond the usual ethic of protection of privacy through anonymity.[8]

Second, Sue made it clear from the first meetings with Chris and Linda that questions from them about her own background were welcomed. Derived from feminist writings on research methods, her assumption was that a reciprocal relationship between teachers and researchers—beyond standard notions of trust and rapport—needed to be explored if epistemologically and ethically defensible research with teachers was to take place.[9] Finally, Sue made a commitment to continue the research work until all concerned felt it had come to conclusion. She felt that this latter point was significant if "exploiting the exploited" was to be avoided.[10]

After the initial data-gathering phase, the process of working through the data together began. This work had two phases, representing a transition from a researcher to collaborative effort, toward a shared effort at "writing our work." At first, Sue shared transcripts of interviews and classes along with summaries and interpretations, presented in the form of letters to Chris and Linda. The transcripts and letters formed the basis of their first writing efforts together—the creation of vignettes of Linda's and Chris's practice. All three discussed a set of transcripts from one of Linda's classes and from one of Chris's classes. Then Chris and Linda each wrote a description of the other's work, the texts were edited together, and each of the two teachers wrote a commentary on the description of her own work. These vignettes were included in a "knowledge-in-use" project monograph, along with other vignettes written by members of the project's writing staff—a group of research staff members and teachers.[11]

This initial phase of writing together seemed to form a base of understanding from which other work might proceed. After this experience with reading and discussing transcripts and writing together, Sue proposed that a more formal analysis and interpretation of the transcribed lessons be done together, beginning with an examination of the categories used in the larger project.[12] Although somewhat unsure of their ability to do the work, and for reasons

which they will later clarify, Chris and Linda readily agreed. In order
to give them a better idea of what the work would entail, Sue provided
an outline of the task and an ethnographer's description of data
analysis.[13] The initial work began with the categories developed in the
overall project, making alterations as a need was seen. They also
looked at the "dilemmas" language from Berlak and Berlak's work to
further refine their understandings of terms which might be useful in
the analysis.[14]

What followed was a whole lot of time together: meetings at
school and Saturday mornings over bagels as they began to talk about
the data. Categories were discussed in relation to specific episodes
from the class transcripts. Additional readings were done at Sue's
suggestion, to provide ways to work through the tensions and
contradictions which emerged between goals aspired to and actual
classroom practices.[15] The "they" of this section was gradually
becoming the "we" of this chapter.

Writing Our Work

This section describes what we found as we analyzed the
transcripts of observations and interviews together. First we briefly
overview what we found in the process of data analysis. General
patterns of selection, organization, and treatment of knowledge
present in the observed lessons are then described, along with
influencing factors noted in postobservation and other interviews.
Finally, we each take a personal look at what was found and the
meaning this project has had for our work.

WHAT WE "FOUND" ON SATURDAY MORNINGS

What will be described here came out of a series of Saturday
mornings together, often supplemented by additional time together at
school. The process was much like the work of any group of
researchers: much time devoted just to deciding how we would
proceed, reading and talking over the transcripts, arriving at
categories, checking to see whether we saw the same things, and
redefining categories where necessary. As in many similar studies,
once this task was accomplished, the actual work of analyzing the
transcripts proceeded smoothly.

While much of what we "found" parallels other studies, a
significant difference here lies in what was done with the "findings."
The latter forms the basis for each of our individual "stories of our

work" that are presented in the subsections which follow. First, we offer a general summary of the knowledge-in-use in the two classrooms, along with a summary of the factors which were seen to affect that knowledge-in-use. A tentative explanation for the contradictions we found between ideals and practices is also offered.

The classes observed were English II, IV, and V, including lessons on Shakespearean plays, a review of a unit of short stories, a segment on short story writing, sessions on nonfictional readings, presentation of original speeches, work on précis writing, and reviewing for final exams. The nature and form of the knowledge-in-use selected for these classes varied. There were some instances in which we could say that the knowledge was clearly the teacher's—for example, Chris's interpretation of a play. Less frequently was the student's knowledge present. For example, during a lesson on a story about Harriet Tubman, a student shared her family's recent visit to local "stations" of the Underground Railroad. On another occasion, students presented their assessment of a talk the previous night by Louis Farrakhan, leader of the Nation of Islam. Social knowledge (for example, personal interactions) did play a role, but this was usually during transitions between or at the end of class sessions. Yet the overall pattern seemed to be primarily standard knowledge within the academic subjects, with several instances in which procedural knowledge (setting behavorial guidelines, collecting homework, etc.) took up a significant amount of class time. Instances of looking at the overall nature of knowledge were not apparent. While the "voices" of Chris, Linda, and their students were seen in the transcripts, they were most often the vehicles for standard and academic knowledge.

In terms of organization, knowledge was most often presented sequentially (e.g., following the plot line), with the teachers relating parts to the whole, specifics to universals, many times using comparisons and contrasts. This organization of knowledge was a clear pattern, explicitly stated to the students. In terms of treatment, there was a clear tendency to integrate knowledge within the subject area and sometimes across to other subject areas. While the overall pattern was to focus on the public nature of knowledge, there were many instances in which either Chris or Linda highlighted the relevance of the topic to the students' lives or used an autobiographical anecdote to make a point clear—instances of personal knowledge. For the most part, knowledge was treated as the content material under study; yet there were blocks of time, especially in the writing classes, when the emphasis was on knowledge as process. In most circumstances, knowledge was treated as revealed, that is, as truth or reality "out there" to be discovered or transmitted, and certain. One clear exception was one of Linda's classes in which there was a lengthy discussion of the Vietnam War, stemming from a short story the class had read. In this segment, the treatment was clearly that of knowledge as created (socially constructed) and problematic.

For all of us, the pattern of the knowledge-in-use that emerged from the analysis was disturbing. It did not match any of our visions of what teaching ought to be. What factors might be influencing this pattern? In the postobservation interviews, both teachers most often indicated their knowledge of the subject matter, their interest in and prior experience with the topic, their personal priorities, and their knowledge of the students as the primary factors affecting why they taught the way they did. While such things as availability of materials and policy decisions were mentioned, both Chris and Linda strongly felt that they taught what and how they wanted to teach, within the broad framework of curriculum guidelines. Textbook availability did seem to play a role, as did the limited ability of students to purchase additional materials, but these were not indicated as primary concerns, nor was the administrative climate. While testing and grading needs were seen as important, one of the classes Linda taught had only teacher-made tests. Both Chris and Linda were sure of *what* they taught; it was the *how* that was most unsettling.

The autobiographical interviews had yielded strong commitments to teaching and to the students. Chris has taught at this school, located in a primarily African-American neighborhood, since it opened, well before it became a "magnet" in the district's desegregation plan. Linda, too, has been at the school a long time. Both Chris and Linda, in postobservation conferences and in informal discussions, had indicated concerns with the changes in teaching they have seen over time. The degree of autonomy they had over their work during their early years of teaching was seen to have been lessened; the number of problems children brought to school had increased.

At Sue's suggestion, we began to consider a possible tension in the teaching practices that she observed. What seemed salient to her were two strong and contradictory tendencies apparent in what she saw. One had to do with the deep commitment and caring that Chris and Linda had for their students. The other was their desire for students to take knowledge at more than face value. What this translated into seemed to be a tendency to trade off "higher-level" thinking for the students' success in school. Neither fear of administration nor fear of loss of classroom control seemed to be salient features. Was it the desire to see children "succeed" which seemed to lead to the "watering down" of classroom experiences and the preponderance of standard knowledge?

As we began to consider our own perspective on what has transpired over the three years of our relationship, these and other thoughts haunted us. In the following pages each of us shares in our own voices what we have experienced and what we have gained from this endeavor.

LINDA'S WORK

I cannot remember a time in my life when I did not want to be a teacher. My mother wanted to be a teacher, but could not afford to go to college. She passed that dream on to me, telling me that there is no job more important than that of a teacher. A teacher's influence, she said, continues long beyond the time spent with the students.

When Sue initially interviewed me, I spoke of the teachers who had influenced my teaching style: my mother, who, in her role as Sunday School teacher, taught me the importance of allowing each individual his or her dignity and sense of value, and that more can be accomplished by firm, kind discipline than by ridicule or harsh criticism; Miss Matthey, who taught me as early as second grade that one's attitudes are affected by how one is treated in the classroom; Mrs. David, who knew that the teacher's attitudes about and selection of materials for the curriculum are as important as the genres one teaches. The list goes on.

It has ever been my hope to pay back those excellent teachers with my own excellence, to carry forward in the spirit in which I was taught. When I began this project, it was my belief that I had been doing just that. This long-standing commitment to the idea of excellence in teacher education programs means that I am usually open to anything which is aimed in that direction. That is one reason why I was interested in Sue's proposition that we join in the research process. An important personal reason why I readily agreed to the project was that I viewed the opportunity to research my teaching methods as a way to verify that I was using the most effective means to educate my students. I wanted to assure myself that I was not doing a disservice to my students and that my teaching was of the highest caliber possible.

The fact that I have always been reasonably confident of my skills in the classroom reduced what I saw as the "risk factor"—that Sue might tell me that I was not a "good" teacher when the research was completed. Even though I did not believe on any real level that Chris and I would be involved much beyond the information-gathering stages, I was still anxious to confirm my expertise in the classroom and to verify that I was doing what I believed I was: sending my students out into the world prepared to participate in it successfully.

When Sue asked Chris and me to participate with her as teacher-researchers, I knew immediately what my answer would be. I also knew that I would have to convince Chris that we could and should join Sue. Chris and I had established a high level of trust in one another over the several years we had been working together; so I felt comfortable with her as a fellow researcher. I believe Chris had similar trust in me. My trust in Sue, however, extended only to the feeling that she would not use anything she learned in a destructive manner. Although she insisted that we would be co-owners of the research, that she would not release any of "our" information without consulting us first, and that she would "stick around" to help us reach closure in our own minds once the project was over, I did not give much credence to her promises. It had been my experience that persons from the university setting who *used* high school teachers and their classes for research purposes made the "noises" that Sue was making, gathered their information, and "faded into the sunset," promises to the contrary notwithstanding. I was prepared for Sue to do the same, but I was interested in participating nonetheless.

So I knew, when Sue invited me to participate in the research, exactly what it was I wanted from the experience. I expected this outside source (Sue) to verify what I hoped was true: I am a master teacher who knows exactly what she is about, and whose curriculum and methods are beyond reproach. As I began the job of reading through the transcripts of Sue's observations in my various classes, I was aided in my interpretations by the readings which she provided. Apple, Ellsworth and Pfalzer, McNeil, and Sirotnik all described the average teacher as one who uses paperwork as a control method, who lectures, who gives students few if any opportunities to formulate opinions or to give meaningful feedback, and whose materials are almost wholly concerned with standard, teacher-controlled knowledge.[16] I was disturbed that this research verified that which I had read on my own, but was certain that I was "none of the above."

Reading over the interviews from November, 1989, I still believed what I had stated:

I have things in my curriculum that aren't stated. And one of those things for seniors is that they will begin to examine their attitudes, and to examine where they are, and where they want to be, and how they're going to get there, and whether or not where they want to go is a good place to go . . . not to intrude my value system, but at the same time, I want them to examine their value systems, and, perhaps, rethink. And if they hear opposing viewpoints on things, it's my hope that they will (interview, November 11, 1989).

What I found on initial inspection of the transcripts was that, while my methods varied, I did a great deal of lecturing. The students in my Shakespeare class were limited almost entirely to responses to questions which tended to require only basic recall, and to teacher-controlled public knowledge that was standard, explicit, revealed, and certain. It was only at the end of a unit (play) that students got to exchange with one another their information, ideas, and opinions about what was going on in the play. Only then did they get to "examine human behavior, focus on difficult material, become conversant with Shakespeare's ideas," things which I had said in the postobservation interview (November 30, 1989) were important in my selection of Shakespeare for an entire semester of senior English. How were they to get a sense of accomplishment from merely reading aloud, with teacher explanations and interruptions?

My other classes were not so steeped in lecture and allowed for student creativity and interaction, perhaps merely because of the materials selected and the nature of the course. The creative writing course was based on writing from teacher-selected models, but students worked in peer-editor groups and relied on themselves and each other a great deal. However, I still appeared to lecture more than 50 percent of the time. The second semester English IV course was based on a collection of short nonfiction pieces. It was during this course that I came closest to doing what I believed I was doing in all my courses: encouraging the students "to exercise their verbal skills, and at the same time examine their attitudes" (interview, March 2, 1990).

I was distressed to see how often, during the course of the transcripts for the classes, I fit into the categories which the researchers had described. Sue suggested that, if I really wanted to know whether I had succeeded at all with what I intended, I ask several of my former students the following question: "If you had to tell someone the five things I felt were most important for you to learn in my class, what would you say they were?" I asked a variety of graduates ranging from the class of 1981 to the class of 1991. The answers which I received led me to believe that somehow I had gotten "my curriculum" across to at least those few. They spoke of such things as my insistence that they have the ability to write coherently and speak articulately, that they be able to read and comprehend well. They also mentioned often the attitudes which they got from my classes: that one can do anything one is willing to work to achieve, regardless of background; that there is no excuse for not doing one's best; that we must have a tolerance for one another; that one must look below the surface of things.

Obviously, I had been doing something right. Just as obviously, it has not been enough, judging from my reactions to the transcripts. Sue did not tell me that I was not doing what I thought I was. She didn't have to. I saw it for myself, in black and white. I still believe in the curriculum which I choose to teach. It is still important to me *what* I teach. I still believe that students' attitudes are challenged and examined, perhaps for the first time, because of the materials I choose for my courses . . . and I *do* choose. There is nothing haphazard or catch-as-catch-can about the things which I choose for my students to read. I am still committed to my "double curriculum" and to my belief that how one treats students is as important as the material one chooses to teach them. (The fact that seniors have not put up any resistance to purchasing their own reading texts has been to my advantage.)

What I have become aware of, and what I have begun to change, are the methods by which I guide students through the materials. That I have changed is evident in the answers I received from the 1991 graduates, students whom I taught after I had begun to examine Sue's transcripts. One student summed up what his classmates said when he stated, "You're not just teaching facts. You wanted us to think, especially in that Shakespeare class. You always wanted to know why. We would give you a perfectly good answer, and you would say, 'Yes, but why?' *Why* was the most often spoken word in that class, and in those discussion groups."

So, I am changing. I no longer spend most of the Shakespeare semester as a lecturer. Just as important, I am no longer looking to others to tell me whether or not I am "on course." I have learned to be an "educated reflective practitioner." I am still learning. I am becoming more aware of the organization and treatment of the knowledge which I make available to my students.

I was not confident, at the beginning of this project, of the extent to which Chris and I would have any real role in the writing of the research, and certainly never imagined that we would play any part in the presentation of our findings. It took what I suspect now was a supreme effort to break through that particular wall of disbelief. That there is shared ownership of our inquiries into Chris's and my teaching methods has long been established as a "given." Now, when Sue says, "We have the opportunity to rework our research" for whatever purpose, I know *we* will rewrite the project, and *we* will spend hours over coffee and bagels on numerous Saturday mornings making certain that everything is done to *our* satisfaction. The trust which took so long to build is now a solid foundation which is taken as much for granted as the understructure of one's house. *When* that happened, I am not quite certain. The "how" of it occurred over time, as Sue welcomed us into her world, took interest in ours, and kept her promises.

It is ironic that I got exactly what I wanted to get out of this project when I agreed to be a partner in it. I learned whether or not I was the teacher I thought I was. The answer, however, was not what I expected. I have been disappointed and discouraged, but (oddly enough) never threatened. I am a better teacher because of my participation, and I expect to continue to grow. This project has, without a doubt, guaranteed that I will be too busy getting better to become "burned out." Had Sue done her research in the traditional manner, this would not have happened. I feel that, although I have benefited immeasurably, the next ten years' worth of students and preservice teachers will learn more and better because I have learned to be a better teacher. That is what makes this kind of research most valuable. Practices must be changed on the "firing line." If teachers tend to teach as they have been taught—as research suggests—we must, then, change the ways those teachers teach. This project has made a beginning.

CHRIS'S WORK

One day, Linda asked me to meet in her classroom. She showed me an application for the teacher education program at the university and said that she needed a cooperating teacher-partner and that it should be me. She knew how I felt about student teachers from UB (University of Buffalo) having heard my horror stories previously. "This will be different and you can do this. I need a partner and you're it." I can honestly say I became involved in the teacher education program because Linda *made me*. I can also honestly say she was right. It *has been different* and I have no regrets.

In 1989 we met Sue. It has been three years since the research began on the knowledge-in-use project. For a long time, I felt inadequate. I particularly felt insecure about my ability to do the research and write the vignettes of our teaching which formed the basis for the *Cases of Wise Practice* monograph. When we began to "write our work," I started to feel a part of the research. Sue treated me as an equal; we did not have a teacher-student relationship. What began as a group of classroom observations and follow-up interviews has evolved into a strong personal and professional friendship.

As we met on Saturday mornings through the fall and winter (1991-1992), discussing the data and categories in regard to the class transcripts, I sensed that we were becoming a team. I felt like a team member. We learned from each other, sharing and understanding, making our feelings known, each interested in what the others had to contribute—three women with similar life experiences and no history of dislike. Sue was the first university person I met who was human. In April of 1992, the three of us traveled to San Francisco to present a paper based on our research together at the annual meeting of the American Educational Research Association. This was the zenith of my teaching career. Before Sue came into my classroom, no one ever asked what I was doing or why. This project has changed what I do in the classroom, and at times, the reflection has made me uncomfortable.

When I began teaching I was very fortunate to have an extremely supportive assistant principal who valued the study of English literature and poetry. Two older science teachers (at that time already in their sixties) took me under their wings and became my mentors. Each day they modeled not just "good teaching" but genuine concern for the children and a commitment to provide the best for their charges. I learned about the need to be flexible and understanding, to prepare lesson plans and how to handle the zillion little details which invade the classroom on a daily basis. Memories of that administrator, Dorothy, and Gladys and Ivah, my teacher heroes, with their patience and helpful suggestions, remain with me today. They cared about a new and inexperienced teacher and gave their time and skill. Because of this experience, I feel the time the preservice teachers spend observing in the classroom is very important. There is much to be learned.

Reflecting on the types of knowledge made available in my classroom, I find that most of it is standard teacher knowledge, usually public, occasionally personal, revealed and certain. Often knowledge is presented sequentially (following a plot line). It may be related to other information the students possess from their previous experience with the subject (e.g., *Julius Caesar* can be related to *Romeo and Juliet*).

I did not find many instances of student presentations of knowledge. However, students are given some input into the selection of knowledge that is taught, depending on age. Decisions are made by the supervisor and department chair who meet with us. Teachers do have a great deal of input into what they teach in their classes.

I seem to pay a great deal of attention to the gender issue. Until I reviewed the transcripts, I was unaware of how really important it was to me. I was raised in a family where women were to be married and have children. Graduating from high school was *fine*. My parents did not. My father went to grade six and had to help out by working. My mother finished grade eight and got married and stayed home with four children. She came from a family of thirteen children; there were five in Dad's. I was the first to go to college out of that entire family. It took me five years (four years of evening school) to finish. I worked days to pay my way. There was money for my brother, however, to go to private high school and to UB; and also for the younger sister.

Perhaps this is why I put so much into teaching literature which represents women as succeeding despite terrible hardship. I put a lot of time into the relationships in *Julius Caesar*, the sexist/chauvinistic marriage of Caesar and Calpurnia, and the more enlightened equal marriage of Brutus and Portia. I'm sure this also influences the autobiographical pieces. This past year I taught Harriet Tubman, Mary McCloud Bethune, Amelia Earhart, Helen Keller, and Anne Frank. Obvious, isn't it? I find that I teach best what I like most— Shakespeare, mythology, women's literature.

I believe knowledge as presented in the classroom is influenced to varying degrees by class size, behavior, student absence, interruptions, and administrative expectations. Each year poses new challenges. Although I feel I am flexible, the students in my classes must complete the novel or play specifically chosen for that grade level. Ideally, it's "read at home and discuss in class." Realistically, it's "read in class and discuss in class" and *perhaps* do homework. Since we do not track, students of various abilities may be found in each class. This often influences what can be accomplished and leads to more compromise and "nurturing" on my part. I try to help without taking the child over. Students often bring serious problems to the class which are unrelated to teaching, but which affect the entire class.

Often, the resolution of those problems becomes the teacher's priority for that period. On certain days, period one is affected by those six to eight students who must see an assistant principal or be put in the Intensive Learning Center and miss the entire class.

In reviewing the transcripts, I have become concerned that I spend too much time on student problems and classroom interruptions. Because of this, there may be times when I am not teaching to my expectations of the students. Although I do not deliberately lower my standards, I can point to instances in the transcripts where I have, especially in classes where achievement ranges from A to F. What is even more discouraging is that I see myself in Linda McNeil's article.[17] Am I simplifying content and reducing demands? Am I controlling the information and trading it off for class controls? On some days, the answer is yes. Does what I make accessible cause them not to read further? Because I often use lists in English class, am I, as McNeil says, "avoiding having to elaborate or show linkages"? Am I impeding my students' ability to express their learning in paragraphs? I didn't think I was. McNeil does. I also had not felt that this controls what is discussed. Hopefully, my students are encouraged to pursue information on their own. Not all will. I have to accept this and go on from that point.

It seems that every time I read Linda McNeil's article, I found something else I didn't like about myself and my teaching. This research has given me back an overwhelming amount of knowledge about who I am and what I do—and I'm not sure I want it! In Dorothy's immortal words: "Toto, this isn't Kansas anymore."

I have taught for a long time—thirty-one years. I thought I knew what I was doing and took pride in the accomplishments of my students. During the research of these past three years, I have been asked not only what I was doing, but why. At times, this reflection has made me feel uncomfortable and even a little threatened. Conversely, it has given me a small place in history.

Although I talk about not lowering my standards and expectations, the transcripts show that on occasion I do. This bothers me. "I have to make up these review sheets." "Who said this on page 14 and who is L.L. on page 29?" "They won't get it if I don't do it and they won't read without this help." So I do these sheets and make them work. I remember memorizing passages from *The Merchant of Venice* in high school. Some students won't even attempt to read. This scenario directly contradicts my statement in my interviews of "loathing spoonfeeding" and my aim of "fostering their independence." Yet, there are students who need more nurturing. Based on my knowledge of the students, I feel this can be done in a nonoppressive way. Often there is no time or a quiet place to read at home. So I read with or for them. There is this real tension between wanting to nurture kids and give them everything they need and making sure you're not spoonfeeding them.

I have reflected on those things I must change. This is very difficult for me. Yet I don't prepare review sheets anymore. Has reflection set me free? Some days I am awash in a sea of interruptions in my classroom. Imagine the surprise—many of them are mine! Do others occur because I haven't given my students enough input? Is there a need to be less in control? I am aware that, because of my nurturing nature, there is a fine line between trying to give my students everything they need and avoiding spoonfeeding them. In the last decade of my career, I have had my teaching "messed with" and it hurts!

SUE'S WORK

Chris's last comment frames well my thoughts on participating in—really instigating—this project. The question of by what right I initiated a project, which I had good reason to suspect, based on my background in "critical ethnographies of schooling," would cause discomfort, continues to haunt me. Others involved in similar work have expressed these feelings. For example, Miller writes:

My fear of imposing myself on our collaborative inquiry emanated from my position as university teacher and thus "expert" according to many traditional conceptions of university-school collaborative projects, as originator of the invitation, and as framer of the initial strands of inquiry that led to our collective studies. Clearly, my desire to acknowledge the attachments that gave point to my work, and my continuing struggle to understand the basis of my own authority as a woman teacher enabled me to at least begin to see that my fears of imposing were situated within structures that often necessitate and reinforce "authoritive discourse."[18]

While I have resolved some of this in terms of realizing that despite my worries about the institutionalized power relationships between university (of which I am now a part, despite my initial and latent affiliative feelings) and schools, both Chris and Linda *chose* to be a part of this project. This recognition of human agency within the oppressive conditions is for me a major outcome of the research.

While I do not pretend that our work is not structured by existing conditions, I am reminded that the possibility for change lies in acknowledging and working against conditions as they appear to be. A mediating factor for me was that I always held out the fear that they would exercise the option I offered initially, to end the research at any time, leaving me, in my untenured status, with years of work and no publication. Yet I also knew that I could always salvage some of this with writings on the difficulties of collaborative work. As Ladwig points out, the potential benefits for academics engaging in collaborative research often greatly exceed those for practitioners.[19]

What seems most important to me to tell is not only our findings about the process within which we began to trust each other, despite our personal and structural risks, but also the emergence of ideas about how research might affect practice, and what happens when one engages teachers in curriculum debate. First, our relationship emerged over time. Linda has made it clear to me how much disbelief there was in my initial claims of "I'll be back. You get to have input in this." Bits of the outcomes of the study continually emerge (e.g., Chris's statement to me, only after going over the first version of this chapter, that she no longer "does" review sheets). We have come to know each other personally (e.g., they hear tales of my children, offer stories of their own with offers of child care help) and empathize. They also know, as I do, that my ten years of public school teaching were not perfect, and that I, too, traded off one interest for another. We have shared autobiographies, transitions from what our families were and are to the worlds in which we now live.

The issue of change in practice plagues me. Chris and Linda have altered what they do in their classrooms. Whether the changes Chris and Linda have made in their practice will have long-term effects on their teaching remains to be seen. Yet both have expressed the strong feeling that the experience of doing the research together has given them a way to look at their practice which might, indeed, sustain them in the next phase of their teaching careers. What instigated those changes? Did the change come about through being able to read transcripts of their teaching? How important was the presence of an outsider, or the presentation of a way of analyzing what they do in classes? What role does the reading of "critical studies" of education play? What role did time play—the fact that we have had three years to get to know and trust each other? I do not know.

What I think I know is that there are tensions and contradictions between what each of us attempts to do in our teaching and what actually plays out in our classes. Whether one such tension exists between a caring and nurturing intent and a need to stimulate critical thought in classrooms is unclear. It does seem to offer an explanation as to why, despite intentions to the contrary, teachers reduce knowledge to easily digestible bits and allow so little student voice. Revealing tensions and contradictions in teaching is not only an academic task. It is also a means to identify spaces where change can occur.

A lot of this text has been written by me, based on our discussions. The reason for this is partly time; as an academic, I have the time to spend drafting our ideas. Some of it is familiarity with academic writing. Yet some of it, too, is knowing that after these three years, Chris and Linda are perfectly capable of and quite willing to tell me where they think I'm either wrong or unclear. As we work through this chapter, our voices increasingly merge, always vigilant for whatever impositional tendencies we see. Our voices become a "we," but as in marriage, the two (in this case three) do not become one, except to reproduce existing lines of power and domination in society. We remain separate and yet together, by choice, by interest, and by friendship.

Looking Backward, Working Forward

Chris and Linda shared this section of a poem which we all feel expresses our feelings upon looking back on the project and ahead to what we still may do:

> Trust flourishes like a potato plant, mostly underground;
> wan flowers, dusty leaves chewed by beetles,
> but under the mulch as we dig
> at every node of the matted tangle
> the tubers, egg-shaped and golden with translucent skin,
> tumble from the dirt to feed us
> homely and nourishing.

> "Doing it differently"
> Marge Piercy

What is gained (and perhaps lost) when we look *with*, and not *at*, teachers? Much has been written of the persistence of lecture or recitation methods of teaching and the lack of opportunities for complex thinking in classrooms today. The critical tradition in curriculum studies has offered insightful explanations for these phenomena, taking into account the organizational demands on schools as well as the broader social context. This has been a small-scale study with a limited number of observations and interviews. Much of the observational data obtained in this study could be seen to sustain conclusions of other research efforts. Yet this study has offered the opportunity to explore instances of curriculum-in-use in two high school classrooms, in a way which afforded greater opportunity to hear teachers' own interpretations of why and how they teach what they teach and to hear their voices.

The study has also given us an opportunity to engage in curriculum debate, across our differences. This chapter focuses a lot of attention on our own personal reactions to the research process. While this is important, it should not detract from our concern with curricular issues. We have not "found" an answer to a perplexing problem in education. We have found lots of questions. How much background knowledge, the characters and plot of the play, the form of a short story, for example, do students need before they can engage in meaningful discussion? How ought one to respond to the fact that many students come to school tired, hostile, and ill-prepared? Each of us has strong opinions, based on our reading and our experiences, and we do not always agree.

The curriculum decisions of two teachers and their practices are seen in this chapter as not of a single seam. They are a complex mixture of competing interests in society, personal experiences, and educational contexts. Teachers' work is neither something to be "celebrated" nor something to be noted as innocent or unknowing participation in the reproduction of social inequalities. It is practice to be interrogated: by scholars, yes, but also by practitioners and with practitioners. This study has given us an opportunity to hear divergent perspectives on persistent issues in curriculum in a new way, one which attempts to privilege none of our perspectives, but to hear them all. We assume that each of us is partially wrong and stands to learn from each other.

NOTES

1. For a description of the overall project of which the work for this chapter formed a part, see Catherine Cornbleth et al., *Understanding Teacher Knowledge-in-Use* (Buffalo, NY: Buffalo Research Institute on Education for Teaching, 1991).

2. Michael W. Apple, *Education and Power* (London: Routledge, 1982).

3. Sandra Harding, ed., *Feminism and Methodology* (Bloomington, IN: Indiana University Press, 1987), pp. 8-10. See also, Patti Lather, *Getting Smart* (New York: Routledge, 1991).

4. For a fuller description of this process, see Susan E. Noffke, "Researching Together: Curriculum Inquiry with, not on, Teachers" (Paper presented at the Twelfth Conference on Curriculum Theory and Classroom Practice, Dayton, OH, October, 1990), and idem, "Speaking For, Speaking With: Reflexive Research for Portraying Knowledge-in-Use" (Paper presented at the Annual Meeting of the American Educational Research Association, Chicago, April, 1991).

5. Cornbleth et al, *Understanding Teacher Knowledge-in-Use.*

6. Sandra Harding, ed., *Feminism and Methodology.*

7. Basil Bernstein, *Class, Codes, and Control,* vol. 3 (London: Routledge, 1975).

8. See Janet Finch, " 'It's Great to Have Someone to Talk To': The Ethics and Politics of Interviewing Women," in *Social Researching,* edited by Colin Bell and Helen Roberts (London: Routledge, 1984), pp. 70-87.

9. Ibid. See also Ann Oakley, "Interviewing Women: A Contradiction in Terms?" in *Doing Feminist Research,* edited by Helen Roberts (London: Routledge, 1981), pp. 30-61.

10. Sheila Riddell, "Exploiting the Exploited? The Ethics of Feminist Educational Research," in *The Ethics of Educational Research,* edited by Robert G. Burgess (New York: Falmer, 1989), pp. 77-99.

11. Jeanne Ellsworth, ed., *Cases of Wise Practice: vol. 1, Teacher Knowledge-in-Use* (Buffalo, NY: Buffalo Research Institute on Education for Teaching, 1991).

12. Jeanne Ellsworth and Laura M. Pfalzer, "Seeking Patterns of Knowledge-in-Use," in Catherine Cornbleth et al., *Understanding Teacher Knowledge-in-Use* (Buffalo, NY: Buffalo Research Institute on Education for Teaching, 1991).

13. Lois Weis, *Between Two Worlds* (New York: Routledge, 1985).

14. Ann Berlak and Harold Berlak, *The Dilemmas of Schooling* (London: Methuen, 1981).

15. These readings included Kenneth A. Sirotnik, "What Goes on in Classrooms?" in *The Curriculum,* edited by Landon E. Beyer and Michael W. Apple (Albany, NY: State University of New York Press, 1988), pp. 56-74; Linda McNeil, "Defensive Teaching and Classroom Control," in *Ideology and Practice in Schooling,* edited by Michael Apple and Lois Weis (Philadelphia: Temple University Press, 1983), pp. 114-142; and Michael W. Apple, "Curricular Form and the Logic of Technical Control," in *Ideology and Practice in Schooling,* edited by Apple and Weis, pp. 143-165.

16. Apple, "Curricular Form and the Logic of Technical Control"; Ellsworth and Pfalzer, "Seeking Patterns of Knowledge-in-Use"; McNeil, "Defensive Teaching and Classroom Control"; Sirotnik, "What Goes on in Classrooms?"

17. McNeil, "Defensive Teaching and Classroom Control."

18. Janet Miller, *Creating Spaces and Finding Voices* (Albany: State University of New York Press, 1990).

19. James G. Ladwig, "Is Collaborative Research Exploitative?" *Educational Theory* 41 (1991): 111-120.

CHAPTER X

Teacher Inquiry as Professional Staff Development

VIRGINIA RICHARDSON

The concept of staff development is changing from what was once conceived of as an externally organized, formal program, toward any process in which a teacher (working individually or in a group) systematically attempts to understand herself, her students, the school context, and/or new practices in order to improve her teaching. The process may be initiated and conducted by the teacher(s) with or without the help of an external facilitator. Within this newer conception, teacher inquiry or action research may be thought of as professional staff development.

In this chapter teacher inquiry refers to an individual or a group of teachers being systematically thoughtful about their teaching, students, and/or contexts. Teacher inquiry may or may not include formal gathering and analysis of data and writing for publication.

The success of teacher inquiry would appear to depend in part on the voluntary participation of teachers in developing their own agendas and maintaining control of the process. Traditionally, however, staff development has been supported by states, school districts, and schools for purposes designed to meet educational goals determined by those who are external to the individual classroom or school. If teacher inquiry is to become supported as staff development, the question to be addressed is how the two conditions of voluntary participation and teacher control of agenda can be maintained. Can a school district promote and support teacher inquiry as staff development without sacrificing the essential elements and desirable effects of a process that has been undertaken spontaneously and voluntarily?

The purpose of this chapter is to examine teacher inquiry as a staff development process. Of particular interest is the question of the form(s) of staff development that best foster teacher inquiry. I will

Virginia Richardson is Professor of Teaching and Teacher Education, College of Education, University of Arizona.

first briefly define teacher inquiry, and then explore three forms of staff development that vary on the important dimension of who controls the agenda, and how teacher inquiry would be conceived of and supported within each form. These three forms may be described as (1) externally set, (2) teacher initiated, and (3) collaborative. I will then present an example of a collaborative staff development project that focused on teacher inquiry.

Teacher Inquiry

Until recently the prevailing conception of the teacher was one who receives and consumes research from academic researchers and incorporates it into her repertoire of classroom behaviors.[1] The current cognitively based conception of the teacher describes a person who mediates ideas, constructs meaning and knowledge, and acts upon them. The ideas may stem from many sources such as staff development, other teachers, readings in research, theory, and literature, or reflection on experience. New understandings are constructed on the basis of these ideas as they interact with existing understandings. It is these understandings that drive the teacher's practices.

However, the knowledge constructed by a teacher on the basis of experience is personalistic and may remain tacit. Teachers make decisions on the basis of a personal sense of what works; but without examining the premises underlying a sense of "working," teachers may perpetuate practices based on questionable assumptions and beliefs. Thus, the concept of teacher as inquirer provides a vision of a teacher who questions her assumptions and is consciously thoughtful about her goals, practices, students, and contexts.

Clift and her colleagues define inquiry conducted by teachers as "a deliberate attempt to collect data systematically that can offer insight into professional practice."[2] Burton, an elementary school teacher researcher, suggests that teacher inquiry involves a teacher in "researching experience." For Burton, the purpose of such inquiry is not to lead to laws of practice meant to predict behavior;[3] nor does it necessarily lead to publication, although it may. It is meant to be useful to the teacher and sometimes her colleagues in their everyday work lives.

Elsewhere, I describe such research as practical inquiry and distinguish it from formal research.[4] Practical inquiry, as described above, is conducted for the purpose of improving one's practice.

Formal research is designed primarily to add to the knowledge base of a larger community. In conducting formal research, one must be cognizant of methodological and rhetorical traditions such that the work is deemed valid and readable by a wide audience. However, there is a relationship between these two forms of research. Practical inquiry may provide the passion, appropriate questions, and the normative foundations of formal research. Thus, practical inquiry that becomes formal research may lead to findings that provide authentic alternatives to teachers as they examine their premises and practices. Our concern in this chapter, however, focuses on practical inquiry, and how to provide help and support to teachers in this endeavor through staff development.

Staff Development and Teacher Inquiry

Recent summaries of the literature on staff development reflect the changing conception of staff development from that which is imposed upon a group of teachers to a change process that may be initiated by an individual teacher. For example, in a review of research on staff development, Sparks and Loucks-Horsley included a major category of staff development called "Individually Guided Staff Development."[5] Cole and Thiessen divided forms of staff development into those conducted *by* teachers in schools, and those conducted *for* teachers and within or across schools.[6]

FORMS OF STAFF DEVELOPMENT

1. *Externally set.* This is still the primary mode of staff development as thought of by school systems. The distinguishing characteristic of these programs is that the processes are developed and implemented by those who are not participants in the staff development, and attendance is often mandatory. These staff development programs take place over several hours, or less frequently over several days. This type of process is sometimes accompanied by coaching, in which an individual, often a teacher, observes and provides feedback to another teacher who is implementing a new practice.[7]

Given the nature of this form of staff development, in which the agenda is controlled by people external to the classroom and participation is often mandatory, it is not surprising to find that few examples of externally mandated teacher inquiry exist. Exceptions are the self-studies that are a part of accreditation processes. Self-studies are group projects in which teachers in a given school examine their programs in relation to their goals and write a report. Externally driven staff development is heavily programmatic, with preestablished agendas and stipulated outcomes. Thus, this approach to staff development would not appear to be useful in fostering teacher inquiry.

2. *Teacher initiated.* Teacher-initiated staff development refers to processes undertaken by a teacher or by groups of teachers for purposes of growth and improvement. This category includes individually determined professional growth (such as taking courses at a local university) as well as group activities (such as study groups either within a school or with teachers from across a district, computer bulletin board networks, and other types of networks such as Foxfire.)[8]

Inquiry within this category is undertaken voluntarily by individual teachers and groups, and the agenda, process, and content are owned by them. If external individuals, such as a university scholar, become involved, the role is one of consultant. The primary purposes of this form of inquiry are to help the teacher understand what is happening to her students and herself and how she contributes to what is happening, to improve practice, and possibly to provide an active voice in educational policy development. Since this approach is seldom institutionalized, and not necessarily undertaken for purposes of publication or presentation at scholarly conferences, it is impossible to determine how much of it is going on. We sometimes see the findings of such work in a published article,[9] hear a presentation at a conference,[10] or hear discussions of the importance of such work, and read statements about the voice of the teacher.[11] There is undoubtedly a considerable amount of teacher inquiry that is not seen in practitioner or scholarly journals. The work is going on in classrooms and schools across the country, however, and is thought to have a strong and positive effect on the day-to-day work of the teacher.

Since this activity is undertaken voluntarily and spontaneously, it is difficult to decide how a system may promote this work within a staff development process. School districts may, however, provide support in the form of substitute teachers and funds for consultants, data collection, and analysis.

3. *Collaborative.* These programs represent a collaboration between two or more individuals, one of whom is the provider or facilitator of the staff development and the others are the primary recipients. For example, a group of teachers and administrators within

a school may approach a teacher educator and work out a mutually agreeable program for the school. This category of staff development also includes organization development programs, teacher centers, and professional development schools.[12]

Most of the examples of teacher inquiry as staff development in the literature are of this variety, and may be viewed as either two-person or group collaborations. In a two-person collaboration a local researcher from a university or another teacher may work with a teacher in her classroom on a problem of interest to the teacher. We often see the results of this research in publications by a single author,[13] or in presentations at conferences by one or both of the collaborators.[14] In group collaborations a group of teachers is engaged in action research with an external consultant available to facilitate the process.[15] There is some contention about the definition of action research. Action research has recently been defined as a process in which a group of teachers explore a curricular, instructional, or systemic problem within their school. A second definition is much narrower and relates to critical theory: a group of teachers (and others related to the school) examine the underlying beliefs and assumptions related to the social and cultural contexts, and experiment with changes designed to emancipate all participants.

Examples of the first type of action research include both Stenhouse's and Elliott's work in England with teachers of science as well as the several collaborative teaching projects funded by the U.S. Department of Education in the 1970s.[16] An example of such a process was conducted by Tikunoff, Ward, and Griffin at several sites in the United States.[17] A researcher, staff developer, and groups of teachers in a school worked together to identify a problem, conduct research on it, and implement a staff development program to deal with the problem.

Examples of critical action research may be found in Carr and Kemmis's book, and in a project being conducted by Paul Heckman and colleagues at the University of Arizona.[18] Heckman's program, for example, involves school, community, and social services people in an examination of the underlying assumptions about how the school operates within the community, and how this translates into what happens in the classrooms. These understandings are used to plan for major reform within the school as well as in the interaction between the school and community and the ways in which the social services operate within the community.

Reflective staff development is a type of action research in which a group of teachers examine their beliefs about the teaching of a particular subject, test their assumptions by collecting data on their students, examine their own practices as well as those of their students, and experiment with new practices in their classrooms.[19] While teachers may meet as a group, they also pursue their individual interests. These staff development processes involve one or several outside consultants who act as facilitators and work closely with the teachers as they examine their practices and experiment with new ones.

The collaborative process appears to be a very useful form of staff development for teacher inquiry. While teachers may be interested in participating in such a process, they may find it difficult to initiate. An important function of the outside facilitator, then, is that of motivating a group of teachers to participate in such a process, and providing and arranging for the initial structure of the group dialogues. The concern about collaborative staff development and research involves issues of power and control in a situation in which a university or other outside expert works with classroom teachers. The relationship must be sensitively handled by all parties, so that the teachers feel equality in participation. This concern is also discussed in chapter 12 of this volume.

Research on Staff Development and Teacher Inquiry

Staff development research has only recently begun to examine processes and effects in ways that are both acceptable as research and useful for practice. Much of the early research on externally set staff development concluded, on the basis of surveys, that teachers generally neither liked such programs, nor used them to improve their classroom practices. Further, evaluations of the programs led to few well-documented results.[20] However, this research was based primarily on self-reports of teachers and did not examine the teachers' classroom actions before and following the staff development process. An exception to this was research conducted as one element of large-scale process-product research programs. In these studies, the staff development programs were "treatments" in experimental studies and were designed to relate certain teaching behaviors to student achievement.[21] This research was summarized by Gage, who suggested that all of these projects, except one, led to changes in teacher behaviors and student achievement.[22] Griffin and his colleagues also used process-product results in a staff development program, but this program focused on training staff developers in the findings of process-product research and in ways of introducing this research to teachers in their districts and schools.[23] Joyce and Showers' work on coaching also provided positive results of externally based staff development that included a coaching component.[24] Analysts combined this literature with that of implementation research[25] and effective schools research,[26] and developed lists of factors that would contribute to the effectiveness of externally set staff development programs.[27] These lists are quite similar, and include the following overarching features:

1. The programs should be context-specific; thus the school is seen as the important unit of change.

2. Teachers and administrators in a school should be involved in all aspects of the process.

3. The process should take place over an extended period of time.

4. The content should incorporate current and verified knowledge.

Of particular interest to us in this chapter, however, is the research on teacher-initiated and collaborative research. While there are few descriptions of teacher-initiated research in the literature, two pieces have had a strong impact on the way many of us think about staff development. Joseph McDonald's article describes three phases in the evolution of the teachers' voices in a group inquiry process in which the teachers controlled the agenda. He suggests that although theory was originally not seen by the group as important or useful, it eventually enhanced their voices.[28] The Boston Women's Teachers' Group provides the second example; here a group of teachers met to discuss the broader implications of the institutional and social structures in which schooling takes place.[29] Their deliberations led to a description of schooling in which teachers' voices have been silenced or turned inward to blame themselves, and "experts" have taken on the role of setting goals and determining methods.

Collaborative action research, on the other hand, has received a considerable amount of attention in the research literature. Tikunoff, Ward, and Griffin, for example, conducted extensive research on their collaborative model that involved a researcher, staff developer, and group of teachers within a school together identifying a problem within their school, conducting research on it, and implementing a staff development program to deal with the problem. They found that the process led to considerable change in teachers' practices, and that the research was considered by a number of experts to be of high quality. Interestingly, when the participants talked to teachers in other schools about the process, these teachers were more interested in the collaborative process than in the specific actions taken by the collaborators in solving the problem in their school.[30] This study was followed by another in the New York City area in which the school context issues were examined.[31]

In addition to changes in professional practice, a number of studies suggest that collaborative action research affects teachers' personal growth and thinking. For example, Groarke, Ovens, and Hargreaves found that teachers became more flexible in their thinking, and a summary of the literature by Noffke and Zeichner suggests that teachers in action research projects increased their dispositions toward reflection and their awareness of their beliefs.[32]

Several researchers have pointed to the difficulty of the role of "outsider" or facilitator. Baird suggests that a conceptual leader is important initially, and Miller and Lieberman conclude that each group requires a leader who is an "idea champion."[33] Oja and Smulyan point to the tension between leadership and democracy in the role of the leader. They suggest that the leader should be strong and should model democratic processes.[34] Short examined her role in facilitating a school-based study group and found that she shared knowledge rather than presenting it, negotiated the personal and group agendas with the participants, and had to establish credibility with the participants.[35] And both Kroath and Elliott suggest the need for broad knowledge of research methodology on the part of the facilitator.[36] It is these and other issues related to collaborative action research that were examined in the study that is described in the next section.

An Example of a Collaborative Teacher Inquiry Project

The Reading Instruction Study was designed to examine the beliefs and practices of teachers of reading comprehension in relation to current research-based practices found in the literature.[37] One element of the study was the development of a staff development process that allowed teachers of grades four, five, and six to examine their beliefs about the teaching of reading comprehension in relation to other teachers' beliefs as well as to findings from research, and to experiment with new practices. The goal of the process was to develop an environment that would allow teachers to examine the explanations for their practices in relation to empirical premises and practices drawn from current research in reading comprehension. Explanations for a particular practice consist of a set of statements of beliefs about teaching and learning that may be placed within the analytic framework of a practical argument.[38]

A practical argument is a set of premises that end in an action. A premise stated by a teacher may be discussed in terms of alternative premises derived from other teachers or from recent research on reading comprehension. In this process, the teacher may alter premises and/or adopt new ones, and consider and experiment with different classroom practices.

The design of the staff development process accommodated both individual and group approaches. In the individual sessions, a videotaped lesson of each teacher's classroom was used to provide a stimulus for a dialogue among the teacher and facilitators about what the teacher does in the classroom. The group-level process was designed as a constructivist activity in which the teachers and facilitators discussed teachers' cognitions and beliefs about their practices, and introduced alternative ways of thinking about and teaching reading comprehension. It differed from externally set processes in that the purpose was not to ask teachers to implement a particular model. Rather, we asked teachers to examine their own theories and practices and to determine whether they wanted to alter them. We worked with them in examining alternative practices, and provided help for them in experimenting with new practices. My colleague, Patricia Anders, and I were the staff developers. This was a long-term process that involved voluntary groups of teachers within each of three elementary schools.

Considerable data on the staff development process and its results were collected, both as an attempt to understand the process and our roles in it, and as a way of modeling the inquiry process. We were conducting inquiry on our own teaching as staff developers as we were encouraging teachers to conduct inquiry on theirs. In the next sections, I will briefly summarize the findings of our research on changes in teachers' beliefs and practices. I will then describe the research on the nature of the process, and the roles of the participants.

Changes in beliefs and practices. Changes in the participants' beliefs were determined by examining the extensive belief interviews given prior to and following the process. These interviews dealt with theories of reading comprehension, learning to read, and the teaching of reading comprehension. Analysis of the differences in the two belief interviews indicated considerable change in participants' theories and beliefs. Most of them moved toward the belief that teaching reading involved placing students in contact with texts that they found interesting and would read, and away from a skills/word approach to the teaching of reading.[39]

Changes in practices were assessed in two ways: one was a self-report as revealed in the second belief interview, and the second assessment was through observational data. A content analysis of the self-reported changes suggested that the teachers felt they changed in the following areas: less reliance on the basal reader; the use of more prereading activities; integration of literature into other subjects; and different practices in grading and assessment. Observations also indicated that teachers changed their practices. Many, for example, began to include prereading activities in which they activated student knowledge, others began to use more literature, and still others began to change their assessment systems.[40] In addition, a recent follow-up study of the teachers indicated that they have moved even further toward a literature-based reading program and the integration of reading instruction into other subjects.[41]

Most striking to those involved in the process were changes in the teachers' feelings of empowerment. At the end of the process, they no longer attributed their use of a practice to external forces such as parents and school board members. They justified their practices on the basis of empirical, value-related, and situational premises that emanated from their own theories and understandings of their classrooms.

The nature of the process. The inquiry process described here asks teachers to become actively involved in understanding and justifying their own practices, to consider directions in which they might change, and to talk about these practices with their colleagues. This requires the development of a highly trusting atmosphere, in which the participants acknowledge their own expertise and are willing to risk experimenting with new ideas and practices.

The staff developers and participants initially found this to be a very difficult process to implement. The introductory distinctions between the university and the school people made the achievement of the equal sharing of power very difficult. In part, this was due to the difference between this inquiry process and the usual staff development programs. The teachers were accustomed to externally set staff development in which the staff developer describes and provides training in a method, strategy, or curriculum that others feel would be good for teachers to implement. While teachers often complain about such programs and resent being mandated to change their practices, they are not required to reveal their inner convictions, and they are often able to ignore the new program in their own classrooms.

Our major problem in implementing the staff development was related to our goal of equal participation. We were interested in reaching a point at which we, the staff developers, were not seen as the only experts in the room, but that all participants could participate equally as colleagues in the inquiry. This suggested a need for an atmosphere that was empowering and emancipatory, such that all participants felt an ownership of the sessions and valued their own practical knowledge and theories. We examined the data carefully to determine whether we accomplished our goal.

In one analysis, Hamilton described three stages of conversation in the group sessions. In the "Introductory" stage, the teachers familiarized themselves with each other. They did not ask many questions, and they politely listened to the conversation. The next stage was labeled the "Breakthrough" stage. This occurred when a person or persons moved through a line of thinking or a way of doing things to a new way of thinking about the topic. The third stage was "Empowerment." In this stage, teachers claimed ownership of the staff development process, and the conversation began to be dominated by the teachers. Hamilton found that there were school effects in terms of how long it took for the participants to reach the empowerment stage, and she was able to attribute these to school context factors such as norms related to how one teacher talks to another about teaching.[42]

At the same time, one cannot look solely to structure and context as the only factors affecting such a process. Certain individual participants also had a strong impact on the process in all three schools. As Cochran-Smith has pointed out:

Data demonstrated that large-scale school restructuring efforts were deeply entangled with the biographies of individual educators, the decisions they made and permitted others to make about the children in their classrooms, and the discussions that occurred (or failed to occur) at the schools.[43]

In another analysis, I examined the discourse in the group sessions in terms of the topics of conversation, who initiated the topics, and the level and type of participation that followed the introduction of the topic. I found that while the staff development processes in the three schools began with considerable "staff developer talk," and it was the staff developers who introduced most of the topics, the discourse shifted toward more teacher talk and discussion and conversation in which the topics were usually introduced by the teachers.[44] These shifts took time and were particularly difficult in one school. The teachers in this school continually attempted to push us to revert to the externally set type of staff development in which we would tell them, as one of the teachers said, "about a neat practice—something you think is a good idea." But eventually all three schools reached what Hamilton described as the Empowerment phase in which the teachers took over the content of the dialogues.

Several other scholars have examined this problem. Ladwig, for example, employs a game-theory analysis to show that collaborative research, as currently practiced, exploits teachers. His analysis suggests that at this time, academic researchers profit from collaborative research more than teachers.[45] However, Ladwig focuses solely on the written products of a collaborative research process—published articles and books—as the outcome of the process. A collaborative staff development process as described above also benefits teachers in terms of changes in ways of thinking, in practices, and in a sense of empowerment.

Elliott examines various conceptions of the outside researcher/ insider practitioner roles and relationships from four dimensions: epistemological, theory-practice, ethical, and political. He concludes that the ideal facilitator (outsider) of "insider research" believes that educational change can be democratically negotiated, and that "insider research can empower teachers to negotiate changes in educational power relations for themselves."[46] We, too, found that it was possible to facilitate changes in power relationships between the staff developers and teachers toward one that was more equal, but that this took time and patience.

The role of the staff developer. We examined our role in this collaborative process, and also analyzed the literature to provide insight from others who have facilitated such a process.[47] The collaborative process described here requires staff developers whose conception of their role is different from the conception of those who operate within the traditional form of staff development. For example, we did not prepare lectures around methods that we thought teachers should implement in class. Nor did we play the role of sole "expert," imparting wisdom in the form of new practices.

Instead, the staff developer in such a collaborative process is one of many experts. All of the participants have expertise related to the content of the staff development. The teachers have practical knowledge based on experience and reflection, and knowledge of the context in which teaching takes place. Often, they have well-developed theories of practice, as well as formal knowledge acquired in graduate courses and workshops. The staff developer's expertise relates to extensive knowledge of formal theory and research in a particular content or pedagogical area, and to process skills related to group discussions. The content knowledge must be deep and held flexibly so that it can be brought to the attention of the group at appropriate points. The staff developer should also be knowledgeable about inquiry processes that help teachers approach their teaching in an inquiring manner.

Manner is also an important element of the role of the staff developer. Freire suggests that, because it is necessary when facilitating such a group process to set up an initial teacher-learner dichotomy, a "self-effacing" stance on the part of the facilitator is essential.[48] This manner suggests that the facilitator is both teacher and learner. The staff developer must also have a genuine interest in and curiosity about the topics under discussion and a personal interest in how the teachers think about teaching.

Thus, I believe it is possible for collaborative research to be conducted in ways that lead to equal power relationships among the participants. However, the role of the staff developer must change from the top-down provider of information to that of facilitator who establishes an atmosphere that is conducive to conversation in which all participants share their expertise.

Conclusions

This analysis of teacher inquiry as staff development suggests that it is possible to help and support teachers who are involved in the process of practical inquiry. However, we must not conceive of this support within the framework of a traditional, externally set staff development program. The assumptions that guide such programs— a preconceived agenda and set of goals, and a deficit model of teacher change—would be detrimental to a teacher inquiry process.

Our analysis also suggests that a collaborative process is a useful form of staff development in which to facilitate teacher inquiry. However, if the process is to be collaborative, close attention must be paid to the power dynamics of the process and the goal of teacher control of the topics. This requires an attitude and a manner on the part of the collaborating outsiders that suggest to the participants that their expertise is worth sharing and their work is valued. We cannot ignore the elements of prestige and power that society has placed on the school district personnel and the academics; nor can we simply "empower" teachers by handing total responsibility over to them—a quite disempowering process. The participants in such a process must work together to examine the control issues and reconfigure the power relationships.

A concluding lesson from this analysis is that school systems need to acknowledge and support the individual teacher inquirer so that she does not end up being ignored and perhaps ostracized by her fellow teachers. Further, the administrator or teacher leader or other facilitator should attempt to help teachers work toward a norm that redefines the role of teaching to include reflection, inquiry, and attitudes of continual change. Publication may be an outcome, but not a necessary outcome, of such a process. This will require a delicate and sensitive approach by the facilitator, who must not simply reward the inquiring, publishing teacher—an act that may cause resentment among her fellow teachers—but work with the teachers as a group in dialogue sessions that explore beliefs and practices.

NOTES

1. See Ellen C. Lagemann, "The Plural Worlds of Educational Research," *History of Education Quarterly* 29, no. 2 (1989): 185-214 for a discussion of the contribution of Judd's work in educational psychology to this conception, and Dewey's alternative conception that is closer to the current views.

2. Renee Clift, Mary Lou Veal, M. Johnson, and Patricia Holland, "Restructuring Teacher Education through Collaborative Action Research," *Journal of Teacher Education* 41, no. 2 (1990): 52-62.

3. Frederick R. Burton, "Teacher-Researcher Projects: An Elementary School Teacher's Perspective," in *Handbook of Research on Teaching the English Language Arts*, edited by James Flood, Julie M. Jensen, Diane Lapp, and James R. Squire (New York: Macmillan, 1991): pp. 226-230.

4. Virginia Richardson, "Conducting Research on Teacher Education," in *Knowledge Base for Teacher Educators*, edited by Frank Murray (San Francisco: Jossey-Bass, forthcoming).

5. Dennis Sparks and Susan Loucks-Horsley, "Models of Staff Development," in *Handbook of Research on Teacher Education*, edited by W. Robert Houston (New York: Macmillan, 1990), pp. 234-250.

6. Ardra Cole and Dennis Thiessen, "In-service Education of Teachers (INSET): An Interpretive Review" (Toronto: Ontario Institute for Studies in Education, 1991).

7. Bruce Joyce and Beverly Showers, "Transfer of Training: The Contribution of Coaching," *Journal of Education* 163, no. 2 (1981): 163-172.

8. Hilton Smith and Eliot Wigginton, with Kathy Hocking and Robert E. Jones, "Foxfire Teacher Networks," in *Staff Development for Education in the '90s*, edited by Ann Lieberman and Lynne Miller, 2d ed. (New York: Teachers College Press, 1991), pp. 193-220.

9. See, for example, Nancy Atwell, "'Wonderings to Pursue': The Writing Teacher as Researcher" (unpublished paper, n.d.); Glenda Bissex and Richard Bullock, *Seeing for Ourselves* (Portsmouth, NH: Heineman Educational Books, 1987); Barbara A. Morgan, "Practical Rationality: A Self Investigation," *Journal of Curriculum Studies* 25, no. 3 (1993): 115-124; Thomas Newkirk and Nancy Atwell, *Understanding Writing*, 2d ed. (Portsmouth, NH: Heinemann Educational Books, 1988); Mina P. Shaughnessy, *Errors and Expectations* (New York: Oxford University Press, 1977).

10. Susan Threatt, "Rejoining the Conversation: Shared Vulnerability and Teacher Research" (Paper presented at the Annual Meeting of the American Educational Research Association, Chicago, 1991).

11. William H. Schubert and William C. Ayers, *Teacher Lore: Learning from Our Own Experience* (New York: Longman, 1992).

12. Terrence Deal and C. B. Derr, "Toward a Contingency Theory of Organizational Change in Education: Structure, Processes, and Symbolism," in *Educational Finance and Organization: Research Perspectives for the Future*, edited by Charles S. Benson et al. (Washington, DC: National Institute of Education, U.S. Department of Education, 1980); A. J. Dawson and Finola Finlay, "Bringing Teacher Education to Remote Northern Canadian Centres: The AHCOTE Story," in *Collaboration: Building Common Agendas*, edited by Henrietta Schwartz (Washington, DC: Clearing House on Teacher Education and American Association of Colleges for Teacher Education, 1990), pp. 32-33; Kathleen DeVaney and Lorraine Thorn *Exploring Teachers' Centers* (San Francisco: Far West Laboratory for Educational Research and Development, 1975); and Jane A. Stallings and Theodore Kowalski, "Research on Professional Development Schools," in *Handbook of Research on Teacher Education*, edited by W. Robert Houston (New York: Macmillan, 1990), pp. 251-263.

13. Dorothy Vásquez-Levy, "The Use of Practical Arguments in Clarifying and Changing Practical Reasoning and Classroom Practices: Two Cases," *Journal of Curriculum Studies* 25, no. 2 (1993): 125-144.

14. Sandra Hollingsworth and Aileen Yamate, "Teacher-research as Counterhegemony: Aileen's Story of Mathematics Instruction in an Urban Middle School" (Paper presented at the Annual Meeting of the American Educational Research Association, Chicago, 1991).

15. Peter Holly, "Action Research: Cul-de-sac or Turnpike?" *Peabody Journal of Education* 64, no. 3 (1989): 71-100.

16. John Elliott, "Developing Hypotheses about Classrooms from Teachers' Practical Constructs: An Account of the Work of the Ford Teaching Project," *Interchange* 7, no. 2 (1976): 2-22.

17. William J. Tikunoff, Beatrice Ward, and Gary Griffin, *Interactive Research and Development on Teaching Study: Final Report* (San Francisco, CA: Far West Laboratory for Educational Research and Development, 1979).

18. Wilfred Carr and Stephen Kemmis, *Becoming Critical: Knowing through Action Research and Prospects* (Victoria, Australia: Deakin University Press, 1986); Paul Heckman, Christine Confer, and Jean Peacock, "A Demonstration of Democracy: Reinvention of Education in a Multicultural and Multilingual Community," in *New*

Educational Communities: Schools and Classrooms Where All Children Can Be Smart, edited by Jeannie Oakes and Karen Quartz, Ninety-fourth Yearbook of the National Society for the Study of Education (Chicago: University of Chicago Press, forthcoming).

19. See, for example, John R. Baird, "Collaborative Reflection, Systematic Enquiry, Better Teaching," in *Teachers and Teaching: From Classroom to Reflection*, edited by Thomas L. Russell and Hugh Munby (London: Falmer, 1992), pp. 33-48; Kenneth Tobin and Elizabeth Jakubowski, *Cooperative Teacher Project: Final Report* (Tallahassee, FL: Florida State University, 1990); Eleanor Duckworth, *"The Having of Wonderful Ideas" and Other Essays on Teaching and Learning* (New York: Teachers College Press, 1987); Virginia Richardson and Patricia Anders, *Final Report of the Reading Instruction Study* (Tucson, AZ: College of Education, University of Arizona, 1990) ERIC ED 324-655; Francine Peterman, "A Teacher's Changing Beliefs about Learning and Teaching" (Doctoral dissertation, University of Arizona, 1991); and Kathy G. Short, "'Living the Process': Creating a Learning Community among Educators," *Teaching Education* 4, no. 2 (1992): 35-42.

20. Kenneth Howey and Joseph Vaughan, "Current Patterns of Staff Development," in *Staff Development*, edited by Gary Griffin, Eighty-second Yearbook of the National Society for the Study of Education, Part I (Chicago: University of Chicago Press, 1983), pp. 92-117.

21. Edmund T. Emmer et al., *The Classroom Management Improvement Study: An Experiment in Elementary School Classrooms* (Austin, TX: Research and Development Center for Teacher Education, University of Texas, 1981), ERIC ED 178 460; Thomas Good and Douglas A. Grouws, "The Missouri Mathematics Effectiveness Project: An Experimental Study of Fourth-grade Classrooms," *Journal of Educational Psychology* 71 (1979): 355-362; Jane Stallings, Margaret Needels, and Nicholas Stayrook, *How to Change the Process of Teaching Basic Reading Skills in Secondary Schools: Phase II and Phase III* (Menlo Park, CA: SRI International, 1983).

22. N. L. Gage, *Hard Gains in the Soft Sciences: The Case of Pedagogy* (Bloomington, IN: Phi Delta Kappa, 1985).

23. Gary Griffin, Susan Barnes, Sharon O'Neal, Sara Edwards, Maria Defino, and Hobart Hukill, *Changing Teacher Practice: Final Report of an Experimental Study*, Report No. 9052 (Austin, TX: Research and Development Center for Teacher Education, University of Texas, 1984).

24. Joyce and Showers, "Transfer of Training."

25. Michael G. Fullan, "Change Process and Strategies at the Local Level," *Elementary School Journal* 85, no. 3 (1985): 391-421; Michael Huberman and Matthew B. Miles, *Innovation up Close* (New York: Plenum, 1984); Milbrey McLaughlin, "Learning from Experience: Lessons from Policy Implementation," *Educational Evaluation and Policy Analysis* 9 (1987): 171-178.

26. Judith W. Little, "Norms of Collegiality and Experimentation: Workplace Conditions of School Success," *American Educational Research Journal* 19 (1982): 325-340; idem, "Teachers as Colleagues," in *Educators' Handbook: A Research Perspective*, edited by Virginia Richardson-Koehler (New York: Longman, 1987): 491-518; Susan Rosenholtz, *Teachers' Workplace: The Social Organization of Schools* (New York: Longman, 1989).

27. Gary Griffin, Ann Lieberman, and Joann Jacullo-Noto, *Interactive Research and Development on Schooling: Executive Summary of Final Report* (Austin, TX: Research and Development Center for Teacher Education, University of Texas, 1983); Gary Griffin, "Clinical Teacher Education," in *Reality and Reform in Clinical Teacher Education*, edited by James Hoffman and Sara Edwards (New York: Random House, 1986), pp. 1-24; Beatrice Ward, "Teacher Development: The Challenge of the Future," in *Beyond the Looking Glass*, edited by Shirley Hord, Sharon O'Neal, and

Martha Smith (Austin, TX: Research and Development Center for Teacher Education, University of Texas, 1985), pp. 283-312; Susan Loucks-Horsley et al., *Continuing to Learn: A Guidebook for Teacher Development* (Andover, ME: Regional Laboratory for Educational Improvement of the Northeast and Islands, National Staff Development Council, 1987).

28. Joseph P. McDonald, "Raising the Teacher's Voice and the Ironic Role of Theory," *Harvard Educational Review* 56, no. 4 (1986): 355-378.

29. Sara Freedman, Jane Jackson, and Katherine Boles, "Teaching: An Imperilled 'Profession'," in *Handbook of Teaching and Policy*, edited by Lee Shulman and Gary Sykes (New York: Longman, 1983).

30. Tikunoff, Ward, and Griffin, *Interactive Research and Development on Teaching Study*.

31. Griffin, Lieberman, and Jacullo-Noto, *Interactive Research and Development on Schooling*.

32. John Groarke, Peter Ovens, and Margaret Hargreaves, "Towards a More Open Classroom," in *Action Research in Classrooms and Schools*, edited by David Hustler, Anthony Cassidy, and E. C. Cuff (London: Allen and Unwin, 1986); Susan E. Noffke and Kenneth M. Zeichner, "Action Research and Teacher Thinking: The First Phase of the AR Project at the University of Wisconsin, Madison" (Paper presented at the Annual Meeting of the American Educational Research Association, Washington, DC, 1987).

33. Baird, "Collaborative Reflection, Systematic Enquiry, Better Teaching"; Lynne Miller and Ann Lieberman, "School Improvement in the United States: Nuance and Numbers," *International Journal of Qualitative Studies in Education* 1, no. 1 (1988): 3-19.

34. Sharon N. Oja and Lisa Smulyan, *Collaborative Action Research: A Developmental Approach* (Philadelphia: Falmer, 1989).

35. Short, "'Living the Process'."

36. John Elliott, "Educational Research and Outsider-Insider Relations," *Qualitative Studies in Education* 1, no. 2 (1988): 155-166; Franz Kroath, "The Role of the Critical Friend in the Development of Teacher Expertise" (Paper presented at an international symposium on research on effective and responsible teaching, Fribourg, Switzerland, 1990).

37. This project was funded by the Office of Educational Research and Improvement, U.S. Department of Education. The coprincipal investigators were Patricia Anders and myself. See Virginia Richardson and Patricia Anders, *Final Report of the Reading Instruction Study* (Tucson, AZ: College of Education, University of Arizona, 1990), ERIC ED 324 655; Virginia Richardson, ed., *A Theory of Teacher Change and the Practice of Staff Development: A Case in Reading Instruction* (New York: Teachers College Press, forthcoming).

38. Gary D Fenstermacher, "Philosophy of Research on Teaching: Three Aspects," in *Handbook of Research on Teaching*, 3rd ed., edited by Merlin C. Wittrock (New York: Macmillan, 1986), pp. 37-39; Gary D Fenstermacher and Virginia Richardson, "The Elicitation and Reconstruction of Practical Arguments in Teaching," *Journal of Curriculum Studies* 25, no. 2 (1993): 101-114.

39. Virginia Richardson, Patricia Anders, Deborah Tidwell, and Carol Lloyd, "The Relationship between Teachers' Beliefs and Practices in Reading Comprehension Instruction," *American Educational Research Journal* 28, no. 3 (1991): 559-586.

40. Mary Lynn Hamilton, "The Practical Argument Staff Development Process, School Culture, and Their Effects on Teachers' Beliefs and Classroom Practice" (Doctoral dissertation, College of Education, University of Arizona, 1989).

41. This project is being funded by the Office of Educational Research and Improvement, U.S. Department of Education.

42. Hamilton, "The Practical Argument Staff Development Process"; Mary Lynn Hamilton and Virginia Richardson, "The Effects of School Culture on the Process of Staff Development," *Elementary School Journal* (in press).

43. Marilyn Cochran-Smith, "Reinventing Student Teaching," *Journal of Teacher Education* 42, no. 2 (1991): 112.

44. Virginia Richardson, "The Agenda-Setting Dilemma in a Constructivist Staff Development Process," *Teaching and Teacher Education* 8, no. 2 (1992): 287-300.

45. James G. Ladwig, "Is Collaborative Research Exploitative?" *Educational Theory* 41, no. 2 (1991): 111-120.

46. Elliott, "Educational Research and Outsider-Insider Relations," p. 165.

47. Virginia Richardson and Gary D Fenstermacher, "The Role of the 'Other' in Teacher Change" (Paper presented at the Annual Meeting of the American Educational Research Association, San Francisco, 1992).

48. Paulo Freire, *Education for the Critical Consciousness* (New York: Continuum: 1983).

CHAPTER XI

Problems and Possibilities of Institutionalizing
Teacher Research

ANN LIEBERMAN AND LYNNE MILLER

Teacher research, like many other promising and significant ideas, has important implications for professionalizing teaching and reforming schools. Perhaps, as some in this volume argue, teacher research can build craft knowledge—from the teacher's perspective—about what it means to teach. We certainly would not argue with the proposition that teachers need to ask questions of their practice, think about what they do, and change their beliefs and behaviors in light of new insight and understanding. The prospect of developing a complex and realistic view of teaching and teachers' understanding of their craft is very enticing, especially for those of us who have struggled with these issues for some time. Yet, there is a romantic and naive quality to this effort, indeed to the entire ambiance that surrounds teacher research. While we support teacher research as a major reform strategy, we do so with caution. For we believe that teacher research cannot stand alone as an innovation, that it must be explicitly linked to organizational conditions that support the transformation of schools. As a solitary innovation, teacher research has a poor chance for survival. As part of a systemic approach to school reform, it may well fulfill its promise. Our intention in this chapter is to explore teacher research and its necessary embeddedness in organizational conditions that support school development and change. We begin by presenting three case studies of teachers involved in research, each representing a different organizational context. We later build on these cases to develop understandings about the relationship between teacher research and the transformation of schools.

Ann Lieberman is Professor of Education and Co-Director of the National Center for Restructuring Education, Schools, and Teaching at Teachers College, Columbia University. Lynne Miller is Professor of Education, University of Southern Maine at Gorham.

Teacher Research: Three Case Studies

CASE 1: KINDERGARTEN READINESS

Janet S. has been an elementary teacher for over twenty-five years; all of her service has been in one small district serving a rural and suburban mix of students. Janet was one of the architects of the district's early kindergarten program, which was designed according to the Gesell Institute's notions of kindergarten readiness and providing "time to grow." The early kindergarten program was developed by a team of teachers who were concerned about the inappropriately young behavior that some kindergartners brought to school and the difficulties these children had in adjusting to school norms and expectations. The program was intended to provide a supportive, nurturing environment for young children who seemed headed for school failure. After one year in such a setting, it was presumed, students would be more ready to enter and succeed in regular kindergarten.

Janet is very active professionally. She is a candidate for a master's degree in institutional leadership. It was as part of her degree program that Janet became involved in teacher research. She enrolled in a qualitative research course and chose as her research topic the socialization of children into early kindergarten. She was particularly interested in how these children interacted with the teacher and each other around a variety of instructional materials. Janet's research project was successful. She collected data that provided insights about her original question. But she also discovered something she did not expect. As she systematically observed the early kindergarten class, recorded field notes, and analyzed them, she was struck by something she had not anticipated. As she watched the children, she recognized that throughout their day they were never exposed to appropriate kindergarten behavior. They were placed with children like themselves; they had no model of how kindergartners were expected to interact with each other nor did they know how to use materials. She realized that the district's program had an underside that neither she nor her colleagues had explored. The program, in effect, isolated the early kindergartners and denied them access to other children from whom they could learn as they grew.

Janet was literally stunned by her finding. She was at once excited about her new understanding and wary of informing her colleagues of what she had discovered. She herself had professed doubt about the research which questioned the effectiveness of early kindergarten. Now she was the harbinger of negative findings. She struggled over how to approach her colleagues about what she had discovered. One of two kindergarten teachers in her school, Janet also had to be concerned about the primary teachers across town, since early kindergarten had become a district policy.

The school district was undergoing its own reorganization and planned to move all of its kindergartners to one site which would become a "kindergarten center" serving all five-year-olds in the district. The center was planned as a stand-alone unit, with no other grade level present on site. The advantage of this move, to Janet's mind, was that it would create a forum for kindergarten and early kindergarten teachers to reflect on their practices and rethink earlier decisions. The disadvantage of the move was that these teachers had never worked together as a team and had to get to know each other and develop their own way of interacting and doing business. Three years later, early kindergarten still exists. Janet is eager to lead in a challenge to that policy.

CASE 2: DETRACKING ENGLISH CLASSES

Elaine R. is in her fifth year of teaching English in a secondary school in rural New England. Through teacher research she has helped move her department from a highly tracked English curriculum to a heterogeneous classroom organization. Her school draws on a range of students whose families include poor people who survive by working in the woods, long-time residents who work in nearby towns as craftspeople, clerks, and factory workers, and native and transplanted professionals who hold high expectations for their children and the education they receive. Elaine, like Janet, began her research as part of a requirement at the university where she was enrolled in a master's degree program.

Elaine's project was to uncover her students' perceptions about how they were placed in their English classes and how these classes were conducted. She asked each of the students to write in response to a prompt, collected the responses, and organized and analyzed them. Her data showed not only that the students in the lower track thought they were "dummies" but also that those in the upper track said: "I'm in this class because I am smart, and that means we don't have to do much work because nobody expects much so we can fool around." What she found was disturbing to her—and quite powerful.

Once Elaine had all her data collected and analyzed, she struggled to find a way to communicate the findings to her colleagues. She knew that most of the teachers in her department believed strongly in the efficacy of ability grouping. Like many teachers, they dismissed research about grouping and depended more on their own experience than on what they perceived as the too theoretical, "ivory-towered" scholarship of academia. As a relative newcomer to the school, Elaine was perceived as being overly idealistic and still too connected to the university. Unlike Janet, she was not an opinion leader in the school.

Elaine consulted with a variety of people before she decided on her strategy. She raised the issue in her university course, discussed it with sympathetic colleagues in the school, read widely about school change, and approached her department chair with her dilemma. The department chair was very interested in her data and was particularly struck by the power of the students' perceptions of their own schooling. He suggested that Elaine take time at the next department meeting to read some student comments and to open the discussion. With some trepidation, Elaine did just that.

The members of the English faculty were very attentive to the words the students had written. Though not ready to discard ability grouping, they expressed an interest in continuing the discussion and in exploring further what their students thought and how other schools were addressing similar issues. Slowly over time, after much conversation, more research, confrontation, and eventually the development of a problem-solving mode of work, the department decided to initiate a nontracked ninth-grade program. They requested and received stipends for their work during the summer to plan their approach. Eventually, they moved to a heterogeneously grouped English program in grades nine through twelve. Now, the English department is an island of change in the school. Other departments continue to place and track students and have shown little interest in doing otherwise.

CASE 3: UNDERSTANDING LITERACY DEVELOPMENT

Sarah and Julie are teachers in a K-3 school that views itself as a "center of inquiry" and takes seriously the idea of teacher research. In fact, the school has so embraced inquiry and professional learning as central to its mission that it has created a new role, that of "teacher/scholar." The teacher/scholar position is a form of in-house sabbatical. It allows a teacher to be released from the classroom for a year to pursue research on a topic of interest to herself and the rest of the staff. The position rotates among the school staff and is funded through the district's regular budget.

The school has been an innovator in using teaching assistants to complement the work of classroom teachers. It was one of the originating members of the local school/university partnership. Its teachers have been actively engaged in discussion with other educators about issues of learning, teaching, and assessment for over seven years. The school's principal, an active participant in the school/university partnership, has promoted teacher leadership and inquiry within the school.

Sarah held the teacher/scholar position the first year it was in operation, and in the second year she shared the role with Julie, a third grade teacher. During the first year, Sarah focused her inquiry on issues of literacy acquisition in kindergarten through second grade. She watched children in classrooms as they selected books to read. She interviewed teachers, did library research, developed field notes and videotapes, and initiated discussions among teachers about their views of how children became literate. As part of her work, Sarah began a "language arts notebook." The notebook provides an opportunity for teachers throughout the school to reflect on children's learning and to share ideas for promoting early literacy development. In contrast to a traditional curriculum guide, the notebook is not viewed as a finished product. Rather, it is a work in progress that engages teachers in ongoing inquiry and dialogue about how children learn to read and write.

As a complement to her work in literacy development, Sarah began an inquiry into ways of assessing what students know and are able to do. Unhappy with traditional measures, she wanted to investigate alternative assessment strategies. She was joined in this line of inquiry by Julie, the third grade teacher with whom she shared the teacher/scholar position. Together Sarah and Julie led the whole school staff in a systematic study of assessment. They began with an examination of student work and engaged their colleagues in discussions of how to determine standards of quality. Teachers met during in-service days and at grade-level meetings as well as during the summer. Teaching assistants assumed responsibility for classroom activities as teachers observed students. Teachers involved students at the classroom level in developing samples of scoring guides, which were also shared with the whole school staff. Over time, Sarah and Julie's leadership as teacher-researchers led to the development of a K-3 portfolio system. Unlike other portfolio projects that collect student work without assessing it, this system sets clear standards for quality work and uses scoring guides for evaluating whether the standards have been met. There is general enthusiasm within the school for this new system and there is interest throughout the district in expanding portfolio assessment through grade twelve.

Based on the success of teacher research at one school, the superintendent and school board are willing to support such research at other sites and to legitimize it through the allocation of resources.

Thus far, one other elementary school in the district has established a teacher/scholar position. Other schools are considering doing the same but are not yet ready to commit to the idea because the supporting conditions are not fully in place.

Teacher Research in Organizational Perspective

Each of these cases is, in its own right, a powerful example of teacher research. In each instance, a teacher posed a problem, collected and analyzed data, uncovered new understandings, and applied what she learned to her home setting. In many ways, the result of these activities demonstrates the efficacy of teacher research and its potential for improving educational practice and expanding our knowledge base about teaching and learning. In our minds, however, these cases cannot be judged as equally successful. They do not represent, to the same degree, a capacity for transforming schools and using knowledge in an ongoing way. We base this judgment on our understandings of the organizational conditions that support and sustain authentic change.

Our work in schools has led us to identify five elements of school organization that promote and sustain change.[1] These are:

- norms of collegiality, openness, and trust
- opportunities, time, and support for disciplined inquiry
- teacher learning in context
- reconstruction of leadership roles
- participation in networks, collaborations, and coalitions.

In the rest of this chapter, we want to demonstrate how these five elements impact on the success of teacher research as a strategy for professionalizing teaching, elevating craft knowledge, and leveraging school reform. In building our argument, we depend on a review of our own work as well as that of others and on an analysis of the three cases described earlier.

NORMS OF COLLEGIALITY, OPENNESS, AND TRUST

Only ten years ago did the issue of collegiality arise as a problem of study. Judith Warren Little's in-depth cases of staff development in six schools in Denver, Colorado, turned the research community to investigating organizational conditions that support teacher growth and change. Her groundbreaking work documented for the first time what actually went on in a school when the principal announced expectations for shared work and modeled behaviors of collegiality, self-examination of practice, and risk taking. Teachers were encouraged to observe each other's work, talk about what they were seeing and doing, and find solutions to commonly defined problems. In the process of encouraging these activities, traditions of practicality, privacy, and isolation were replaced by shared ownership of issues and problems of practice, a willingness to consider alternative explanations, and a desire to work together as colleagues.[2]

Understanding collegiality and experimentation was a conceptual breakthrough leading to a fuller appreciation of what it takes to change a school culture. This insight was followed and enhanced by the work of Susan Rosenholtz, who examined the workplace conditions for teachers in sixty schools and how those conditions differentially affected teachers' beliefs about schools, teaching, and their own growth and development. She found that there was a strong relationship between the structures, norms, and patterns of interaction in school cultures and the potential for teacher growth.[3] Where teachers worked in more collaborative settings, they reported that teaching was a complex craft and saw professional learning as a never-ending process. In isolated settings where there were barriers to collaboration, limited collective goals and little support from the principal, teachers reported that their professional learning was limited to their first two years of experience. Both of these studies document the connection between the roles of principal and faculty and the building of trust between and among faculty as well as the necessity for some structure that provides for continuous discussion of teaching problems. But they also raise tough questions about how this trust gets built, why such commonsense ideas do not happen more often, and how difficult it is to promote conditions of colleagueship that find their way into changed and improved conditions for students as a result of this changed culture.[4] Building such norms takes time, patience, and the creation of other conditions including the simple providing of time, support, and opportunities to share.

Our first case is a good example of the promise and problems associated with teacher research as a solo enterprise. Janet clearly developed a deep insight into her own teaching. She made an extraordinary discovery that what appeared to be a good solution to providing a better start for "young kindergartners" had effects which might prove more detrimental than beneficial. She found that instead of waiting to put students in ability groups or in tracked classes, teachers were actually isolating, labeling, and grouping children as they entered kindergarten. She had, in effect, uncovered evidence that undermined the best intentions of her colleagues. But her knowledge was private and she lacked the mechanism to share, discuss, and use this knowledge for more informed district practice or policy.

Janet had learned the power of doing her research, but she lacked the power to act on her newfound knowledge. Her growing confidence as a researcher and her potential influence as an intellectual leader with her colleagues were thwarted by the lack of either a districtwide or schoolwide collegial group where inquiry was shared and not merely a course requirement. Like many teacher researchers, Janet became more—rather than less—isolated from her colleagues because she had information that was important for the group, but she had no legitimate way to share it. Her isolated knowledge required a structure for collegial exchange.

Janet may be able to create a culture of collaboration at the new kindergarten center. This will take time. As Janet becomes more enmeshed in her new school culture, she stands a good chance of assuming leadership among her colleagues because of her experience, knowledge, and reputation. In this role, she must be mindful that her unique experience in teacher research must be duplicated for her colleagues so that together they can begin to make changes in policy as well as practice.

Elaine's case is similar to Janet's in that her research was initiated through graduate coursework. Unlike Janet, however, she had a mechanism of support for her work through her department. Within that structure, she had colleagues who listened to her findings and responded to her evidence. Together they developed a response to the issue of ability grouping in English. This is a good example of how secondary schools build professional community and colleagueship.[5] While at first blush this case seems more promising than the previous one, it is not without its problems. Most of the conditions of support for teacher research were in place for Elaine, but they were in place at the department level, not at the school level. The department functioned as an isolated subculture within the total school setting. English teachers continued to struggle alone in their department. The struggle might become energy-depleting: it is difficult to build and fight simultaneously. The English department will need to confront the school culture and work to transform it if they want to ensure the survival and success of their own insights and innovations. This case describes the power of a "balkanized" school culture,[6] typical of high schools. The English department is one among many groups, each teaching a piece of the student without a coherent way of thinking and working toward overarching goals for the school as an organization.

The third case, Sarah's and Julie's, emerges as our most positive example of teacher research within a collaborative culture. Unlike Janet's case, here an established culture based on inquiry, collegiality, openness, and trust is in place. And unlike Elaine, Sarah and Julie work in a culture that is not balkanized but extends to the entire school. The big idea of creating a school as a center of inquiry is being implemented by small steps. The establishment of the teacher/scholar role draws on the developing needs, interests, concerns, and talents of teachers in the school. Its rotational nature ensures that a large portion of the faculty had access to it.

The initial line of inquiry that Sarah pursued became shared by the rest of the staff through one-on-one interaction, group discussion, and the development of the "language arts notebook." Knowledge was not private, but public; it was not isolated, but shared. When Julie assumed half of the teacher/scholar role, she and Sarah could share their classroom as well as their research activities. It is noteworthy that the conditions were in place to allow for their reinvention of the teacher/scholar role so early in its history. Other teachers in the school became engaged in the language arts and assessment inquiries, in part, because they already had a common language and a willingness to trust each other and to work jointly. Teachers developed and deepened their professional learning through the daily engagement with colleagues that was already in place. In this case, unlike the other two, teacher research is not an add-on or an isolated experience; nor is it struggling for survival inside the larger school community. Rather teacher research is at the center of the school's ongoing commitment to inquiry-based practice and is embedded in the dailiness of its life.

OPPORTUNITIES, TIME, AND SUPPORT FOR DISCIPLINED INQUIRY

Disciplined inquiry into teaching and learning is critical to successful school improvement efforts. Finding the time and creating the opportunities to talk, to plan, to create, and to use knowledge are essential. Yet, finding time is the major problem confronting faculties who want to avoid routinization and to continue professional learning. Schools involved in major reform are finding ways to think about and solve the problem of time. Some faculties are making use of the "retreat" as a means of thinking through large issues of organization, curriculum, and assessment, while others are learning to bank time (by making class periods shorter, adding a period) to be used as blocks of time for teacher work. In some places there is a serious negotiation of the union contract to expand the work day, provide pay for workshop attendance, and redefine what a teacher does. Some places have provided time during the school day for planning and working through problems of teaching and learning. One of the most notable examples of this is Central Park East Secondary School in New York City, where on Wednesday mornings when students do their community service the teachers meet for several hours to plan their work. In other schools, teachers are grouped into teams with common planning time. The possibilities for inventing or seizing time are limitless.

Opportunities for inquiry take many forms. Departmental, whole faculty, and grade-level meetings that have always been a part of school life can be redesigned to fit new purposes.[7] Small reading groups, often called "dine and discuss" groups, can also be developed as ways of legitimizing teacher discussion and inquiry. Summer work for which they receive stipends can also allow teachers to concentrate and to consolidate academic year learnings. Finally, staff development can be redefined to move away from structured workshops and "one size fits all" presentations and move toward inquiry projects, dialogue, and planning.[8] It is these kinds of deliberate opportunities, either in the form of new inventions or adaptations of existing structures, that promote professional growth. They need to be seen not as add-ons or special events, but as part of the school day, week, and year.

An examination of the three cases shows how important time and opportunity for disciplined inquiry are for successful teacher research. As she was conducting her research Janet's work environment offered no time for her individually or for her colleagues collectively to engage in inquiry. She did her work on her own time, as part of her coursework which was outside the parameters of her job.

Elaine's case provides a good example of how an already existing structure, in this case the department meeting, can be redefined as an arena for inquiry, debate, and decision making. The summer work with stipends also provided Elaine and her colleagues with support for preparing to use their new knowledge. Finally, the experience of Sarah and Julie demonstrates the kind of extended supports that promote inquiry as a transformative strategy. They could draw on grade-level meetings, in-service days, summer work with pay, and teaching assistants. They also created opportunities through the "language arts notebook" and portfolio development. In fact, the teacher/scholar position itself is a wonderful example of a new opportunity, designed to meet the needs of a particular staff.

Teacher and student learning are inextricably connected. While the object of student learning is related to the mastery of a particular field of study, the object of teacher learning is the learning process itself. Teachers may attend workshops and read about new approaches, but it is not until they are in real classrooms with real students that their professional learning takes hold. Teachers need to make new practices their own and they can only do that when they are grounded in the social realities of their own work. Teacher learning is not generic.

Some approaches to instruction, curriculum, and assessment are more compatible with this notion of "teacher learning of content in context" than others. In general, these are constructivist approaches which view students as meaning makers and teachers as facilitators of understanding. Process writing, whole language literacy development, mathematics as a symbol system learned through manipulation, discovery and hands-on science, and authentic assessment are representative of constructivist pedagogy. In all these cases, there is the opportunity—though not the guarantee—for teachers and students to become partners in learning and inquiry.

The Foxfire approach is an exemplar of this kind of teacher learning. With its roots in John Dewey, Foxfire ultimately requires that teachers reframe their conceptions of teaching, learning, content, and process. As one Foxfire teacher states:

I am a very creative teacher. Parents and students will attest to that. I've been sharing my creativity with students for years. What I have become aware of is that everyone knows about *my* creativity, but I know little or nothing about my students' creativity. It's hard to let go of a career of being on stage, especially when students have loved being in my classroom, but I have to share my classroom. It has to become a place where the creativity of everyone can blossom. The first years of moving out of the limelight have been difficult, but exciting. It has changed how I perceive myself as a teacher and it feels good.[9]

This kind of teaching is hard work. It demands a great deal in terms of time, commitment, and capacity for reflection and self-criticism. We are just now becoming aware of what authentic teacher learning entails. As another Foxfire teacher explains:

We've all thought long and hard about what constitutes good learning and teaching. We take that thinking into our classrooms and we use it. It has become a standard for our practice. When you reach it, you're ecstatic. It can be very hard when you don't. Some days I wonder privately if I have the stamina and courage it seems to take to keep pushing toward that standard. Once you've seen what kids can really do when they're empowered, you can't go back to old practices. Yet, there are times when I wish I could.[10]

In our three cases, we see powerful examples of teachers learning in the context of their work. It was only when Janet watched her own students that she began to question the wisdom of early kindergarten. She had read the relevant literature on the topic, but had dismissed it as contradictory to her own experience. She was changed, not solely by newfound knowledge, but by her own work within the context of her professional life. Now that Janet has new insights into her own practice, she holds herself to a standard she cannot meet, given the policies in place. Her professional life is at once more engaging and less satisfying.

Elaine, Sarah, and Julie also demonstrate what happens when teachers systematically look at their students and themselves. The knowledge they acquire is seen as legitimate, not only by themselves, but by their colleagues as well. It seems clear that teacher research is synonymous with teacher learning. It promotes one of the conditions that sustain change. However, as our previous discussions show, teacher research is a necessary but not a sufficient condition for school transformation.

RECONSTRUCTION OF LEADERSHIP ROLES

Leadership is another key element in promoting and maintaining school change. Whereas in traditional school settings leadership is hierarchical, bureaucratic, centralized, and formal, in the schools we envision leadership is neither limited nor defined by rank or role. Sergiovanni makes a useful distinction between technical/managerial conceptions of leadership and the notion of cultural leadership.[11] Cultural leaders exercise "power to accomplish" rather than "power over people and events"; they seek to diffuse leadership rather than consolidate it. Principals who become cultural leaders are able to encourage teacher initiative and inquiry because they are not threatened by it.

It is helpful to have some concrete examples of this kind of leadership in action. Norma Goddard is a principal in rural New England. She leads her faculty by modeling the norms of inquiry and openness to new ideas that she espouses. When teachers report on classroom practices, she asks them why they do what they do. When teachers voice a concern about curricular consistency, she invites them to talk together, to raise questions for each other, and to seek acceptable solutions. The school has become a place where uncertainty is valued and where new ideas are translated into programs and approaches for children. In a California school, Nancy Chiang leads her faculty in a collaborative research project with a university professor on the topic of standardized tests. Together they generate a list of questions, keep journals, make observations, collect data, meet regularly, reflect on their findings, and reach conclusions about how the uses and abuses of standardized tests affect children. Such is the work of cultural leaders.

But leadership cannot be the exclusive domain of principals. Teachers must assume the mantle as well. Teacher leadership can be contrived, the invention of administrators who pay lip service to the rhetoric of site-based management, or it can be authentic. What distinguishes one from the other is the degree of freedom teachers have in defining their roles and in setting their own agendas. Teachers lead from their strengths[12] and they lead about things that matter.[13] They lead as classroom teachers, as curriculum builders, as demonstration teachers, as team leaders, as staff developers, as assessment specialists, and as student advocates. In a transformative culture, leadership is "dense"[14] and it permeates a school. It is always evolving and emerging.

In the three cases, there are varying degrees of cultural leadership on the part of administrators. In Janet's case, the principal does not have any presence. Although Janet looks to her colleagues as potential sources of support, she does not include the principal as an active player in her desire to rethink policy. The principal seems to be invisible and this makes Janet's work that much harder.

Elaine, on the other hand, does look to a formal leader for counsel and assistance. The English department chair shows persistence, support, and strategic intelligence; and he offers all of these as resources. Though Elaine has less experience as a teacher and less stature in her school than Janet, she has a better chance of institutionalizing her work because of the leadership of her immediate supervisor. What Elaine and her department lack, however, is the strong leadership of the school's principal. It is the absence of this leadership that helps keep heterogeneous grouping an idiosyncrasy of the English department and not a consistent practice of the whole school.

Again, we find Sarah and Julie in the most advantageous position for having their work institutionalized. Their principal is an active promoter of inquiry, colleagueship, and change. She developed the teacher/scholar position and continuously supports it. She shares power and knowledge and seems unthreatened by teacher leadership and expertise. She promotes the schoolwide support that Janet and Elaine lack.

While all three of the cases demonstrate the power of teacher leadership, it is only in the third case that teacher leadership is complemented by cultural leadership at the level of the principal.

NETWORKS, COLLABORATIONS, AND COALITIONS

The final element in a culture of inquiry extends beyond the school itself. Support systems that connect schools and school people across districts are another necessary ingredient in establishing and sustaining new ways of thinking about and doing one's work. Networks, collaborations, and coalitions have many forms, but they are similar in that they provide opportunities for sharing ideas and perspectives and for supporting and promoting experimentation, questioning, risk taking, leadership, and professional learning. These organizations tend to be alternative in nature, share a common purpose, exchange information and psychological support, are voluntary, and are based on equal participation of all members.[15]

Networks often take the form of regional partnerships involving school districts and a local university. The Southern Maine Partnership is an example of this kind of organization. It is a member of the National Network for Educational Renewal, a national coalition of school/university partnerships. Teachers and administrators meet regularly to discuss educational ideas and to act on new initiatives. In the past two years, they have dealt with such diverse issues as equity, grouping practices, teacher leadership, assessment approaches, restructuring schools, the new math standards, early literacy acquisition, and teacher education. Their power is derived from their self-direction and self-generation. Teachers from the Southern Maine Partnership comment on this power when they say:

The Southern Maine Partnership is to me a place where thinking is at the cutting edge. At the same time, there is remarkable collegiality such that people can enter the conversation at any time, no matter what their background.

It has been effective because it is rather loose, and is directed by participants. It's teachers who are raising the questions. The Partnership has dignified the role of teachers, not only in providing a forum for our voices and needs, but in many small gestures that show caring and respect for practitioners.[16]

Administrators also recognize the unique opportunity that such an organization can offer:

Sometimes we superintendents end up dealing so much with the business end of schools that not much of our time and energy gets spent on the real reason we're here. For me and for people in my district, the partnership has helped focus on learning—both our own and that of children.[17]

Networks can also be national in orientation and link regional collaborations with each other. A new example of this kind of organization is the National Center for Restructuring Education, Schools, and Teaching (NCREST) at Teachers College, Columbia University, in New York City. NCREST provides the opportunity for educators from across the country to exchange ideas, to meet around topics of interest, and to develop policy statements about common concerns. Its affiliates represent urban, suburban, and rural constituencies. Its power lies in its ability to connect people who might not otherwise communicate and to develop a national agenda about school restructuring. Like regional networks, NCREST reaches out beyond narrow boundaries and creates new sources of support, information, and challenge. Networks, collaboration, and coalitions enable schools and school people to extend their fields of vision and to legitimate their development as cultures of inquiry.

Only one of the cases has any mention of involvement in networks or other like groups. For Sarah and Julie, their school dates its participation back to the inception of a local school/university partnership. Teachers as well as the school principal have been actively engaged in dialogue about schooling with educators from across the region. The partnership connection encourages an outward orientation for the school staff and helps preserve an infusion of ideas. It is ironic that the case that needs a network the least is the one that has the most access to one. Or it may be the case that its involvement in the partnership helped ready the school for its ongoing transformation. Unfortunately the case does not provide enough information to evaluate this hypothesis.

The other two cases would be well served by membership in a network. Janet's concern about early kindergarten placement could benefit from dialogue with other primary educators outside her school and her district. Such interaction could provide the moral support she needs to continue her work. Engagement in such discussion may help influence her immediate colleagues as well. Similarly, Elaine and her department members could benefit from discourse with like-minded secondary teachers. Such opportunities to compare notes and exchange practices would considerably diminish the isolation the department experiences within the school. As with Janet, Elaine and her colleagues need to find sources of support outside their specific context to help energize them for the struggles they face within. The power of networks to support and promote teacher research and sustain its impact has been considerably underestimated and undervalued and has only now become an important topic of study.[18]

Teacher Research as a Vehicle for School Reform

The three cases we have used are examples of how teacher research looks when it takes place in different contexts. The cases all show the connections that teachers make in their own learning when they ask questions and collect evidence through observation, or by eliciting information from their students and peers on important issues of academic and social learning. As a powerful means for teachers to inquire into their own practice, teacher research may be unequaled. But these cases also point to the necessity to see teachers and teaching as embedded in the particulars of a school culture and a district culture, each of which has the power to enable or inhibit the development of individuals and collectivities. Organizational conditions of collegiality, opportunities for disciplined inquiry, teacher learning in the context of work, an enhanced view of leadership and partnerships, coalitions, and networks all play a role in building a learning community. Without these conditions, teachers as individuals can have powerful learning experiences, but they will continue to be solo players rather than members of an ensemble. It is as part of a community where learning is not limited or private but is available and accessible and where inquiry takes place over time as an integral part of the culture of the school, that teacher research can become a significant lever, not only for powerful learning on the part of the teacher, but as a center for the transformation of the whole school.

NOTES

1. Ann Lieberman and Lynne Miller, "Teacher Development in Professional Practice Schools," *Teachers College Record* 92, no. 1 (1990): 105-122.

2. Judith W. Little, *School Success and Staff Development: The Role of Staff Development in Urban Desegregated Schools* (Boulder, CO: Center for Action Research, 1981).

3. Susan J. Rosenholtz, *Teachers' Workplace: The Social Organization of Schools* (New York: Longman, 1989).

4. Judith W. Little, "Assessing the Prospects for Teacher Leadership," in *Building a Professional Culture in Schools*, edited by Ann Lieberman (New York: Teachers College Press, 1988); idem, "The Persistence of Privacy: Autonomy and Initiative in Teachers'

Professional Relations," *Teachers College Record* 91 (Summer, 1990): 1-37; Marilyn Cohn and Robert B. Kottcamp, *Teachers: The Missing Voice in Educational Policy and Practice* (Albany: State University of New York Press, 1992); Ann Lieberman, Ellen Saxl, and Matthew B. Miles, "Teacher Leadership: Ideology and Practice," in *Building a Professional Culture in Schools*, edited by Ann Lieberman (New York: Teachers College Press, 1988), pp. 148-166; Milbrey McLaughlin, "Strategic Sites for Teachers' Professional Development," in *The Struggle for Authenticity: Teacher Development in a Changing Educational Context*, edited by Peter Grimmett and J. P. Neufeld (New York: Teachers College Press, forthcoming).

5. McLaughlin, "Strategic Sites for Teachers' Professional Development."

6. Michael G. Fullan and Andy Hargreaves, *What's Worth Fighting For? Working Together for Your School* (Toronto: Ontario Public School Teachers Federation, 1991).

7. Michael G. Fullan, Barrie Bennett, and Carol Rolheiser-Bennett, "Linking Classroom and School Improvement," *Educational Leadership* 47, no. 8 (1990): 13-19; Milbrey McLaughlin, "Strategic Dimensions of Teachers' Workplace Context" (Paper presented at the Annual Meeting of the American Educational Research Association, Boston, 1990); Meg Sommerfield, "More Planning Time Urged for Front-line School Reformers," *Education Week*, 9 December 1992, p. 8.

8. Lieberman and Miller, "Teacher Development in Professional Practice Schools."

9. Marilyn Wentworth, "Field Notes" (Gorham, ME: Partnership Teacher Network, University of Southern Maine, 1992).

10. Ibid.

11. Thomas Sergiovanni, "The Theoretical Basis of Cultural Leadership," in *Leadership: Examining the Elusive*, edited by Linda T. Sheive and Marion B. Schoenheit (Alexandria, VA: Association for Supervision and Curriculum Development, 1987), pp. 116-130.

12. Lynne Miller and Cynthia O'Shea, "Teacher Leadership: Portraits of Practice," in *The Changing Contexts of Teaching*, edited by Ann Lieberman, Ninety-first Yearbook of the National Society for the Study of Education, Part 1 (Chicago: University of Chicago Press, 1992), pp. 197-211.

13. Patricia Wasley, *Teachers Who Lead* (New York: Teachers College Press, 1992).

14. Sergiovanni, "The Theoretical Basis of Cultural Leadership."

15. L. A. Parker, *Networks for Innovation and Problem Solving and Their Use for Improving Education: A Comparative View* (Washington, DC: Dissemination Process Seminar IV, National Institute of Education, 1979).

16. Southern Maine Partnership, *Prospectus* (Gorham: University of Southern Maine, 1993).

17. Ibid.

18. Ann Lieberman and Milbrey W. McLaughlin, "Networks for Educational Change: Powerful and Problematic," *Phi Delta Kappan* 73, no. 9 (1992): 673-677.

Section Five
CONVERSATIONS AND CRITIQUES
OF TEACHER RESEARCH AND
EDUCATIONAL REFORM

Introduction

The concluding section of the volume reflects upon the others and questions not only the nature of the teacher research movement with its epistemological, sociopolitical, and professional critiques of how and by whom educational research is conducted, but the forms of discourse it might take and the effects it might have on educational transformation. Rather than closing with impressions of the "findings" of this work, the authors in this section preserve the postmodern "voice" of this volume by raising new questions about current understandings of teacher research and future imaginings.

CHAPTER XII

Teachers' Voices in the Conversation about Teacher Research

SUSAN THREATT (ORGANIZING AUTHOR), JUDY BUCHANAN,
BARBARA MORGAN, LYNNE YERMANOCK STRIEB,
JAY SUGARMAN, JAN SWENSON,
KAREN TEEL, JEANNE TOMLINSON

This chapter takes the form of a conversation among us—eight teachers from across the country—and is our collective, negotiated response to the request that we write "a chapter from the practitioner point of view on teacher research" for this yearbook. In addition to points of view, the chapter attempts to convey a promising set of norms for teachers' exchanges and to explore a genre that might productively become more commonplace. How we teachers actually make sense of our experiences in schools and what we need to do for ourselves should be both recognized and validated—by ourselves and by others in relationship with us. Though we do learn from each other through talk, we do not generally have the opportunity to talk with each other about the implications of "researching" our own classrooms. We believe there is much to talk about. Enabling, constructing, and presenting this conversation has been a personal, practical, social, political, and symbolic act, not only about content, form, and process, but about desire and opportunity as well.

In some respects, of course, this text violates the conventions of both chapter and conversation. Each of us has been able to make suggestions, to edit our own written text as well as its placement, and to approve the final version. It is, however, a conversation "heard"* and reported by one of its participants, Susan Threatt. Though we are multiple voices and all have something to say, we speak uninterrupted by spontaneous interjection, sometimes in juxtaposed monologues,

---

*Participants were asked to pose questions with which the group might begin its exchange. Each participant chose particular questions from the compiled set of questions, wrote responses, and suggested possible "topic turns." The "conversation" was constructed from the material with those choices in mind.

and sometimes in dialogue. Though we respond to each other's questions, we do not speak in each other's company, except for that which we "know" about each other as fellow teachers. Not all of what we want or have to say has been expressed or is preserved. The constraints of time, space, and tradition have played as much a part in this conversation as they do in our everyday life in schools. However, this conversation is a beginning, at least among the eight of us. Hopefully, people who read it might be able to experience a little more realistically what it would be like to interact with us were we actually together as a faculty. Because we have been so long anonymous in educational literature, we introduce ourselves before we begin our conversation.

Judy Buchanan works on special assignment to the Philadelphia Writing Project, a site of the National Writing Project, and has been an elementary classroom teacher in Philadelphia for seventeen years. Since 1978 she has been a member of the Philadelphia Teachers' Learning Cooperative, a teacher collective which meets weekly to discuss issues of classroom practice through the use of the Documentary Processes developed at the Prospect Center in North Bennington, Vermont. She currently serves as a director of the Philadelphia Writing Project and has worked in teacher development programs of that project in Philadelphia since 1987. While she has shared her work locally with other teachers for quite some time, it is only recently that she has been writing about her work and speaking to groups of teachers nationally. She has written several articles on teacher research including "Listening to the Voices" in *Inside/Outside: Teacher Research and Knowledge*, edited by Marilyn Cochran-Smith and Susan L. Lytle (New York: Teachers College Press, 1993).

Barbara Morgan teaches fifth grade at Corbett Elementary School in Tucson, Arizona. Growing up in a small Kansas town, she began teaching herself Chinese while in high school. Though she graduated in the bottom 5 percent of her class and was admitted to a state school which "had to take everyone," she eventually graduated from the University of Kansas with a bachelor's degree in Chinese language. For two years during her undergraduate studies she lived in Taiwan, where she studied history and taught English. After graduation, she studied at the Folklore Institute of Indiana University. Barbara has taught in public school for six years and has investigated her practice using the frames of practical rationality (*Journal of Curriculum Studies*, in press) and performance-centered folklore. She will finish her doctorate in Teaching and Teacher Education at the University of Arizona in 1993.

Lynne Yermanock Strieb has been a first and second grade teacher in Philadelphia for twenty-one years and now teaches second grade at the

Greenfield Elementary School. She has also taught a graduate course in early childhood curriculum at Chestnut Hill College, and as a Fulbright Exchange teacher she taught four-year-olds in an Infant School in West Midlands, England. She is a founding member of the Philadelphia Teachers' Learning Cooperative and participates in the North Dakota Study Group on Evaluation. She is a cooperating teacher in START (Student Teachers as Researching Teachers) and a teacher-consultant in the Philadelphia Writing Project, both at the University of Pennsylvania. She has led workshops on writing, book making, record keeping, classroom research, and teacher groups. During the 1991-92 school year, she did research on folklore as a Readers Digest/National Endowment for the Humanities Teacher-Scholar. Among her many published writings are *A Philadelphia Teacher's Journal* (1985). Lynne connects her involvement with teacher research to her keeping a record and journal during her career as well as to her involvement with Pat Carini and the Prospect Center (Vermont) Summer Institutes for Teachers since 1973.

Jay Sugarman teaches fourth grade at the Runkle Elementary School in Brookline, Massachusetts, and also serves as an Adjunct Associate Professor at Simmons College in Boston. Interested in providing forums for teachers and administrators to discuss their roles as educators, Jay founded *Reflections*, the Brookline school system's educational journal in 1984. Since 1986, he has produced and hosted a local cable television show entitled "Video Open House: Teaching in Brookline." During 1988-89, Jay served as a field test coordinator for a Stanford Teacher Assessment Project on teachers' literacy instruction portfolios. He has written several articles about teachers' portfolios and continues that interest as the Vice Chair of the Middle Childhood/Generalist Standards Committee of the National Board for Professional Teaching Standards. Jay has received awards for his teaching from *Learning Magazine*, the Christa McAuliffe Fellow Program, and the Massachusetts Council for the Social Studies. Jay got involved in teacher research for one of the primary reasons he "got interested in teaching as a career—the exploration of ideas and how people think about different things." From 1988 to 1991 he served as program chair of the Special Interest Group on Teachers' Voices in the American Educational Research Association.

Jan Swenson is a second-year teacher of fourth grade at Merion Elementary School in Merion, a suburb of Philadelphia. She chose teaching as her life's work after ten years in law and business. She completed her master's degree in elementary education through the University of Pennsylvania Graduate School of Education's START Program in August 1991. While at the University of Pennsylvania, Jan received the 1991 Outstanding Elementary Education Student Award and was one of a group of authors who wrote "Leaving the Script Behind," a chapter in *Inside/Outside: Teacher Research and Knowledge*, edited by Marilyn Cochran-Smith and Susan Lytle

(1993). She also participated as a discussant on a panel about teacher research at the 1992 Annual Meeting of the American Educational Research Association in San Francisco. Jan got involved with teacher research when she "changed careers and chose a particular university program that blended with (her) thinking that teaching is a social and political act."

Karen Teel is on a year's leave from teaching history at Portola Middle School in Richmond, California. She spent the first thirteen years of her career in the Richmond School District's suburban schools, first as a teacher of world history and United States history in a junior high school and then as a high school French teacher. After a two-year leave with her family in Tokyo, Japan, Karen decided to return to graduate school at the University of California at Berkeley and to focus her study on adolescent behavior and student motivation and learning. During that time, she became convinced that many children in urban schools are neither understood nor recognized in terms of their particular intelligences, strengths, and talents. After four years, she decided to return to a Richmond District urban middle school classroom "to become a teacher researcher." One of her papers on her work was presented at the 1992 Annual Meeting of the American Educational Research Association and she has recently completed her doctoral dissertation on her classroom research.

Jeanne Tomlinson teaches and consults at Holt (Michigan) High School. She first taught in a three-room schoolhouse in Knapp, Wisconsin, in what she remembers to be a "caring learning community for all." She then substituted for three years in a center-based program for challenged students, ages three to twenty-six. Eventually, she completed the Vocational Rehabilitation Counseling Program at Michigan State University and went on to teach in a self-contained program for secondary students eligible for special education services. She later became a resource teacher, first at Mason Middle School and then at Holt High School, where she now enjoys collaborating with her colleagues in the Professional Development Schools Program at Michigan State University. Inquiry into the full inclusion of her school's most challenged students is her current interest. Jeanne traces her involvement with teacher research to when she "team taught with a regular education teacher who relished having a colleague in the classroom from whom to learn and with whom to risk" and to her involvement in projects of the Professional Development Schools Program.

Susan Threatt (organizing author) teaches social studies at Monte Vista High School in the California Bay Area's San Ramon Valley Unified School District. Though she has been there for much of her twenty-seven-year career, she has also taught at different grade levels in other schools, in different communities and countries, with students and faculties challenged by a variety of circumstances. Susan has served as discussant on three panels at meetings of the American Educational Research Association and in 1991 presented a paper entitled "Shared Vulnerability: Rejoining the Conversation on Teacher Research." She is currently chairperson of "Teachers' Voices," a Special Interest Group of the American Educational Research Association. She became familiar with the notion of "teacher as researcher" after she returned to graduate school in 1988 and took a course of the same name. In that particular course she felt that she "could finally and openly ask questions that meant something" to her. Susan is now finishing her doctoral work at the University of California at Berkeley.

The Conversation

The conversation is organized by some of the questions we posed for ourselves and begins with a discussion of our different definitions of the ambiguous term "teacher research" and what we see as its purposes and goals. It moves on to what teacher research might offer in terms of the development and use of different forms and processes, to how teacher research might become a part of teachers' lives in school, to our particular work, to conjecture about how our research has influenced our practices, and to a discussion of teacher research issues on the horizon. Because we want to interpret our own talk, the chapter ends with our commentary.

WHAT ARE OUR DEFINITIONS OF TEACHER RESEARCH?

Jeanne: I'm thinking of a teacher with whom I team teach. After a year of working together in a new project combining English and history, I suggested we develop an interview for students and parents. I had several questions about how positive the experience had been for me and several students in the classroom. We had taken risks and really thought differently about many things—content, assessment, grouping, the roles of teacher and learner. We spent a long time developing the interviews and left for summer vacation with a plan to call the students and parents and complete our questionnaire. I relished the conversations I had had with the students and returned in late summer to compare our discoveries. When I caught up with the teacher I had worked so closely with, he informed me that he had had one of our secretaries complete his interviews. *I couldn't believe it!* He really saw no worth in reflecting about our teaching together, and clearly did not see his role as a teacher-researcher. I learned from that experience that not all teachers are curious about their time spent with students. I think for this particular teacher, research is something completed in ivory towers by stuffy university types who don't know what the "real world" is about. For this person, research and teaching didn't fuse.

Lynne: Is there such a person as a teacher who doesn't do research? Can one be a good teacher without doing research? What view of teaching does being a researching teacher imply? Can one be considered a researcher without sharing one's research? I want to use a very broad and inclusive definition of teacher research, a definition that includes inquiring into classroom practice in a variety of ways, spoken as well as written. When people hear I'm a first grade teacher their eyes glaze over; when they hear that I write about my teaching or that I do classroom research, they are much more interested. That doesn't make me happy. It is my *teaching* that I want valued more than the writing and publishing. At the same time, I believe it is partly through the sharing of stories about classrooms, *in our own words*, that teaching and teachers will come to be valued by the public at large.

Judy: Lynne's question is at the heart of the matter for me. I do think that we, as teachers, should think carefully before adopting any new labels which describe our work. Often the label arrives so quickly and a "movement" is defined with a label attached before we have had any time to think about what new ideas are being put forth. The words themselves can convey images which create new dilemmas for teachers. If some teachers are "just" teachers and others are "teacher-researchers" what does that do to the world of teachers? The word "research" gets in the way for some people because of the many images it holds and the relative privilege the title "researcher" connotes in our society as opposed to the word "teacher." How do we talk about new ideas without categorizing people as they experiment, explore, try out, investigate, struggle, fail, and succeed in the process of learning new ideas and trying out new practices, including the practice of "research?"

Jan: In my graduate program, we were steeped in the notion that teacher research is "systematic, intentional inquiry." I am intentional, all right. It's the "systematic" part that I worry about. What does "systematic" mean? Is my reflection, by itself, enough? Do I need to document it in some way? When I ask myself some of the "big" questions that we grappled with in my graduate program last year (for example, about multicultural and gender issues, power and control, learning styles), I'm not recording my inquiry in any way—I just think about the issues. I left off writing in my journal in January because there wasn't enough time in my day. I fall into bed at 10:30

after planning and replanning my lessons for the following day, and I feel guilty that I haven't been keeping my journal up-to-date, or that I haven't done something else (except an occasional visit to the Teachers' Learning Cooperative). Am I not "doing teacher research" if I am not writing in my journal, or constructing "big" teacher-researcher questions? Is my own self-inquiry too short-sighted or concerned with minutiae? Is constant questioning of myself, my internal reflection, and oral discussion with colleagues considered "teacher research?"

Karen: I've tried to differentiate between a teacher and a teacher-researcher. I definitely think they are different and that the researcher part of the teacher enriches the teacher's perspectives in many different ways. Teacher-researchers look at classroom experiences in ways that teachers do not. Teacher-researchers must step back from their experiences, look at them, and make some sense out of them. They are interested in change, in improving the learning experience for their students. Teachers often move ahead with their plans without really understanding the impact of their teaching on the students.

Jay: For the most part, I believe they are synonymous. As long as there is a long-term commitment to inquiry then I feel comfortable using either "teacher" or "teacher-researcher." Good teachers continually question, observe, and analyze teaching and learning behaviors. However, most of us need support to undertake a more formal analysis of teaching and learning in our classrooms. Teachers can't just be asked or expected to conduct research as an add-on.

Susan: Thinking that "teacher" and "researcher" are synonymous terms encourages a particular political and social relationship and suggests epistemological questions. That teachers and researchers are indeed engaged along similar paths—that we wonder about things, that we have our particular processes by which we understand and know, that we make public in some way what we understand to people other than ourselves, that our beliefs and our knowledge shape what we do and that what we do affects other people—means that teachers and researchers can empathize with each other. In other words, they have a better chance of understanding each other, or at least of being willing to work together. Synonymy and similarity, from this point of view, might have a practical function. They quite possibly might serve to draw people together in a collaboration in which real differences do not divide, but rather contribute, and where differences in status dissolve and do not separate or demean as they have historically.

Barbara: Why teacher as anything? Can't we legitimately speak simply as teachers? How about researcher as teacher? It seems to me that teaching is a better common ground than research. If you mean research to be something like "exploring an environment in order to understand what is going on," then research is basic to teaching (and to almost everything else for that matter). That's not how I think of research. I think research is (1) an attempt to step back from what one is doing/seeing and (2) to come to some analytical conclusions (however tentative) which one (3) wishes to share with an audience outside of the research setting. A "reflective practitioner" would need to complete steps one and two. Many of my colleagues who are much better teachers than I am stop here and cannot understand why I pursue step three. I wonder sometimes if they don't consider my efforts to "communicate with an audience outside the research setting" not only irrelevant but counterproductive in that it uses energy which could be spent on my classroom and my children.

Jan: If there can be multiple purposes for teacher research, for example, for public consumption, for private use, and for professional use, then it must be important and valuable for each purpose. I seem to use my own reflection to inform my own practice right now, and I find it extremely valuable as a means to weigh other options. For instance, I often find myself asking myself why I want to present a language arts lesson in a certain way. Is it the best way for the kids to learn what I want them to learn? Through the process of this examination, I may come up with a better pedagogical method. If a teacher does this kind of thing all the time—the "extra layer" of work—how could she or he possibly write it all down, much less publish it? Besides, at least from my perspective as a new teacher, the results of my own inquiry have consequences in my classroom that are more important to me than publishing.

Karen: I cannot imagine why teachers would do research in their classrooms and then keep their findings to themselves. It takes a great deal of extra time and energy to keep records of classroom experiences and analyze them. The insights teachers gain from this kind of systematic inquiry would be very useful not only to the teacher but to other teachers in the school. The problem is finding time to share. A teacher-researcher could type up latest findings and share a copy with other teachers. Those teachers interested in discussing the findings could arrange a meeting time. I guess I believe that research should be "made public" because it is valuable knowledge that should be shared so that our students can benefit. For example, at the end of my second year of teaching urban school children last year, I presented my work to our faculty at my school. Since then, I have spoken with members of the faculty individually about my classroom research and we have compared our experiences.

Barbara: I think that those of us who tend toward the silent "making do" often do not effectively resist the stupidities of policy and institution. To act in this way harms children. However safe we keep them for the time they stay with us, we cannot protect against damage done by schooling. We must enter the conversation because we are closest to the children, and we have the possibility of bringing the children's voices into the conversation too. We have not spoken enough. We need to speak not as "raw data" but as analytical women (and men) who have rigorously considered their environment and are ready to add new interpretive frames.

Lynne: If research implies "making public" in some way, then doesn't writing research (that is, sharing one's findings) add an additional burden to the work of teachers? I guess I might as well say it: to me, teaching and researching are inextricably bound up, while I see the writing and publishing as being separate. Not only do we have to teach, but we are also under pressure to make our findings public. Is this fair to us? There are times in people's lives when (to quote Jan) "constant questioning of myself, my internal reflection, and oral discussion with colleagues" *must* be enough. Not everyone has time to write. Not everyone likes to write. Not everyone feels comfortable sharing her or his work in writing. Why should Jan, a new teacher, feel guilty because she hasn't been keeping her journal up to date? Though I enjoy writing and have had my work published, I believe it would be a sad day if all teachers (new or experienced) were forced to write in journals and in essays in order to be considered good teachers. We just have to make sure that those who want to do it get the support they need.

WHAT ARE SOME OF THE OTHER PURPOSES OF TEACHER RESEARCH?

Jay: Teacher research is a dynamic form of teacher development. Teachers are engaged in inquiry on a day-to-day basis versus sitting in a staff room at 3:00 p.m., probably listening to some new buzz-word topic which is usually not of interest or even relevant to them— especially given the one-shot nature of current staff development activities. Teacher research occurs over a period of time which helps sustain teacher interest. It helps make teaching exciting, especially for veteran teachers. It seems to give these teachers a shot in the arm, a new sense of purpose when they are put in control of investigating issues related to their teaching and their classrooms. It seems only natural that teacher education be the place where this type of inquiry begins and is modeled, encouraged, and expected. Learning about teaching is an ongoing process. From this perspective, teacher research can be viewed as a means of learning to teach—learning to look, ask questions, take risks, be open to inquiry. Teacher research is also an attempt to see and make visible what's already going on. It's a vehicle for teachers' voices to be heard in order to inform practice—for the benefit of students, as well as for the professional development of teachers. Teachers are put into the role of learners about the teaching/learning process.

Lynne: Unless the work is done to benefit the teacher-researcher herself or himself, I don't think it's worth doing. Doing research in my classroom benefits me because the more I write, the more I observe and the better I am able to teach. Research also benefits other teachers. When we read the work of others, we learn what others (children or teachers) are doing. People who have used my journal tell me that it gave them ideas for their own classrooms, that they felt less isolated after reading it because they recognized themselves in the descriptions and the stories, and that they learned from my analyses. They might reject my ideas and my ways of doing things, but they benefit from thinking about them.

Karen: Since I share my research methods with my students, they've become more familiar with the idea of research. As for other teachers, teacher educators, and university researchers, the more I share my findings with them about classroom dynamics, teacher-student relationships, and effective teaching strategies, the more insights they will have into these important features of a teacher's classroom experience. The more information we collect about classroom experiences the deeper our understanding will grow. University researchers can use teacher research as a check against their more theoretical notions of teaching, motivation, and learning.

Susan: What about our associations with university-based researchers—as objects and subjects and collaborators? Despite my excitement at having other people to talk with—people with unique perspectives and interesting and sometimes valuable information—in some ways, at this point, those relationships seem to me to have a colonial flavor to them. The more friendly and equanimous the relationship, the harder it is for me to explain that feeling and perspective. I realize I must not forget that I am studying at a university now myself. In fact, it was at a university that I became involved in the discussion about teacher research. But it seems to me that someone else is having the discussion we need to have for ourselves and that someone else benefits in an economy that rewards their making sense of our work.

Lynne: As for research that is a collaboration between university and school teacher-researchers, both should benefit. Most important is that the teacher feel empowered by the presence of, and the associations with, outside researchers, not belittled or patronized in any way. For example, if a researcher is a participant-observer in a classroom, it could be difficult for the teacher if the researcher has a strong idea of what the "right" way to teach is and the teacher believes she doesn't live up to that "right way."

Susan: We could put the shoe on our own foot here. What about the sense we make of our students and who participates in that making sense? What about the children? What about the parents of the children we teach?

Lynne: I don't know if there should also be, or can always be, some benefits to parents as a result of research in their children's classrooms, or how that would work. I know that when I was involved in a study of beginning readers, though the parents weren't interviewed about their children's literacy, I personally informed parents whose children were being observed in my classroom what we had observed about them. I gave them the written descriptions of their children. To my mind, that study was conceived in an extremely respectful way, in a way that benefited both the researchers and teachers. I'm certain that if it were being done now, the parents of the children being observed would have also been included beyond giving permission to proceed with the study, and would have also benefited from it.

WHAT NEW FORMS OF RESEARCH CAN TEACHERS, AND PERHAPS STUDENTS, CREATE OR LEGITIMATE?

Susan: I don't think we've done enough work in explicating or validating the ways we teachers already inquire and make sense in our classrooms or the ways in which we already communicate what we know. I do not happen to agree that we are a "less theoretical" group.

Our "theoretical discussion" is carried on differently, more embedded in material from the contexts in which we work, in descriptions of the classroom dynamic, in what we do and say. While I don't advocate bypassing research from the university or the social science laboratory or excluding others from collaboration, I think that we already have some particular mechanisms and forms in place and those should be identified, developed, and used. I also think we should be wondering just how other literacies, other research traditions, and other conceptions of knowledge affect our own—and our practice.

Lynne: I'm thinking of forms of teacher research that do not involve writing a finished product. I think we can learn a great deal from interviewing or being interviewed, and then discussing the transcripts of those interviews. Jan, I can imagine how valuable it might be to a new teacher like you to read a transcript of an interview with you about your teaching and, further, to sit down with a group of teachers to analyze it; and you wouldn't have all that pressure to write a finished product. Judy and I have been members of a teacher's learning cooperative which is starting its fifteenth year, and the work we do there offers us insights that influence our thinking and our work. We use the collaborative, oral, descriptive processes developed at the Prospect Center to do inquiry. These processes include observation and description, followed by questions and recommendations by the group. Through these processes we form new knowledge about our classrooms, the children, and their work. We save the notes from our meetings, and some people have used these notes as the basis for research papers. The potential for further use is great. Including interviews and group inquiry as research helps broaden the definition of teacher research.

Barbara: I would also be interested in making legitimate alternative methods of teachers' communication. But I think it is potentially dangerous to call all teacher communication "research" because the term "research" is not neutral. To accept this term is to make ourselves vulnerable to its history and implied power structures. I think the term "research" should be reserved for a formal product that is written for a potential audience of teachers and others. Let's preserve the informal, conversational way we communicate with one another. Implied in the perspective that research is somehow valued over teaching is that in order for teaching to be valued it should start looking a lot more like research. I think this would be a big mistake. We must stop begging for others to empower and value us. We have power and value. Others, and we ourselves, must come to terms with that. We do not need to be scientists, researchers, doctors, lawyers, or any of those other things our mothers wanted us to be. It is not that we need to comply with others' visions of our work. We have been entirely too compliant. Instead, "legitimacy" and "status" must be rewritten to include us. I am offended by some of the metaphors university researchers come up with in their analysis of what we are about.

WHAT ARE SOME WAYS WE CAN IMAGINE TEACHER INQUIRY OR TEACHER RESEARCH BECOMING A PART OF TEACHERS' LIVES IN SCHOOL?

Jay: One of the most important factors to help make this a reality is that teacher inquiry needs to be valued by both the school administration and the school community. While some teachers do find ways to reflect upon their practice within their current teaching situations, the vast majority of teachers need a restructured school day for this to happen with any consistency and at a level that will be of benefit to themselves and their students. I just made a presentation last week to my faculty about the use of teacher portfolios as a vehicle for reflecting about their practice. Most of the teachers at the meeting were very interested in somehow documenting and reflecting about their work which are two of the potential benefits of developing a portfolio of one's teaching. One of the suggestions to help make this successful is that the principal find coverage (that is, arrange for released time) for these teachers every six to eight weeks so they would be able to discuss the different aspects of their teaching that they are documenting in their portfolios. Another key factor is that the faculty of the school has to be interested and in a sense ready for this to happen and to be a part of their lives. Partly this depends on the personalities of the teachers and how they get along with each other; another aspect is where people are in both their personal and professional lives.

Lynne: The more formal discussions I began to describe could become models for teachers to set up structures to discuss their work systematically and intentionally. Talking is what we teachers do anyway; it is one of our strengths. We could make some of our talk more formal; we could set aside time during the school week to hold these formal discussions; we could decide ahead of time on a focus for each discussion; we could train ourselves to chair those meetings using procedures that help us to hold to the topic; we could save the notes of these discussions to make them available to be referred to and used.

We should insist that schools provide support to make these things happen, and if they did, we'd have gone a long way toward including more teachers in research. And we might discover that some of those teachers would become interested in writing about their practice for the benefit of themselves and others.

HOW HAS BEING INVOLVED IN TEACHER RESEARCH CHANGED OUR PRACTICES AND WHAT ARE WE WORKING ON AT THIS TIME?

Jeanne: For many years I studied and thought about how students learn. Over time, I gave very little thought to the perceptions the students had about their own learning. What I have learned from the teacher research I have been a part of has created much pain for me. Through interviews with students eligible for special education services, I have gained new insights into their feelings about themselves and the message the process of special education has sent. I have felt that my intentions have been right, but I have been going about it in the wrong way. I work hard to help others understand what I am learning. I work hard to include students traditionally tracked, pulled out, sorted. I work hard to include myself. I work hard in finding ways to provide advocacy for all kids. Teacher research allows me to change my practice based on a change within.

Jay: It has helped me better formulate my thoughts about some issues and has made me anxious and intimidated in other areas. Sometimes, the more you know the more you begin to realize how much you don't really know; you feel you're not doing all you could be doing about something. Overall, it's helped me make more explicit the connections I make between instruction, assessment, and curriculum. Being involved in teacher research has helped me learn a lot from my colleagues. Having similar interests has brought me together with peers to discuss and explore topics.

Susan: It has helped me get back in touch with what it might be like to be a student, to be curious, to run up against convention, to learn how to navigate systems, to risk saying and writing about what I think and feel, to risk the evaluation and judgment of others. Because I am more in touch with that part of myself, I think I have been able to make changes in how I proceed in the classroom in terms of the design and enactment of lessons, my verbal responses to students, how activities are organized, and my compassion for their—no, *our*—particular situation and predicament of being in school. Being involved in teacher research has helped me check out the discrepancies between what I think I am about in the classroom and what I actually do with my students. I think I might have missed more of those discrepancies without that involvement. My students see me as a learner and we all ask questions about our learning, about knowledge, and about school.

Jeanne: I want to know how students eligible for Special Education view themselves as learners. What impact do these perceptions have within the classroom? Do these perceptions change depending on how students are grouped? What role does the process of special education play in the development of these perceptions? How can these perceptions be shared with teachers, especially Special Education teachers? How do we reconcile basic philosophical differences when we all have good intentions? My focus is shifting. I've got the sense of how students see themselves as learners. Now, this year, as we include some extremely challenged students in "regular" education, I'm wondering what the impact will be on students and adults who have not experienced this diversity in the classroom.

Karen: I want to understand cultural diversity. Since I am Caucasian and live in the suburbs, I am different in many ways from the students in my urban classroom who are primarily African-American. I want to know who my students are and what their needs are. How can I meet their needs? What kinds of changes would I like to see in my students by the end of the year? I also want to know what they will get from their experience in my classroom. How will I be able to tell that they have changed? How can I describe the student change I see or share it somehow with outsiders? I want to know how and why I change over the course of a year. I want to know who I am in the classroom, why some students' behavior bothers me and what I can do about it? Do I reach out to the community and how do I do that and with whom? How can I legitimate all the different kinds of success in my classroom?

Susan: One of the teachers who was invited to write in this conversation eventually decided not to join us. As she explained it to me, she wanted to focus on her own personal inquiry regarding her own classroom, did not see herself as a teacher-researcher per se, and did not feel she could or wanted to contribute to a discussion about teacher research at this time and in this way. I asked her permission to include this description and her questions in this chapter. I think she represents many teachers in relationship to teacher research—as a movement and as a frame for teaching. She confirms our sense that, though some teachers do not join a movement or decline to participate in a particular discussion, they are nonetheless asking important questions. She asked whether she should teach values and, if so, which ones. She asked about an education for character, how group work can be made to work effectively, and what she should do about violence in our society. She wanted to know what to do about homeless children and how she could help develop self-esteem in children and how she could get the community to support that goal. She wanted to know how to help parents help their children. She wondered how to get kids to think instead of passively watching TV, what she must do to make a class a community, how she can "empower" kids and give them the tools so that they can make a difference.

Lynne: Last year, I noticed that the children in my class were creating groups segregated by gender and I wrote about it in my journal as I wrote about other issues and events. What I did *not* do last year was to start out by saying, "I'm going to study gender issues in my classroom," and to limit my observations and notes to that. My colleagues and I discovered, in my journal entries, some of the ways both the children and I addressed the issue of gender, and how I reflected on it. During the coming year, in addition to the usual wide-ranging description that I write, I'll try to pay closer attention to gender to continue that study. I described each incident regarding gender in relation to the rest of the classroom. In general, I am interested in how teachers go about choosing things to focus on when deciding to do "research." There is a difference between research that involves describing a context fully, and another kind in which a teacher comes up with a question and sets out to collect only data which she thinks relate to that issue. I want to avoid ways of doing research that lose the complexity and richness of either the issues or the children or the classroom.

Judy: I am struck by how hard it is to talk about teacher research apart from the students we teach. This is what makes the teacher part of teacher research so important and also what makes it so hard to figure out how to deal with the big questions of time, support, purposes, and audiences for this work. Teachers need time to talk about their classrooms with other teachers, both within their school communities and across communities. Time is in such short supply for teachers that the very notion of teacher research makes some people angry. I must admit I have a hard time envisioning school life differently from the hectic pace it is today.

WHAT ARE SOME OTHER ISSUES ON THE HORIZON
FOR US TO CONSIDER?

Lynne: My primary job is teaching in an elementary school. That's different from teaching in a university where professors are expected to write and to give papers, and where they are given time and secretarial help to do so because it's considered to be part of the job. When I am asked to give a paper at a conference, I worry about leaving the students. I don't mind having to ask for permission from the school district to speak at conferences, but it is rarely given and I must go through the humiliating experience of getting someone of a "higher status" to intercede for me when my request is refused. Finally, being invited to speak at a conference has become a prestigious undertaking for many teachers. Does that count more than teaching in their minds? Is that what we want? Does such a system encourage good teachers to want to leave classrooms? What I'm saying is that this issue is much bigger than we think (or at least bigger than I thought).

Judy: One issue I see is the issue of critique of teacher research—which I would like to see within our own community and not just outside of it. I would like to see us develop ethical guidelines and standards and also structures for sharing our work; ways to include raising questions and asking about difficult issues within teacher research. But that requires that teacher-researchers have forums, such as this one, for raising the issues and opportunities and time for struggling with them.

Barbara: I wonder if doing research distances us from our nonresearching colleagues.

Susan: I wonder about that too. There seems to be an "us" and "them" in many schools. Sometimes it's the people who attend all the district workshops or the quiet solitary souls, the people who support the principal, or the detractors, the mutterers, and the back-row folks at faculty meetings. Sometimes it's this team or that team, this department or that department. Sometimes it's the first wave, second wave, or third wave groups, the young ones or the older ones, the conservative disciplinarians or the purportedly laissez-faire. Sometimes it's an academic group or a vocational education group. On the other hand, teachers have always been much like yaks in a circle—very protective of one another as a general group, for some historic and very valid reasons. What if my study needed to include information about another faculty member? What if my study questioned the adopted strategy for developing literacy in my school? What if my study questioned policy and/or looked at particular events, or suggested the dissolution of borders between sets of subject matter, or challenged prescribed behaviors? How will my being a teacher researcher affect my status or my conception of my status, and how will that affect those helpful friendships and alliances I've made for other reasons and along different lines? In any case, I see the tradition of teaching as containing several unresolved issues where new direction could most certainly clash with expectations and the usual practice. I don't think any of this description prohibits or should prohibit moving forward. I just know that is the lay of the land and it will have to be dealt with in some way.

Jan: Being a student teacher in someone else's classroom, and in the company of a very experienced teacher, how much could I admit and ask about substance and style when I was so unsure of myself? How could I relax and develop, in a natural way, my own teaching style and my own sets of conclusions? As a student teacher, can you really disagree with your cooperating teachers when you are essentially in debt to them? They write letters of recommendation for you and give feedback to the university. The cooperating teacher/ student teacher relationship is, after all, a political one, and there are tensions between styles and philosophies. During your first year of teaching and if you are in a formal mentor/mentee relationship, what happens when the mentee is better equipped to teach than the mentor? How is expertise established? How can we genuinely ask and answer our own questions given the politics and notion of expertise involved in schools?

Lynne: I wonder what happens to a teacher who prefers to work alone rather than to collaborate with others in research and in writing about her findings? Also, making public one's findings implies that teachers belong to intentional communities, in which, even if we don't publish our research in writing, we share what we have learned from our own and others' practice in some way. Is this fair to ask of all teachers?

Barbara: I want to ask: have any of you had trouble gaining access to your own classrooms for your research? I had some amazing difficulties with this. It led me to ask: who owns my teaching?

Lynne: I'm glad that in social science research the question of "ownership" of classroom research is currently being addressed. Whose name goes on the article about a classroom when a university person is doing research there? Is a thank you to the classroom teacher in the "Acknowledgments" enough? Or should there be negotiations beforehand so that both the university person and the teacher know what each will "get out of the research?" What happens if they disagree about such things as methodology, theory, the description of the classroom, and the interpretation of the data? It is my conviction that the teacher should be involved in designing the project with the university researcher, should be given access to all the notes, information, and knowledge gained by the researcher, should be consulted about descriptions of the classroom, and perhaps should be able to participate in and/or respond to any of the interpretations of her classroom or the children.

Susan: The same caution and concern can be framed in terms of our relationships with students as well. A senior in my psychology class once said to me, "What I would tell you as a teacher is different than what I would tell you as a researcher." As a unit of study I had asked students to photograph their school lives and write narratives to accompany their photographs. I was after a way to learn about how my students perceived their school experience as well as a way to incorporate their perceptions about their world as course content, as material they might develop and examine to learn about their own experience. Students were as concerned about their relationships with their fellow students and the adults in their world as teachers are in regard to relationships in their professional lives. So, one of my questions is about my ethical responsibilities to students who see things that way, who see those roles as perhaps conflicting. I wonder how that concern shapes what I can know as well as what I can talk and write about and to whom I can communicate what I have understood.

Barbara: You ask about the ethical ramifications of teacher research. I worry about this too. I do see the teacher and researcher roles as separate. Unfortunately, in my case they often occupy the same time and space. Susan, you teach older students. At least they thought to confront the issue. I teach younger students and I have to chart the course myself and I am very unsure. For example, I read in a student's writing some reference to violence at the hand of a stepparent in her life. The writing was elicited for research. The student knew this and willingly wrote for an audience other than just me. But I know things as "teacher" about this student's history which have a definite bearing upon my interpretation of her writing. That part of the student's history was not, and I think should not have been, shared with the "researcher." To further complicate things, I think this student might want to share her experience with a wider audience. She has discussed this possibility with me. Her parents, on the other hand, seem less open. Whose wishes do I follow? What are the consequences for each? I'm still thinking about this one. So far I have presented the writing with a qualifying statement. I put it in and I'm uncomfortable. I take it out and I feel I'm sanitizing my children's world.

Lynne: My anecdotal records on the children in my class are for me, and I don't give them to the parents to read in their unedited form. Is it okay to write things in those records which I would not share with parents? Can I then use the information in them in oral inquiries with other teachers without asking permission, having changed the child's name? Can I use a child's work in an article if I have changed that child's name and masked her or his identity, but have not gotten permission from the parent? Can I use excerpts from my records on students (having changed their names) without asking permission to do so? I teach younger students. It is commonplace right now for older students to be brought into a teacher's research in some way. Is this important for younger students? How much should we tell them? How much do we involve their parents? Certainly a big project needs permission, but what about our own record keeping which might sometime later be used in an article?

Susan: You mentioned that the questions and issues of "ownership" of classroom research are currently being addressed in terms of the relationship between university/school collaborators. It sounds as if the relationship between teachers and students bears similar sets of concerns and we've already begun to touch on this. How have you involved your students in your own research to date?

Jay: One of the things I usually do at the beginning of the school year is to interview the children with regard to their thoughts about reading and the reading process. Together we review their responses. Later as a class we look at the range of responses and try to make some generalizations. Once we've done these things together, I have them interview several adults: a teacher or someone at school and one parent at home. When they've completed these tasks we put them on chart paper and begin analyzing them together—hoping to learn more about how people at different levels think about reading and the reading process. I have my students in my elementary methods course conduct oral histories of veteran classroom teachers. We spend several sessions sharing the responses they received and then trying to make some generalizations from the information. I hope to write this project up in the near future. As I am writing these two examples, the question about the "validity" of teacher research is running back and forth through my head. I'm not sure if what I've listed would be considered "valid research." It's the type of question and conversation I tend to avoid. Why? Maybe I'm more interested and concerned with the reflective process rather than agreeing on a definition of the term.

Karen: I think the fact that teacher-researchers are asking questions and making it known that they don't have all of the answers is a positive influence on the students. The systematic investigation into confusing and very complex issues demonstrates to the students a way of thinking and acting stemming from uncertainty and an interest in learning more about a topic. The students should be exposed to as many quests for knowledge and understanding as possible. During the last two years as a teacher-researcher in my classroom, I continually encouraged my students to share their views on various topics, emphasizing the value of each student's opinion. As part of my classroom research, I documented changes in the students' willingness to contribute to discussions and the changing nature of their contributions.

Susan: I wonder what it would mean to investigate the possibility, even to implement a policy, of involving students and fellow faculty members in our research in much the same way that some of us think we ought to be involved in university research. How far could we take that idea, given the nature of the world in which we currently live? I wonder what it might mean for our teaching methodology, the curriculum, the subject matter, and our roles to consider students as researchers and learners with us and to actually develop a teaching policy and methodology to carry that out. I also wonder what that would mean in terms of what knowledge is and how and what we understand. In a world that expects a particular kind of expertise from teachers as well as the enactment of a particular role in reference to a particular conserved knowledge, what is teacher research going to do in terms of our relationship with the communities in which we live and work?

Commentary

At the end of this "conversation," each of us reflected upon its process and its content. Several of us agreed with Barbara who commented that each one of us could have written a chapter on her or his own and that "a chapter called 'teachers' voices' sounds more like a choral program than a writing task." We worried with her that "because we had not settled upon a central focus, the chapter might appear superficial and inadvertently reinforce some of the stereotypes about the relative position and intellectual competence of university researchers and K-12 teachers."

The final version of this conversation for publication only hints at the rich complexity we began to share with each other. Its construction remains unfinished and it is a cacophonous work in some respects. Teachers are not all of one mind. However, even though we note that this conversation is but a beginning, that it proceeds in fits and starts, and that it is both supported and endangered in this particular context, we hear particular threads and tensions which may become part of our future conversations.

We all identify the need, recognize the importance, and reserve the opportunity to talk as teachers about our own work, its processes, knowledge, ethics, norms, and standards. We all feel a responsibility to our students, to our colleagues, to our communities and to the role of teaching in our lives. We share the perspective that teacher inquiry is vital and essential to teaching.

We notice that the traditional continuum which posits theory and practice at its nether ends is deeply embedded and interwoven in our discussion. We are not currently in agreement, however, about the nature of their relationship and whether or how it is problematic; nor are we collectively certain about the value of reconciling their differences. Some of us think that such a continuum tends to make our discussion dichotomous, resulting in dilemmas that are difficult to confront, challenge, process, and render. We look for paradigms which might more fully admit our world to view by reconciling those dichotomies.

We also notice that the more we enter a world beyond the classroom—through "teacher leadership roles" and graduate study—the more we adopt a language not of the classroom. It is often bureaucratic, policy-laden, or specialized in ways that exclude many of us as teachers from the discussion on teacher research. On the one hand, our emergent "bilingualism" gives us greater control over the institutional environments in which we work and allows us to talk with people in other worlds; on the other hand, it could impede our talk as teachers in the particular settings in which we work.

We have deeply felt ethical concerns and questions that rise in the perceived discrepancy between the role of teacher and the role of knowledge maker. We think conventions about anonymity, participation, and confidentiality must be reexamined—including conventions that govern the asymmetrical relationship between university-based researcher as knowledge maker, teacher as knowledge maker, and student as knowledge maker.

We see our differences in terms of writing to know and writing to publish—a dispute about whether one can "know" one's practice without struggling to write about it, and a dispute about whether one owes any obligation to others to share one's research. The choice may well be publish or perish for others. For many of us, the dilemma seems to be publish *and* perish. Rather than adding writing onto the already accumulated obligations that fill a teaching day, we suggest the displacement of some of the other configurations with which we deal—such as traditional staff development—as well as a restructuring of school relationships, curriculum, and time.

Finally, we realize that we live and work together in a social context, in social relationship with our fellow teachers, with our students and in our community. "Going public" calls upon us to take stances that aren't as easy to change as are positions taken in moment-to-moment actual conversation, or as easy to channel and control as when we close our classroom doors. If we are to talk and write together, we need to ask what modes, conceptions, processes, and agreements move us forward? For us, the question of going public involves questions of development, of responsibility, of role, and of professional community.

CHAPTER XIII

The New Teacher

JONAS F. SOLTIS

Twenty-five years from now, this NSSE yearbook either will be forgotten like so many of its other well-intentioned predecessors or it will be cited by many as a major landmark in the history of the emergence and transformation of a more sophisticated and richer conception of teaching and schooling in the last quarter of the twentieth century. I know what I hope will happen, but my best guess is that the odds are against it. Major revolutions in educational thought and practice are few and far between in human history and the dominant forces and practices of our time are well entrenched.

In spite of such a pessimistic prediction, but in line with my hope for real change, I would like to use this final chapter to explore and celebrate what the editors and authors of this Yearbook have done here and now as they have invited its readers to think about the possibility of an educational reformation which, if it is to happen, will require a major shift in mind set and the conversion of many well beyond the readership of this NSSE Yearbook. I am using the Kuhnian language of conversion and gestalt switch here to underscore how radical a conceptual, social, cultural, and material revolution this needs to be if it is to succeed.

Like the progressive education movement at the beginning of the twentieth century, it must capture the imagination of a vast number of people as a radical *new* form of education and teaching and not just a reform or readjustment of existing practice. Also like progressive education, it must be part of and consonant with a larger set of forces at work in the social, political, and intellectual world. Lawrence Cremin, in his aptly titled history of the progressive education movement, *The Transformation of the School*, put this part-whole relationship quite well when he said:

Jonas F. Soltis is William Heard Kilpatrick Professor Emeritus of Philosophy and Education at Teachers College, Columbia University.

Actually, progressive education began as part of a vast humanitarian effort to apply the promise of American life—the ideal of government by, of, and for the people—to the puzzling new urban-industrial civilization that came into being during the latter half of the nineteenth century. The word *progressive* provides the clue to what it really was: the educational phase of American Progressivism writ large. In effect, progressive education is a many-sided effort to use the schools to improve the lives of individuals.[1]

Do we have anything comparable today? Perhaps. There have been a number of serious challenges to our taken for granted views of the world and how people live in it, many of which have filtered down and reached into the lives and culture of ordinary people. Consider, for example, the feminist critique, pluralism and multiculturalism, critical theory, the ecological view of the environment, democratization of new and old nations, the peace movement, and most especially postmodernism in its many forms and manifestations. Something seems afoot that bespeaks a possible radical transformation of society and our basic assumptions about knowledge, others, and what are desirable ways to live our individual and collective human lives.

Not yet named, there are a number of sympathetically connected ideas, slogans and themes embedded in this potentially transformative era. Consider for example, *emancipation, edification, nurturance, relational, conversational, dialogical, voice, qualitative, ecological, intersubjective, caring, deconstruction, interpretation, construction,* and then add your own favorite words of the new vocabulary. What it seems the editors and authors of this yearbook have done is to locate the ideas of teacher research and educational reform in this stream of postmodern consciousness transformation.

Paraphrasing Cremin and inserting a few new words might help give some substance to this claim. A historian of the future might write about this period saying something like this:

Actually the transformative movement in education began as part of a vast humanitarian effort to apply the promise of a democratic form of life—the ideal of each individual and every group developing their capacities to find and live a good life—to the puzzling new postmodern global village that came into being during the twentieth century. The word *transformative* provides a clue to what it really was: the educational phase of a larger transformation of consciousness, of political awareness, of our limited concept of knowledge, and of a vision of equity and humanness that included an effort to use the schools to improve all individuals and societies.

Between the lines of all the essays in this volume is an almost palpable hopefulness that teaching and schooling will not only take on a new form, but a much better one—one that will radically transform the work of teachers, the lives of their students, and the functioning of society.

Each of the essays in this volume also contributes its own perspective on the essential characteristic of the emerging concept of teaching. Variously calling it teaching as research, as inquiry, as learning, or as reflective practice, the authors attempt to capture the essence of a new way of thinking and talking about teaching by using an all-encompassing label, a core metaphor, or a captivating slogan. Many of the authors recognize the dangers inherent in this essentializing, however. Like the slogans and metaphors of the progressive education movement such as "learning by doing," "teach the child not the subject," "education is growth," almost any practice imaginable can be justified. Every metaphor fails at some point, every label limits thought, and every slogan invites abuse.

What is essential, then, is to find a way to transmit an understanding of the deep and complex new meaning of teaching and schooling as it is being formed and formulated currently without locking it prematurely into a potentially harmful or distorting label, metaphor, or slogan. We might do better, then, to talk about the "new teacher" or the "newly emerging concept of teaching and schooling" without characterizing it initially in a way that does not invite additional discussion and curiosity about what it is. I will adopt this strategy.

The New Teacher: A Portrait

In this section I want to set out a collective portrait sketch of significant features of the new teacher as they have been painted by the various authors in this volume. I use the term portrait intentionally. No portrait is the one and only true representation of an individual. Each good portrait captures some of the signaling features of the individual that make him or her uniquely who he or she is and directly recognizable by viewers. Some painted features are not crucial but merely helpful, like the portrait of a college president in academic rather than everyday attire. Thus while everything put into a portrait is intended to play its part in portraying the person portrayed, not everything in the portrait is essential to all portraits of that person. It is only a sketch of some important dimensions of the new teacher I am after here and so I will leave many helpful details out. Moreover, and in reality, each new teacher may differ from others in specific features, but the similarities and family resemblances along certain dimensions will be more important than the differences in recognizing the new teachers as belonging to a new breed no matter at what level—primary, secondary, or tertiary—they teach.

One of the characteristics of the new teacher which the metaphors of researcher, inquirer, learner, and reflective practitioner try to convey is the idea of genuine intellectual engagement in what he or she is doing, has done, or will do as a teacher. Intellectual engagement should be read here in its broadest sense to include the use of such powers as the creative and imaginative, the analytic and critical, the practical and idealistic, the interpretive and appreciative, and wisdom in judgment. The metaphor of researcher suggests systematic study; that of inquirer, a willingness to question and seek answers; that of learner, one who takes from experience important ideas to use in future; that of reflective practitioner, one who thinks back on his or her actions and judges their successes and failures with an eye to improving practice. There is more in each of these metaphors, of course, but I am only suggesting here a way to see them each and all as trying to convey the same thing—a qualitative dimension of the new teacher that requires genuine intellectual engagement in one's practice in an effort to do it well.

There is another characteristic of the new teacher which belongs in the portrait. He or she is not a loner. This is the relational dimension. While the primary focus is on improvement of one's practice, there is much that can be done in and learned from collaboration with other teachers, university and school people, and one's own students. There is a genuine caring that permeates these relationships. It is not just the improvement of one's practice that is paramount. It is engaging with others for their sake as well. Giving to and sharing with others is as important as receiving and improving one's self and one's practice. Sharing the values, standards, and appropriate "sacred stories" of a new teacher culture cements a collective sense of solidarity, support, and altruistic purpose.

Finally, there is the characteristic of social-ethical sensitivity. Some might call it the political dimension. The new teacher sees his or her practice embedded in a larger social context where power, dominance, and social injustices exist. The school as a social institution serves social purposes whose worth and moral goodness need to be consciously and conscientiously appraised. School practices and pedagogical actions may carry with them the unintended consequences of reproducing undesirable and unjust social prejudices and arrangements. The new teacher must cultivate a nose for the unintentional curriculum and a sense of moral obligation to right its wrongs in a way consonant with fundamental democratic values of equality and justice, and human values of nurturance and love.

There is more that can and should be added to this composite, three-dimensional sketch. But at least the main features now have been given a place on the canvas. The details, the subtle colorings and shadings, the background, the structures needed to support the telos of the new teacher, all need to be filled in and many have been by the various authors of this volume. We are in their debt for the richness of the portraits they have given us.

Pragmatism

Epistemology. What a formidable word! At the heart of the concerns of many of the authors in this volume who advocate the view that the new teacher should be a researcher, an intentional, systematic inquirer, or a reflective practitioner is a nagging worry over how such a teacher's knowledge claims are to be legitimated. What is the new teacher's *epistemological* warrant?

If only the authors had merely asked how can teachers examine their own practice in ways that will inform their attempts at understanding and improving that practice, the ogre of epistemology might not have appeared. But the editors and authors of this volume know that we have all been imbued with the myth of science as the only legitimate form of knowledge and the idea of educational research and scholarship as the only legitimate provider of knowledge for guiding practice. They also know that there will be many who believe that without a justifying epistemology an individual's knowledge claims should be held suspect. They clearly recognized that the new teacher needs to have a philosophically respectable epistemology to fend off critics. Fortunately, there is one available!

That epistemology comes out of the American pragmatic tradition and carries the weight of such recognized philosophers as Peirce, James, and Dewey. The version I will sketch here comes mainly from Dewey, who quite fittingly was not just an epistemologist but also, as we all know, a major philosopher of education.[2] In a way, I am only resubmitting here ideas Dewey offered educators many years ago. Too few realized the import of those ideas then. Too many today have not become acquainted with them in their professional education.

Pragmatism is a theory of knowledge (an epistemology!) based on an evolutionary view of the human mind as a very useful adaptive biological/psychological mechanism for the survival of the species. On this view, meaning, knowledge, and truth are ideas applied to human experience and success in dealing with the world, not to abstractions or absolutes. Peirce viewed humans as adaptive organisms who had evolved a belief-doubt system for functioning in the world to satisfy survival needs.[3] Beliefs were human "habits" for operating in the world which were acquired through action on the world. For example, moving closer to a fire produces the sensation of warmth and the belief that fire is a source of heat. This, in turn, produces the "habit" of moving closer to the fire when one is cold. Doubt, for Peirce, is the failure of habit to produce the desired expectation and thus upsets belief. The organism is upset; it is thwarted in meeting its needs and so seeks to end the state of "doubt" by finding an action that will serve as the basis for a new habit that will allow it to achieve its goal and so "fix" a new belief. Beliefs for Peirce are knowledge but not absolute truths; they are fallible modes of operating on the world in pursuit of human purposes.

William James, in his version of pragmatism, focused his attention on individual human beings and the way in which they fixed their beliefs about God, the moral life, and their fellow human beings.[4] For James, one's personal philosophy had to make a "definite difference" in one's life and the way one lived it. As a psychologist, James was interested primarily in lived experience, and how that experience formed habits, which served to help individuals to operate purposefully, effectively, and meaningfully in their environment. In this way he tied meaning and truth to the "usefulness," "practicality," "workability," and "cash value" of our beliefs about the world and to the success and failure of our expriences in it. Knowledge was a set of beliefs that we as individuals use to deal with our everyday world.

Unlike many of the classical philosophers who preceded him, but like his contemporary James whom he knew and read, Dewey also did not search beyond the realm of ordinary experience to find some more fundamental and enduring reality as a basis for knowledge.[5] Dewey believed that it was in everyday experience that thinking begins, knowledge is acquired, and the solutions of problems (practical, social, and philosophical) are to be found and tested. Like Peirce and James, his view of human beings and mental life was biological and evolutionary and this provided the cornerstone for his description of habit, intelligence, thinking, and growth. He believed that it was through experience and purposeful action that our understanding of the world was acquired, used, adjusted, and added to in future experience.

PURPOSE, THOUGHT, AND ACTION

The key to understanding Dewey's epistemology is the role that purpose and consequences play in thought and action. Human beings naturally have needs, desires, and interests that they seek to satisfy by action in and on the world. Sometimes such actions are haphazard or trial and error; sometimes just a repetition of routines. As our species evolved, however, we have learned that purposeful action regulated by foresight, planning, the use of past experience, monitoring, and tending to novel conditions pays off more often than not in successfully producing consequences that satisfy our initial purposes.

For example, imagine two prehistoric men, both hungry, one who haphazardly traverses an area hoping to come across some game and the other seeking and finding a game trail and lying in wait for his prey. Both no doubt will be successful sometimes and sometimes fail to achieve their purpose. But the hunter acting on foresight, thought, and planning will probably go less hungry in the long run. He, we might say, is the more knowledgeable or the more intelligent hunter. His purposeful action has been informed by what he already knows, by imaginative planning, and by the use of intelligence in connecting knowledge, ideas, and action.

Moreover, when the consequences of his action benefit him with food, he has good reason to believe that his strategy may work again. Indeed he probably will try it in future with an eye both to testing its validity and to satisfying his need for food. If it fails, he will look for reasons for its failure and not just give up what was once a good idea. He may come up with a new and better strategy: looking for a watering hole to wait for animals to come to him or designing and setting snares on the trail when he cannot be there in person to wait for game.

INTELLIGENCE AND KNOWLEDGE

From this simple example we can see that the use of intelligence in purposeful action often results in a gain of knowledge and the generation of new ideas even though getting and affirming knowledge are not ordinarily the main purposes of such action. Knowledge that is a by-product of action and tentative is no less legitimate than knowledge that is directly sought after and seemingly settled, however. Knowledge acquired in action may or may not do effective work when called on in future situations but it gains in warrant the more it serves our future purposeful actions well. It has a legitimacy-in-use.

To some, this may sound like the underpinnings for a budding description of the beginnings of empirical science. In a way it is. Dewey and especially Peirce were very impressed with the natural origins of scientific thinking and the long evolution of its development into a crowning achievement of the use of human intelligence. For Dewey, however, it was not that science was the best model for human thinking. Rather, it was that this very effective form of human thinking, this "method of intelligence" which serves as the model for logic and science, should also be taught and used in everyday life in its basic form.

What we have in Dewey and in the hunter example, then, is an epistemology that shares some key features with the epistemology of the scientific mind set that dominates our view of educational research and legitimate knowledge. But there are also some very crucial and important differences. In both, for example, hypotheses are generated and empirically tested; replication and similar results increase confidence in the validity of the hypotheses, and knowledge is generated from such doings. However, knowledge which is the goal of scientific observation, experimentation, and evaluation is not what the pragmatist's epistemology of intelligent human action is about. It is about securing through action and thought what is desired and desirable. It is using intelligence to achieve our purposes by thinking about what we are doing before, during, and after doing it. When that happens, one has warrant for certain knowledge claims that may or may not be universal or generalizable, but that nonetheless have proved themselves to have efficacy in a local situation of purpose, meaning, and action.

Pragmatism in Teaching

Imagine a new teacher with purposes and interests of the following sorts: getting students to appreciate poetry, to see the power of words and symbols to communicate feelings and inchoate meanings, to enjoy the rhythm and play of words, to develop self-confidence and the ability to express themselves, and to learn to communicate with others via a special genre of human expression. These purposes and interests become the contextual parameters for generating ideas, making choices, and judging many aspects of one's teaching, including the effectiveness of the poems chosen for study, the goodness of fit of the activities, assignments, and modes of evaluation designed for students, and the pertinence of the moves, responses, and changes made in actual classroom attempts to achieve these purposes. Each purpose provides a guiding vision of what one wants the consequences to be for students. These visions also provide the means both to assess progress toward these goals and to generate new ideas and new purposes along the way when some things turn out differently in practice than was anticipated in thought.

There is a dynamic quality to this use of thought in action. There is constant "reflection," "inquiry," "research," and "learning" going on even though none of these labels fully captures the richness of this process. This is an epistemology of the purposeful use of human intelligence in ongoing experience.

It is not some recipe or method for getting or legitimating knowledge that makes possible the fuller use of one's intelligence in practice. It is constant attention to what one is doing with an eye to what one hopes to accomplish and inventing new ways to go about it. This requires many sorts of knowledge as well as empathy, imagination, skill, creativity, and critical reflection.[6] One also needs knowledge of alternative ideal purposes to choose from, enhanced understanding of complex, connected, and compatible aims (like the new teacher of poetry above), frameworks for interpreting various aspects of practice, a reservoir of practical experience to draw from, models of good practice, intimate and deep knowledge of subject matter, and understanding of the developmental stage that one's students are at and who they now are as unique individuals and much, much more. Basic, however, is one's own evolving knowledge of how to be a good teacher. Teaching is always a becoming. To paraphrase Dewey's definition of growth, teaching for the new teacher is the constant reorganization, reconstruction, and transformation of one's experience. It is developing one's philosophy of teaching and of education as well. And, to paraphrase William James, one's philosophy must make a *definite difference* in the way one lives his or her professional life.

THE RELATIONAL DIMENSION

In treating the issue of epistemology, we have focused attention primarily on only one dimension of the portrait of the new teacher, genuine intellectual engagement in the educational process. Of course, some teachers have done this for years. For them, there is nothing new about the pragmatic development of their knowledge about teaching except perhaps to find out that pragmatism is a legitimate and legitimating epistemology. More often than not, however, such teachers struggle alone to develop and improve their practice, seldom if ever sharing with others the fruits of their hard-gained knowledge. The new teacher, on the other hand, has been painted as one who openly reaches out to others. So we should turn to the relational dimension of the image of the new teacher in order to explore some of the potentials and problems of community, communication, and collaboration with others.

The potential to learn, to grow, and to develop as an individual teacher and to transform the profession as a collective is very great when viewed from the relational perspective. We must, however, begin with the primary relation, a teacher to his or her students. Many of the authors in this volume, especially the teachers and those with feminist leanings, recognize the primacy of this relation. It is at the heart of the educational process. They recognize that students are unique individuals with developing minds and emotions that teachers need to understand and respect. How teachers relate to their students—as caring, interested, fellow human beings or as cool, disinterested authorities—is as or more important for the potency of the new teacher than what subject matter is being learned. This message of relation runs through many of the essays and for good reason.

Militating against teachers establishing genuine caring relations with their students is the impersonal, bureaucratic, hierarchical structure of our schools which have been designed ironically to provide for the fullest education of the greatest number of individuals as possible. Sheer numbers of students, however, can easily overwhelm a teacher who sees relation to individual students as individuals to be a fundamental element of good teaching.

We also have seen that this same structure in the schools militates against the development of community, cooperation, and the sharing of teachers' knowledge with one another. The call by Lieberman and Miller to build a culture of collective and collaborative teaching in our schools recognizes the need to radically restructure the teacher's workplace; the call for collaborative resonance by Cochran-Smith does the same for teacher education; and the call by Clandinin and Connelly for "restorying" and "reimagining" the "sacred stories" of hierarchical roles and relationships also speaks at the cultural and not just the external social/material level of the kind of change required to nurture and support the new teacher. And the voices of the teachers themselves in Susan Threatt's group show how difficult it is to realize in thought and action the posture of the new teacher.

Can such deep and radical transformations be brought about in schools that physically have been built to support another view of schooling and teaching? Can they come about in a social-cultural world that encourages excessive individualism, control from above, and a cost-benefit accountability for a very narrow range of learnings? The pessimist has much to support his position. Still, the optimists in this volume have an appealing vision of what might be. For example, Richardson describes staff development as collaborative inquiry; Noffke, Mosher, and Maricle show how teachers and university people can not only collaborate but can communicate as well; and Atkin adds the potential of the teacher to play a role in affecting policy.

UNIVERSITY-SCHOOL COLLABORATION

While there may be some hope, the case that can be made for the possibility of university-school collaboration is not much better and perhaps is even worse than that for changing the structure and culture of the schools. We also have been reminded of the deeply entrenched power relation hierarchies of professor over teacher, researcher over practitioner, theory over practice in the Miller-Hollingsworth exchanges and the essay by Lytle and Cochran-Smith. Not only does this status relation disadvantage the teacher trying to become the new teacher; it also disadvantages the academic who wants to collaborate as an equal but whose own political culture requires and encourages the posture of expert and disinterested researcher. Many of the other essays in this volume also have thoughtfully examined problematic aspects of this status relationship.

Genuine collaboration will not only require new teachers in new school cultures and structures, but also new teacher educators, new cultures in schools of education, and altered university structures. For academics, changing the culture and structure of the schools may look like a very difficult task, but not totally impossible. However, the possibility of changing their own milieu has got to look much harder if not outright impossible, and for good reason.

Just as teachers feel that they have little status and power in the schools of today, education faculty *know* they have less status and power in their colleges and universities. While certainly not as vicious or harmful as the deep-seated and pervasive effects of bias regarding race, class, and gender in our society, the members of an education faculty endure a similar kind of repressive treatment in the academic community. They are viewed as less than respectable scholars by their liberal arts colleagues. The kind of work required by a teacher education faculty to bring about the education of the new teacher will look like academic suicide to the liberal arts faculty, deans, and presidents. It is doubtful that those in power would support such a radical change in what a college- or university-based scholar is supposed to be and do. In fact, many faculty in colleges of education would likely agree with them. I may be overly pessimistic here, but the weight of power, tradition, false consciousness, bias, and history is, as we all know, a heavy impediment to real change.

There may be one good thing that could come out of this bias against education in the academic community, however. (Ironic, isn't it, that academics hold education in low esteem?) It could help teacher educators to know a little of what many others who are worse off suffer by way of repression, inequity, fear, and a sense of inferiority and powerlessness. This, in turn, might be used to find ways to develop more sympathetically the social-ethical sensitivities of the new teacher, one of the most important aspects of the portrait presented in these pages. The great contribution of the feminist critique and critical theory in education has been raising the consciousness of teachers about what else is learned in school and what needs to be attended to in order to work at relieving social injustices. The chapters by Zeichner and Welch help us to see that education for democracy in a multicultural society is more than political education; it is an education in living together and honoring the democratic values of equity, respect for persons, and justice. The new education professor and the new teacher will find that many in the university as well as in society do not hold these truths to be self-evident. He or she will have to work to make them a genuine part of their students' education.

Imagine a School

Let us suppose for the moment that all the problems the pessimist has posed in this essay have been surmounted and the era of the new teacher has arrived. What would schools, teachers, and teacher education look like? We have been given powerful and provocative glimpses of this possible future by many of the authors of this volume.

Let me end my essay with an imaginative summary of the brave new world of education that they envision.

Kyesha, a beginning teacher, has just joined the faculty of the Hopeful County Middle School. In tandem with completing her BA in history at State U, she worked in her junior, senior, and fifth year in the Department of Education where she also earned a Master of Arts in Teaching degree. That program not only included education department courses at the college, but also increasingly involved her in participation and internship at the university-town sponsored professional development school.

What Kyesha liked most about this direct experience in the school for all of her three years was her growing understanding of what was meant by the term "new teacher" that she had heard bandied around at the college as if it were something special. It was. She knew she still had much to learn about teaching, but she had been given a good start at how to reflect on her own practice, what the sharing of ideas about teaching could bring to and from others, and how important one's teaching can be in the lives of students who live in a pluralistic and not always a just society.

She also found that working with professors as a teacher was very different from studying with professors at the college. The education department professors seemed to be real human beings interested in her and in what she did with her students, what she really thought about education, and what it ought to be. The things Kyesha and her professors read and talked about together gave them a common language and multiple conceptual frameworks for exploring and reflecting on what happened in the classroom. In fact, sometimes she had all she could do to get back "her" classroom after the professor or her mentor-teacher got their hands on it to try out something they were working on. Kyesha definitely wanted to develop a similar relationship with her own students. It made learning meaningful.

Besides the pure enjoyment of working with her students, she thought the next best was having the chance to talk seriously and at length about what she was trying to do and how it was or wasn't working out with other teachers who had a wealth of experience and knowledge to share with her. Being a "new teacher" meant being in communication with others.

After graduating from State U, she was delighted to find the Hopeful School because there were so few such schools in the state. It was only three years ago that Hopeful had declared itself a "School for the New Teacher" with the strong backing and approval of the Board of Education. She couldn't believe her good fortune to have been hired there. Hopeful was really different from the middle school she had gone to only ten years ago.

Students arrived for breakfast around 7:00 a.m. Faculty and administrators also ate with them in the cafeteria and often found themselves helping with a difficult homework problem, checking up on how a sick father was doing, exploring options for summer work for those turning sixteen and doing just about anything else that might come up in the informal atmosphere of breakfast together before classes. (The same thing happened at lunch.)

Classes began at 8:00, and ran to 11:15 with a short midmorning break. Lunch began at 11:30, but by 12:30, both students and teachers (especially those teachers who had chosen to do team teaching) were doing some last minute preparation and review for afternoon classes that ran from 1:00-4:15. Teachers taught either morning or afternoon classes (not both) and used the nonclass time for working either independently or with others on what was officially called "research" but really was reflecting on and working at one's teaching and the understanding of one's students and trying to find ways to do both better. There was never enough time at school for all of this and so many teachers carried work home and tried to fit professional writing in on the weekends or vacations. The Board knew it was getting its money's worth because it saw how hard the teachers worked and how much the students liked being in school.

The teachers also had the opportunity to talk to each other about their teaching and their "research," to collaborate with staff developers from the college nearby, developing new ways to examine what they were doing as teachers and to explore with fellow teachers ways to structure nonclass aspects of Hopeful's program. That's how they came up with the community breakfast idea. They've also been thinking about involving their middle school students in a tutoring program for elementary students. This would give their students a chance to be teachers themselves. A community service program is also in the planning stage.

Even though it was new, the teachers' library had some excellent books on education and numerous books, articles, reports, journals, and videotapes done by teachers. A book discussion group formed and met over lunch each Monday. There was also an educational issues group that met weekly. It seemed that there was so much more for the "new teacher" to think about, do, and reflect on with others. Kyesha was thankful for the time that had been built into the system to do it.

Even so, she was finding it hard to keep up her writing in her own journal.

Journal writing had been an important part of her experience in her teacher education program. She had found it to be so powerful that she has asked her students to keep a journal in her history classes reflecting on what certain aspects of the history they are studying say directly to them as individuals. This is one of the best ways Kyesha has found to really get to know her students. She is thinking of writing up her reflections on this experience to share with other teachers who have not yet used journal writing as a pedagogical tool, and depositing her journal in the teacher's library which is computer-linked to other libraries.

There is so much more going on in Hopeful: college course opportunities for those who want to learn more about their subjects, about education, or about things that might be helpful as they take a turn at administration. At Hopeful, there are no career administrators. Teachers select leaders from their own ranks for a three-year term at the end of which the leader returns to teaching. There are opportunities to share experiences with teachers elsewhere through computer networks and in-house desktop publications. Professors from the nearby college of education also come to visit and learn from the teachers' research. There are all-school activities that provide opportunities for teachers to be with students in meaningful, nonacademic settings both on and off campus. Kyesha is just beginning to get to know about these things and wonders what else tomorrow may bring. One thing she is sure of; tomorrow will always bring something that makes teaching one of the richest, most interesting and challenging occupations one could ever hope to engage in . . . if one is a *new teacher*!

Conclusion

What will the future bring? A better question is what will people who believe in the concept of the new teacher do to make the future different from the past? History is made by people. It doesn't just happen. They will have to work at it.

Even the pessimists who feel powerless can opt to struggle against the powers that be rather than sit back and say I told you so. And the optimists? They can continue to spread their visions and try to convert others as well as roll up their sleeves to work at whatever seems pragmatically useful for achieving their shared purpose of creating new school structures and educating the new teacher.

Someday there may be many Kyeshas, and Hopefuls, but we must do more than just be hopeful that this will come to pass. As pragmatists, believers in the idea of the new teacher must act on the world trying to achieve their purposes, learn from their experiences, and try again and again, using all the imagination and creativity they can muster with no guarantee that they will succeed.

NOTES

1. Lawrence A. Cremin, *The Transformation of the School: Progressivism in American Education 1876-1957* (New York: Alfred A. Knopf and Random House, 1961), p. viii. (Italics in original).

2. It also comes from parts of the entry "Dewey, Pragmatism, and Education," which I wrote for the forthcoming *International Encyclopedia of Education*, 2d ed., edited by Torsten Husén and T. Neville Postlethwaite (Oxford, UK: Pergamon Press, forthcoming).

3. Charles Hartshorne and Paul Weiss, eds., vols. I-VI, and Arthur W. Burks, ed., vols. VII and VIII, *Collected Works of Charles Saunders Peirce* (Cambridge, MA: Harvard University Press, 1931-1953).

4. William James, *Pragmatism and the Meaning of Truth* (Cambridge: MA: Harvard University Press, 1978).

5. The synopsis of Dewey's view of pragmatism sketched here is drawn mainly from my reading and interpretation of three volumes by John Dewey: *Democracy and Education* (New York: Macmillan, 1916); *How We Think* (Boston: D. C. Heath, 1933); and *Logic: The Theory of Inquiry* (New York: Holt, 1938).

6. Ideally, the new teacher's pragmatism should be what Cleo Cherryholmes calls "critical pragmatism." In his book, *Power and Criticism: Poststructural Investigations in Education* (New York: Teachers College Press, 1988), Cherryholmes distinguishes between "vulgar pragmatism" and "critical pragmatism" (pp. 151-152). Vulgar pragmatism only seeks efficiency in doing without questioning the political, social, or philosophical assumptions that underwrite atheoretical practices and social reproduction. Critical pragmatism requires critical reflection, interpretation, and reconstruction of practice in light of an examination of the taken-for-granted background of practice.

CHAPTER XIV

Epilogue

MEMORANDUM TO: Hugh Sockett
FROM: Sam Hollingsworth
SUBJECT: Researching the experience of this volume

    I would like to end this volume with a note to you reflecting upon the years we have collaborated to bring it about, and the progress of the teacher research movement during that time.

    As you'll recall, I began my academic career by teaching a course on "teaching as research" at the University of California (Berkeley) in 1986. Because few current American resources and examples were then available in the literature to use in the course, I broadened my search to find others who were also interested or were working with teacher researchers. With the help of Walter Doyle at a Division K business meeting at AERA the next year, I gave a brief talk on my perceived importance of teacher research to teaching, teacher preparation, and studies of teachers' knowledge. I asked others who were interested in teacher research to contact me, and followed up with a similar request in the Division K Newsletter. I received only two responses. One of them came from you, and we began a collaborative association which led to this volume.

    Since that time, groundbreaking work has appeared in the *Educational Researcher* by Cochran-Smith and Lytle on the place of teacher research as a field of inquiry, along with similarly important work on narrative inquiry by Connelly and Clandinin. Zeichner and Noffke have written about teacher research in preservice teacher preparation. Richardson writes of the role of teacher beliefs in educational research. Lieberman and Miller describe the cultures of supportive school organizations that would sponsor teacher leadership. Both you and Soltis have raised philosophical questions about the nature of the educational knowledge base. Such scholars as Miller and Welch have pointed out the personal, relational, and cultural nature of the school curriculum. I have called attention to the feminist groundings of the teacher research movement. Many classroom teachers, including Threatt, Sugarman, and others, have

261

drawn attention to teacher research within AERA. All of those efforts seem to have converged over the last four years to create a space for substantive conversations on teacher research. The time was right for you and me to pull together a variety of essays written by those educational scholars to show the experiences, the values, and the difficulties of teacher research.

In chapter 1 we opened this volume with a historical review of the contributions of teacher research. We suggested that it could reform education by:

1. reducing the gap between research and practice;

2. demonstrating the problematic nature of "outsider" knowledge in directing teachers' work;

3. emancipating educators from the positivist "domination of thought" through their own understandings and actions;

4. establishing the centrality of teacher-selves in research, challenging the privileged view of traditional research's "objectivity," and, therefore, hierarchies of knowledge; and

5. showing how teacher researchers come to trust their own abilities to construct knowledge, to become meaning makers, and to improve their practices.

My reflective query on the progress made toward the educational community's endorsement of those contributions is prompted by an idea from Jonas Soltis as he closed the last chapter: All of us who have contributed to this movement have worked to promote the promise of teacher research without any guarantee of success. Are we succeeding?

As I prepare these remarks I am just returning from seven months of collaborative teacher research projects in international schools in Asia. I mention that background as it currently gives me another set of cultural lenses to use in reflecting upon the progress over the last four years. The challenge of changing the relationship of educational research and theory to practice through the centrality of the teacher (the first four contributions of teacher research listed above) is certainly a feature of cultural and societal norms. Soltis clearly pointed out the difficulty of developing a radical transformation in American education in "a social-cultural world that encourages excessive individualism, control from above, and a cost-benefit accountability for a very narrow range of learnings." Honoring the position of the teacher and the role of education in society is much better supported in other cultures with Confucian heritages, such as I found in Asia. Yet, even without the support of Confucian values, I would agree with Soltis that American society is moving with others—and with a certain degree of struggle—into a postcolonial, postmodern world. Within that global framework it is clear from the literature outlined above, which raised paradigm-shifting questions and reinterpretations of experience, that progress has occurred. Though the first four contributions of teacher research are not yet uniformly acknowledged, there is at least some awareness that neither a position of control nor autonomy will suffice to direct American education.

While I've been in Asia, we have inaugurated a new President of the United States who promises a greater economic and institutional commitment to education for all American children. While those promises are yet to be realized, our national funding agencies have directed a small amount of economic support for teacher research during the previous administration. Additionally, at least on experimental and rhetorical levels, there is institutional support for shared leadership and decision making in programs labeled "site-based" and "collaborative." In this volume, we've noted that progress through concrete examples of such work by Atkin, Connelly and Clandinin, Lieberman and Miller, Welch, and others. Cochran-Smith and Zeichner have reminded us of such changes at the university level. There are many other school-university partnerships not fully represented in this volume, such as those at the University of California at Davis and Michigan State University.

At the same time, it is clear that much more institutional support and change is needed to recognize the contributions of teacher research to educational reform. I agree with Soltis in his suggestion that "genuine collaboration will not only require new teachers in new school cultures and structures, but also new teacher educators, new cultures in schools of education, and altered university structures." However, as Soltis pointed out, "History is made by people. It doesn't just happen." Societal and personal change are reciprocal. To see how teacher research might impact school cultures, therefore, it is also important to look at personal change.

The central contribution of teacher research to educational reform, in my opinion, has occurred in its fifth contribution: "showing how teacher researchers come to trust their own abilities to construct knowledge, to become meaning makers, and to improve their practices." Many authors, including the teachers in chapter 12, have noted the personal element of growth, awareness, improved teaching, and professionalism as a result of the teacher research movement. The change in my own teaching and personal development, as well as that of teachers with whom I've worked, has been clearly delineated in our writing across these years. The personal relationships and conversational opportunities formed across this work have been the most significant form of support for changes in our teacher-selves. I'm reminded again of Glesne's image which we cited in chapter 1: "Buoyed by trust in themselves, [teacher-researchers] gather confidence to take new risks. The impact expands like concentric circles around the stone thrown in water." Such change supports the feminist challenge that teacher research offers—and promises that the first four contributions of teacher research will be recognized along with the fifth. Although I am aware of the "backlash" against the feminist movement by American men and women who suggest that control of women and "women's professions" by men is more "natural" or "comfortable" than the struggle for equitable positions for men and women, I have consistently noted the personal growth in both male and female teacher researchers. For me, it is the single clear message which supports the challenge and the risk of this work.

Across the years I've also noticed many of the cautions that Threatt and her colleagues, Zeichner, and others warned us about regarding the uses and abuses of institutionalizing teacher research. Even given the strong examples cited by Welch and by Noffke, Mosher, and Maricle in this volume, whether or not teacher research always results in "higher quality" or more equitable forms of teaching is indeed questionable. Large numbers of children are still "left out of the rewards" of teacher research. For teachers, it does sometimes create new hierarchies, add new burdens, and isolate teacher-researchers from their peers. Mary Dybdahl, a California teacher with whom I've worked since 1986, is currently a teacher research group leader in her working-class school. Her peers now look to her for guidance and approval as they used to look to outside "experts." She has had to learn how to foster self and peer trust among those with whom she works in order to retain her "teacher" status among her colleagues. Through my ongoing relationship with Mary and other teachers, I've learned that some teacher research collaboratives within a school site are more about control and power than they are about instructional change. Most teachers will have to struggle, as Zeichner, Threatt, and others point out, to get recognition for their work.

The insightful comparisons of personal awareness and recognition and institutional support made in this volume by Lieberman and

Miller have also been made clear to me over the years we've collaborated to produce the book. Though we're moving away from professional knowledge as a "rhetoric of conclusions" to "the spirit and content of inquiry," we have a long way to go to see "teaching . . . as a form of inquiry and . . . research . . . as a form of teaching." I've seen an increasing need, as have Lytle and Cochran-Smith, for "more public knowledge of the profession through both case studies of individual teacher researchers . . . and case studies of teacher-researcher groups that function within schools or as part of university-sponsored programs and school-university programs." I've also learned to appreciate that teacher research alone is not enough to create the transformative vision we've outlined here. We also need self-reflective studies in administrative and institutional organizations. The political and social connections between students, teachers, administrators, school boards, university faculties, and governmental agencies cannot be overlooked.

While I was in Taiwan I learned that the government of the Republic of China routinely conducts research to understand how teachers could improve their instruction *within the educational system*. The result has recently been a recommendation, not to increase or measure teachers' knowledge from the outside in, but to change the institutional structure of school to allow teachers more professional time to reflect, collaborate, and research. Now both elementary and secondary teachers have three blocked hours during the school day for their professional work. Additionally, much of the schools' administrative work is conducted by teacher leaders. Although it would be difficult, given the societal values we hold in the United States, perhaps the teacher research movement here could also contribute to a revised vision of educational reform by expanding its boundaries from teacher as researcher to administrator as researcher and economic/legislative agencies as researchers. We might look at our educational system as a whole, and expand our conception of educational reform—from "improving teachers' knowledge" and ways of evaluating it to improving the conditions for career-long reflective study, professionalization, and a respect for learning within educational institutions. Such a vision might indeed find this yearbook twenty-five years from now, as Soltis suggests, "cited by many as a major landmark in the history of the emergence and transformation of a more sophisticated and richer conception of teaching and schooling in the last quarter of the twentieth century." Our children, our country, and our world are worth the risk of such a vision.

Memorandum to: Sam Hollingsworth
From: Hugh Sockett
Subject: Reply

I share your guarded optimism, hope, and commitment. I share also many aspects of the vision, especially that of fostering self-reflective studies in institutions other than schools and universities. However, the crux of the movement and momentum described in our first chapter is the increasingly emancipatory power it provides for individuals, primarily in their quest for self. I think you will agree.

Yet should we not have reminded ourselves more often than we did, in our own work and as we developed this book, just how daunting is the problem of change? The characteristic phrase, "change is difficult," usually ignores the personal predicaments that its advocates find themselves in. It is not simply the business of how we do things differently or encourage others to reflect and change. The opposition is fearsome. The actions of those who are either changing themselves or seeking to support change can attract not just professional hostility, but personal aggression, vindictiveness, jealousy, and envy. Bureaucratic weapons are used by opponents to diminish the freedoms of individuals. So, those who embrace teacher research within educational reform need to develop the practical virtue of courage, alongside the honesty, care, and compassion which the work itself demands. It can be a lonely business.

Yet loneliness is what we expect in the stereotypical researcher—ploughing the lone furrow, single authorship of a paper or dissertation, teaching alone, and learning alone in a library carrel. We have neglected for too long this question: How can we put the conception of the team into the institutional infrastructure for learners? While you have been in the Orient, I have been working with a team to build a new kind of teacher-research Master's program based on recruitment in teams. American culture may rhetorically hail individualism, and there is a sense of the growing importance of cooperative learning. That is even important in modern American business culture. It seems to be ignored in university structures where it really matters—in the structural paraphernalia of the degree. To my mind, the central agenda for institutional change is to break the notion of the university being in contract with the individual, qua student, and to install teams at every level. Of course, the very word "team" sounds trite. But it represents the notion of mutual support, with common goals, born of profound trust and mutual understanding.

So I agree that the self-confidence among teacher-researchers is a crucial contribution in the emerging epistemology of practice. While the groups, large and small, which are now so much a part of the landscape of movement in teacher research, are exciting and promising, the institutional change necessary to protect (and maybe enhance) that change has to be ambitiously conceived. I think we can find ways to offset the harshness of the institutionalization to which Zeichner, Threatt, and others refer. The transformative vision has to be worked out in a deconstruction of the traditional mechanisms and structures of academic-student relationships and their reformulation within the five characteristics of teacher research which we believe we all share. That way I think we can get personal, institutional, and social change working in harness, not at odds.

We have presented to our readers a rich vein of thought and activity. We have tried to picture teacher research as an emerging and powerful human conversation. We are also offering an invitation to join that conversation and to find new institutional ways in which the reconstructed relationships can find a properly educational form.

Name Index

Subject Index

Action research: definitions of, 190; factors favoring use of process model of, in U.S., 6; Lewin's ideas about, 3; recreation of, in U.K., 5; revival of, as teacher research, 4; role of facilitator in collaborative forms of, 193; two types of, 190-91; use of, in curriculum projects in the 1950s, 3-4. *See also* Teacher inquiry, Teacher research

American Association of University Women, report of, on *How Schools Shortchange Girls*, 127

American Educational Research Association, special interest group in, on Teacher Research, 12, 72, 98

Bay Area Writing Project, 8, 12

Boston Women's Teachers' Group, 8, 77, 192

Center for Applied Research in Education (University of E. Anglia), 5

Classroom Action Research Network, 5, 72

Collaborative research, between schools and universities: difficulties encountered in, by school teachers and by university researchers, 93-94, 98; obstacles to establishment of, 255-56; political nature of, 86-87; possibilities of, for reconstructing the "sacred" theory-practice story, 93-94; promise and possibilities of, 88-89; risks for university faculty in, 99

Collegiality: problems arising in teacher research in absence of, 210-11; studies of, as a factor in school change, 209-10

Critical praxis, purpose of, in teacher research, 8-9

Cultural leadership, role of, in promoting change in schools, 215-17

Curriculum reform (Britain): challenges to control paradigm of, 6; "process model" of curriculum innovation as a means for, 5, 6

Curriculum reform (U.S.): emphasis in, on talented students, in 1960s, 4; faltering of, in 1980s, 4-5

Educational reform: changing emphasis in proposals for, 1-2; place of research in "control paradigm" for, 2; teacher autonomy and decentralization as alternative to control paradigm for, 2

Educational research, limited impact of, on the educational enterprise, 104

Frankfurt School, 8

Gender equity, in teacher research, 121-39

Handbook of Research on Teaching, 71

Holmes Group, 13

Horace Mann-Lincoln Institute (Teachers College, Columbia University), 3

Hughes-Hart Educational Reform Act (California, 1983): provisions of, 108; purposes of, 107-8

Inclusive dialog: definition of, 53; examples of silencing of, in multicultural classes, 53-55; techniques used to foster, 60-62

In-service professional development, role of various participants in teacher-research based program for, 42-43. *See also* Staff development, Teacher research

Knowledge-in-use, study of, 166-184: findings from, 170-73; methodology of, 168-70; reflections of academic participant in, 181-83; reflections of teacher participants in, 173-81; theoretical framework for, 167

Lesson planning: criticism of, 154; decreasing use of, by experienced teachers, 153-54; dominance of, in written discourse about teaching in teacher education programs, 153; challenges to, in research-oriented student teaching, 155

National Board for Professional Teaching Standards, 1

274

INFORMATION ABOUT MEMBERSHIP IN THE SOCIETY

Membership in the National Society for the Study of Education is open to all who desire to receive its publications.

There are two categories of membership: Regular and Comprehensive. The Regular Membership (annual dues in 1994, $30) entitles the member to receive both volumes of the yearbook. The Comprehensive Membership (annual dues in 1994, $55) entitles the member to receive the two-volume yearbook and the two current volumes in the Series on Contemporary Educational Issues.

Reduced dues (Regular, $25; Comprehensive, $50) are available for retired NSSE members and for full-time graduate students *in their first year of membership*.

Membership in the Society is for the calendar year. Dues are payable on or before January 1 of each year.

New members are required to pay an entrance fee of $1, in addition to annual dues for the year in which they join.

Members of the Society include professors, researchers, graduate students, and administrators in colleges and universities; teachers, supervisors, curriculum specialists, and administrators in elementary and secondary schools; and a considerable number of persons not formally connected with educational institutions.

All members participate in the nomination and election of the six-member Board of Directors, which is responsible for managing the affairs of the Society, including the authorization of volumes to appear in the yearbook series. All members whose dues are paid for the current year are eligible for election to the Board of Directors.

Each year the Society arranges for meetings to be held in conjunction with the annual conferences of one or more of the major national educational organizations. All members are urged to attend these sessions. Members are also encouraged to submit proposals for future yearbooks or for volumes in the series on Contemporary Educational Issues.

Further information about the Society may be secured by writing to the Secretary-Treasurer, NSSE, 5835 Kimbark Avenue, Chicago, IL 60637.

RECENT PUBLICATIONS OF THE NATIONAL SOCIETY FOR THE STUDY OF EDUCATION

1. The Yearbooks

Ninety-third Yearbook (1994)
Part 1. *Teacher Research and Educational Reform.* Sandra Hollingsworth and Hugh Sockett, editors. Cloth.
Part 2. *Bloom's Taxonomy: A Forty-year Retrospective.* Lorin W. Anderson and Lauren A. Sosniak, editors. Cloth.

Ninety-second Yearbook (1993)
Part 1. *Gender and Education.* Sari Knopp Biklen and Diane Pollard, editors. Cloth.
Part 2. *Bilingual Education: Politics, Practice, and Research.* M. Beatriz Arias and Ursula Casanova, editors. Cloth.

Ninety-first Yearbook (1992)
Part 1. *The Changing Contexts of Teaching.* Ann Lieberman, editor. Cloth.
Part 2. *The Arts, Education, and Aesthetic Knowing.* Bennett Reimer and Ralph A. Smith, editors. Cloth.

Ninetieth Yearbook (1991)
Part 1. *The Care and Education of America's Young Children: Obstacles and Opportunities.* Sharon L. Kagan, editor. Cloth.
Part 2. *Evaluation and Education: At Quarter Century.* Milbrey W. McLaughlin and D. C. Phillips, editors. Paper.

Eighty-ninth Yearbook (1990)
Part 1. *Textbooks and Schooling in the United States.* David L. Elliott and Arthur Woodward, editors. Cloth.
Part 2. *Educational Leadership and Changing Contexts of Families, Communities, and Schools.* Brad Mitchell and Luvern L. Cunningham, editors. Paper.

Eighty-eighth Yearbook (1989)
Part 1. *From Socrates to Software: The Teacher as Text and the Text as Teacher.* Philip W. Jackson and Sophie Haroutunian-Gordon, editors. Cloth.
Part 2. *Schooling and Disability.* Douglas Biklen, Dianne Ferguson, and Alison Ford, editors. Cloth.

Eighty-seventh Yearbook (1988)
Part 1. *Critical Issues in Curriculum.* Laurel N. Tanner, editor. Cloth.
Part 2. *Cultural Literacy and the Idea of General Education.* Ian Westbury and Alan C. Purves, editors. Cloth.

Eighty-sixth Yearbook (1987)
Part 1. *The Ecology of School Renewal.* John I. Goodlad, editor. Paper.
Part 2. *Society as Educator in an Age of Transition.* Kenneth D. Benne and Steven Tozer, editors. Cloth.

Eighty-fifth Yearbook (1986)

Part 1. *Microcomputers and Education*. Jack A. Culbertson and Luvern L. Cunningham, editors. Cloth.

Part 2. *The Teaching of Writing*. Anthony R. Petrosky and David Bartholomae, editors. Paper.

Eighty-fourth Yearbook (1985)

Part 1. *Education in School and Nonschool Settings*. Mario D. Fantini and Robert Sinclair, editors. Cloth.

Part 2. *Learning and Teaching the Ways of Knowing*. Elliot Eisner, editor. Paper.

Eighty-third Yearbook (1984)

Part 1. *Becoming Readers in a Complex Society*. Alan C. Purves and Olive S. Niles, editors. Cloth.

Part 2. *The Humanities in Precollegiate Education*. Benjamin Ladner, editor. Paper.

Eighty-second Yearbook (1983)

Part 1. *Individual Differences and the Common Curriculum*. Gary D Fenstermacher and John I. Goodlad, editors. Paper.

Eighty-first Yearbook (1982)

Part 1. *Policy Making in Education*. Ann Lieberman and Milbrey W. McLaughlin, editors. Cloth.

Part 2. *Education and Work*. Harry F. Silberman, editor. Cloth.

Eightieth Yearbook (1981)

Part 1. *Philosophy and Education*. Jonas P. Soltis, editor. Cloth.

Part 2. *The Social Studies*. Howard D. Mehlinger and O. L. Davis, Jr., editors. Cloth.

Seventy-ninth Yearbook (1980)

Part 1. *Toward Adolescence: The Middle School Years*. Mauritz Johnson, editor. Paper.

Seventy-eighth Yearbook (1979)

Part 1. *The Gifted and the Talented: Their Education and Development*. A. Harry Passow, editor. Paper.

Part 2. *Classroom Management*. Daniel L. Duke, editor. Paper.

Seventy-seventh Yearbook (1978)

Part 1. *The Courts and Education*. Clifford B. Hooker, editor. Cloth.

Seventy-sixth Yearbook (1977)

Part 1. *The Teaching of English*. James R. Squire, editor. Cloth.

The above titles in the Society's Yearbook series may be ordered from the University of Chicago Press, Book Order Department, 11030 Langley Ave., Chicago, IL 60628. For a list of earlier titles in the yearbook series still available, write to the Secretary, NSSE, 5835 Kimbark Ave., Chicago, IL 60637.

280

2. The Series on Contemporary Educational Issues

The following volumes in the Society's Series on Contemporary Educational Issues may be ordered from the McCutchan Publishing Corporation, P.O. Box 774, Berkeley, CA 94702-0774.

Academic Work and Educational Excellence: Raising Student Productivity (1986). Edited by Tommy M. Tomlinson and Herbert J. Walberg.
Adapting Instruction to Student Differences (1985). Edited by Margaret C. Wang and Herbert J. Walberg.
Aspects of Reading Education (1978). Edited by Susanna Pflaum-Connor.
Choice in Education (1990). Edited by William Lowe Boyd and Herbert J. Walberg.
Colleges of Education: Perspectives on Their Future (1985). Edited by Charles W. Case and William A. Matthes.
Contributing to Educational Change: Perspectives on Research and Practice (1988). Edited by Philip W. Jackson.
Early Childhood Education: Issues and Insights (1977). Edited by Bernard Spodek and Herbert J. Walberg.
Educational Environments and Effects: Evaluation, Policy, and Productivity (1979). Edited by Herbert J. Walberg.
Educational Leadership and School Culture (1993). Edited by Marshall Sashkin and Herbert J. Walberg.
Effective School Leadership: Policy and Prospects (1987). Edited by John J. Lane and Herbert J. Walberg.
Effective Teaching: Current Research (1991). Edited by Hersholt C. Waxman and Herbert J. Walberg.
From Youth to Constructive Adult Life: The Role of the Public School (1978). Edited by Ralph W. Tyler.
Improving Educational Standards and Productivity: The Research Basis for Policy (1982). Edited by Herbert J. Walberg.
Moral Development and Character Education (1989). Edited by Larry P. Nucci.
Motivating Students to Learn: Overcoming Barriers to High Achievement (1993). Edited by Tommy M. Tomlinson.
Psychology and Education: The State of the Union (1981). Edited by Frank H. Farley and Neal J. Gordon.
Radical Proposals for Educational Change (1994). Edited by Chester E. Finn, Jr. and Herbert J. Walberg.
Reaching Marginal Students: A Prime Concern for School Renewal (1987). Edited by Robert L. Sinclair and Ward Ghory.
Research on Teaching: Concepts, Findings, and Implications (1979). Edited by Penelope L. Peterson and Herbert J. Walberg.
Restructuring the Schools: Problems and Prospects (1992). Edited by John J. Lane and Edgar G. Epps.
Rethinking Policy for At-risk Students (1994). Edited by Kenneth K. Wong and Margaret C. Wang.
Selected Issues in Mathematics Education (1981). Edited by Mary M. Lindquist.
School Boards: Changing Local Control (1992). Edited by Patricia F. First and Herbert J. Walberg.